Floyd Brewer

Bethlehem Diary
Stories & Reflections: 1983-1993

ARCHED BRIDGE CARRYING THE YELLOW BRICK
ROAD OVER THE NORMANSKILL. NORMANSVILLE.

MARK L. PECKHAM
AUGUST 6, 1987.

BETHLEHEM DIARY EDITORIAL COMMITTEE
Teresa Buckley, Editor in chief

Published Under the Auspices of the
BETHLEHEM BICENTENNIAL COMMISSION

November 1994

Copyright 1994 by the
Bicentennial Commission
Town of Bethlehem, New York

Library of Congress
Cataloging-in-Publication Data

ISBN 0-9635402-1-1

Printed by the
Hamilton Printing Company
Rensselaer, New York

Manufactured in the
United States of America

Cover jacket: Adams House Hotel,1838;
original painting by David Coughtry, who
grew up in Bethlehem and has painted
many area scenes.

Title page: Original sketch of the
Normanskill Bridge in Bethlehem
by the well-known local artist,
Mark Peckham, who did most
of the sketches for this book.

Dedicated to
my wife, Coleen,

whose patient advice
keeps me on a steady course.

Floyd Brewer

Floyd I. Brewer
Senior author
Delmar, New York

Acknowledgements

The idea to publish excerpts from the Bethlehem diaries received considerable encouragement and support from members of the Bicentennial Commission. The late Ann Patton offered counsel and direction in the early stages. Former Town Supervisor Kenneth Ringler, present Town Supervisor Sheila Fuller, and members of town board established guidelines and a financial structure for getting the project off the ground. Significant help with business arrangements was given by Judith E. Kehoe and Richard S. Webster. Commission members are especially grateful to Town Clerk Kathleen A. Newkirk and her assistants, C. Terri Picarazzi and Gloria Johnson, for their long-term commitment to marketing the book and keeping the records.

Barbara Mladinov, Marie S. Carlson, and the Bethlehem Public Library staff provided invaluable resource assistance as did Richard and Mary Ahlstrom of *The Spotlight* staff. Additionally, we were fortunate, indeed, to have Thomas Knight handling most of the photo development work, a major reason why so many of the pictures in the book are sharp and clear. Significantly, desktop publishing came of age in Bethlehem under the master hand of Charles D. (Chuck) McKinney, who designed the book and prepared camera-ready copy on his trusty Macintosh LC computer, with assistance from Barbara Stoddard.

Finally, five experienced, volunteer editors met regularly over a period of two years, reading the voluminous diaries, and selecting a balanced group of entries to print. Joseph Allgaier, town historian; Teresa Buckley, layout/copy editor for the *Times Union* ; Kristi Carr, director of information for the Bethlehem Central School District; Susan Graves, managing editor of *The Spotlight*; and Ryland Hugh Hewitt, a retired University at Albany professor, were all uniquely qualified to edit and arrange the information in a readable manner. This is one more in a long line of examples of the excellent work of volunteers in the town of Bethlehem.

J. Robert Hendrick, Jr., chairman
Bicentennial Commission
Delmar, New York

Introduction

The life of a town is a product of the people who live in it. When the Bethlehem Archaeology Group began digging at various sites around town in 1981, the members found artifacts of Indian cultures and the remnants of past inhabitants of the town. Unfortunately, they found no diaries to aid them in documenting the lives of early residents. To fill the void for future historians, retired professor Floyd Brewer began a diary in 1983 and filled eleven large books with his musings through the town's bicentennial year in 1993.

This was no simple chronicle of the weather and local events. He examined the factors that had shaped his life, the changing relationships with his wife and family as they grew older, innovations and inventions that marked new ways of going about everyday tasks, his contributions to town history, and his feelings about state, national, and international events that shaped his world.

We are an information-oriented society. Television, telephone, fax, and computer modems all keep us abreast of current affairs. But how much of this will translate into knowledge for future archaeologists/historians? Brewer kept his diary to ensure that written records of at least one man, one family, and one town, in one time, would be on the record for all to use. Access to the complete diaries will be available to journalists, historians, and other scholars through the Bethlehem Public Library in 1995 and later.

For the present, the Bethlehem Diary editorial committee has selected a representative group of excerpts from the diaries to be read by anyone interested. To some readers, this will be a glimpse of a different way of life, for others it will seem very familiar. For all, it will be a pleasurable journey with a man who is leaving one career and embarking on another.

Teresa Buckley
Editor in chief
Delmar, New York

Background

An eleven-year odyssey during the preparation of *Bethlehem Diary* began with feelings of frustration in early 1983, regarding the almost total lack of similar information needed for documenting selected chapters in a planned bicentennial history. I resolved then and there to make sure that historians of the future would have access to at least one man's view of life in Bethlehem during the period leading up to and including our bicentennial year. There was no plan to publish excerpts from the diary until 1990, and the information included in the early years is more personal and family-centered. Entries recorded during 1990-1993 are more Bethlehem-centered.

It has been a labor of love as well as a therapeutic experience, an eleven-year think piece about the meaning of family experiences and events in Bethlehem, a town of about 28,000, a few miles southwest of Albany, New York. It was an effort to consider the impact of government policies and social systems on one small family, with occasional extrapolation to other families and groups.

The editorial committee has chosen to publish a selected group of excerpts that seem quite representative of the total diary to me. Better still, the editors included snapshots of their own diaries during 1993, our bicentennial year, giving readers a broader picture of life in Bethlehem.

Floyd I. Brewer
Senior author
Delmar, New York

Contents

Contents (continued)

1 *Nineteen Hundred Eighty-Three*

Floyd Brewer started keeping a daily journal in March 1983. He was scheduled to retire that spring from his position as associate professor, Department of Counseling Psychology, at the State University of New York at Albany and he wanted, in particular, to track his finances as he moved from the working world. He hoped he would be able to continue a life-style that allowed for some travel for himself and his wife, Coleen, a homemaker.

With adequate funds and sound health, he was looking forward to a "second career" in archaeology, a field where he'd already had some experience yet wanted more knowledge. He intended to devote much of his extra time in retirement to the fledgling Bethlehem Archaeology Group, started just the year before but already with plans to write a history of Bethlehem for the town's bicentennial—still ten years away.

Stupid Letter
April 7

A letter was placed in my mailbox at the office today—a notice that I would not be considered for a merit increase next year. Well—how about that! Stupendous stupidity. What would I do with an increase when I'm not on the payroll?

They're trying to find a way to let me buy my swivel chair from the state. Red tape galore. I'd like to take it with me since it's the only chair I've ever used that fits me perfectly.

My Wednesday evening Introduction to Counseling class decided to have a semester-end party for my last class at the State University of New York at Albany. I've been thinking about doing a "Trends in Counseling" lecture. Big changes have come to pass in thirty-five years: psychiatrists have receded in importance; the Hinkley trial (President Reagan's assailant) pushed them farther down the ladder. Psychologists are on the upswing but still make the headlines for their far-out behavior. Counselors, unprotected by law, are being sued more frequently. Behavioral methods are being used heavily.

Aerial view of State University of New York at Albany, ca. 1993. Main academic podium, four residential quadrangles. Physical Education Building and Recreation and Convocation Center in foreground.

Program Criticized
April 11

This was a long day—up at 6:00 A.M., home after archaeology class at Hudson Valley Community College at 10:00 P.M. Faculty in the Counseling Psychology Department at SUNY Albany were angry over the American Psychological Association's reviewing team report on our Ph.D. program (which has just completed three years of provisional operation and was hoping for permanent approval). The committee recommended continuance of provisional status. The chairman (Don Biggs) feels that their report is full of errors. The truth is likely that some of their criticism stung and is perhaps partly on target. Faculty agreed to try to get a reversal on the floor of the next APA meeting.

Class at HVCC tonight was much more interesting. I ran through 250 years of history at our Nicoll-Sill project and related artifacts we've unearthed to owners of the building in different time periods. Florence and Peter Christoph, historians in this area, followed me with a detailed sketch of the people who lived in the house. We are literally writing a new chapter in our town's history since much of what we've pulled out has never been written before.

Master's Program in Classical Archaeology
April 15

Jeffrey [son] called tonight. He's attending a conference in New York City and staying with Tina and Selma Zomback, Beth's [his wife's] aunts. He's coming for a visit with us Sunday noon through Monday.

This was a quiet day. I rearranged the furniture in my den downstairs and did some correspondence. There was a lot of time to think.

Also, it was a good time to finish the application for SUNY Albany's master's program in classical archaeology. I wonder if they will take someone as controversial as I seem to be? Some professional archaeologists in the area feel I am committing four cardinal sins: (1) teaching without formal training in the field; (2) directing a major historical site excavation; (3) supervising a laboratory; and (4) leading a private archaeology group.

I'm going to fight for what I believe in; they'll have to stop me—I'll never quit. If they succeed, I'll just try another route.

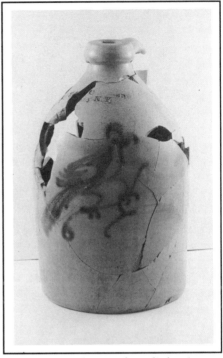

Reconstructing history from little pieces— American stoneware jug, ca. 1809-1833, Nicoll-Sill site.

At Last We Can Dig
April 23

Finally, the weather allowed us to dig at the Nicoll-Sill site. After helping Ann Jacobs (assistant field director) get set up in the grid nearest the house, I took two members of my HVCC archaeology class a few hundred feet away to the Vloman Kill bank grid and we began to search for major trash pits.

It was a beautiful day, sunny but cool— exactly the kind of day to dig. Most of

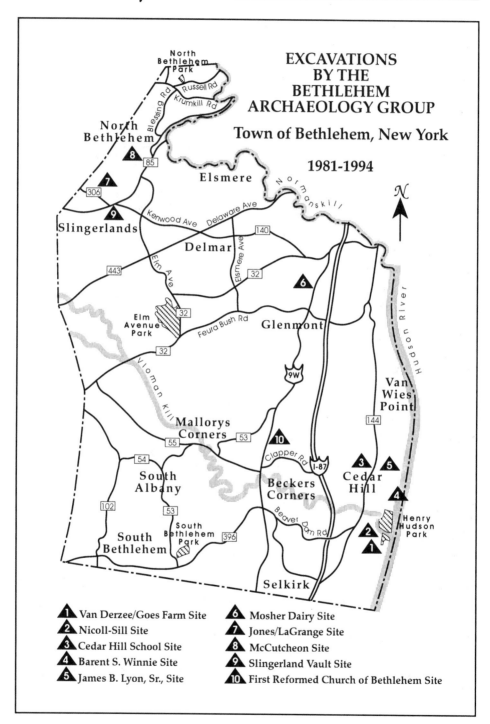

**EXCAVATIONS
BY THE
BETHLEHEM
ARCHAEOLOGY GROUP**

Town of Bethlehem, New York

1981-1994

North
Bethlehem
Park

Russell Rd

Krumkill Rd

Blessng Rd

North
Bethlehem

8

85

7

306

9

Elsmere

Normanskill

Kenwood Ave

Delaware Ave

Slingerlands

Delmar

140

443

Elm Ave

Elsmere Ave

32

6

Elm
Avenue
Park

32

Feura Bush Rd

Glenmont

32

Vloman Kill

9W

Hudson River

Van
Wies
Point

144

Mallorys
Corners

55

53

10

54

Clapper Rd

I-87

3

5

Cedar
Hill

4

South
Albany

Beckers
Corners

102

53

Beaver Dam Rd

2

Henry
Hudson
Park

South
Bethlehem
Park

1

South
Bethlehem

396

Selkirk

1 Van Derzee/Goes Farm Site
2 Nicoll-Sill Site
3 Cedar Hill School Site
4 Barent S. Winnie Site
5 James B. Lyon, Sr., Site

6 Mosher Dairy Site
7 Jones/LaGrange Site
8 McCutcheon Site
9 Slingerland Vault Site
10 First Reformed Church of Bethlehem Site

us wanted to dig so badly that we took only a half hour for lunch.

Collectively, hundreds of artifacts were uncovered today. No major trash pits were found, but we have hopes for tomorrow. They're important since we have only one skimpy inventory on the Nicoll-Sill house and know almost nothing about the life-style of the famous occupants of the house in the 1700s and 1800s.

The Cost of Living
April 30

This diary was started three months before retirement to see if our quality of life is somewhat the same three months after retirement. I'll examine one dimension each week for the next several weeks and look at the same dimensions six months from now to see how things have changed.

Finances

Annual Income:

SUNY Albany	$32,748
(full-time salary)	
HVCC	$4,200
(part-time salary)	
Book review	$125
	$37,073

Overall, we have an adequate income for the kind of life-style we're comfortable with; however, we'd both like to travel more, and we'd both like to spend more on recreation, week in, week out. Everything else seems adequate.

Career-End Feelings
May 4

My last class at SUNY Albany, ECPY601A, Introduction to Counseling, was a pleasant affair. There was some good food and wine plus individual meetings with each student—an appropriate way to end a clinically oriented class.

Would I have had an interesting, well-paying career in higher education without the World War II GI Bill? Probably not. Education at the college level had been generally limited to the wealthy and the middle class in this country prior to 1940. The GI Bill changed all that. Additionally, a liberal social agenda in the Kennedy and Johnson administrations in the 1960s fueled opportunities for the lower middle and lower class members of the population. Through earning a doctorate, I literally transported myself from lower class to middle class. Could this happen in China or Russia? Not likely.

I have never been very class conscious but, occasionally, life's events raise it as an issue. I'm much better off than many who live in this town. I feel OK about it because I worked hard to get here.

Recreation
May 7-9

Another main dimension in the quality of life is clearly recreation—or fun

5

in living. Although we budget only $25 every two weeks and put it in an envelope called "recreation," we bootleg additional money for this purpose.

• We usually go out to dinner on Saturday night. Tonight's dinner at the Shanty in Delmar was $19.25 including tip. So we have only $5.75 left in the envelope. Next Saturday evening (if we didn't have a special trip planned, as we do next week) we would scrounge another $8 or $10 from the grocery and miscellaneous envelopes and a little from our personal allowances and go out for dinner again, to a cheaper place.

• About every other month we substitute a movie for dinner at a cost of $6-8.

• There are usually two short (weekend) trips a year to places like Boston, financed from the checking account.

• Another two weekends a year (on average) are used for visiting relatives. Without fail we have visited Coleen's sister, Joan, and her family in Southington, Conn. Also, we regularly visit my sister Janet and her family in Houlton, Maine, and, occasionally, my brother Calvin, his family, and my sister Edris and her children in Westminster, Mass.

• We regularly entertain our good friends, particularly John and Doris Gold and Ralph and Muriel Wood...and they entertain us in return...on an average of every other month.

• Mark comes over for Sunday dinner about twice a month; occasionally the three of us go out to dinner. He'll be here for Mother's Day today.

• We've been going to the Albany Symphony occasionally and have recently bought season tickets...so next year we'll be going eight or ten times. Our friends, Ralph and Muriel Wood, also have season tickets.

• We like window shopping a lot and frequently visit the shopping malls after dinner out. Most of our shopping needs (outside groceries) are filled at one of the area's malls. We like the Mohawk Mall in Schenectady best although we go to Colonie Center on Wolf Road more often, simply because it is more convenient. We usually buy some items on each trip. Watching the people is half the fun.

• Overall, and throughout the year, we like small-group activities. Coleen does a lot of things (for fun) in small groups at the Delmar Presbyterian Church. I like groups connected with archaeology and history.

AIDS
June 18

A disease known as acquired immune deficiency syndrome, probably caused by a virus, is striking fear in the hearts of many around the country—particularly the homosexual community. So far, it has struck 1,552 people around the United States and 597 have died. It is usually fatal.

Since 70 percent of the victims are homosexuals, it is thought to be transmitted by either sexual intercourse or, possibly, by contaminated needles—since 17 percent have been intravenous drug users.

The United States Public Health Service has named it our number one enemy since it could claim 100,000 victims within three years at the present rate and as many as 1.6 million within five years.

Small wonder some nurses are refusing to care for AIDS victims, some funeral directors are refusing to embalm them, and transportation officials are refusing to transport them.

Our Neighbors
July 5-7

One reason we decided to stay in Delmar is our neighbors. Most of them are cordial (and helpful). We try to be the same but, on occasion, patience is strained.

Larry and Judy Fink live immediately behind us on Lansing Drive. They and their son, Matthew, are fine but their dog Brandy—a red setter—is a pain. She barks too much. I kicked her once last year (clearly the wrong thing to do) and both Larry and Judy were angry about the incident. However, they are now taking their dog in after she barks three or four minutes, so there has been a big improvement. We talk but, predictably, are not good friends.

Helen Nickel across the street on Lansing Drive, a head nurse at Albany Medical Center Hospital and now fifty-six years old, is a good friend. We talk a lot and she comes over for coffee a lot. She has a high school age son, Jeffrey, and another son, Douglas, who works at a local motel, living home. Jeff is still feeling the effects of his Mother and Dad's divorce some eight years ago and is pretty demanding at times. A daughter, Susan, is married and living in Norfolk, Va. Another son, Stephen, is just finishing a two-year degree program at Hudson Valley Community College and hopes to improve his job status. Helen's friendship means a great deal to us.

John and Janice Skilbeck and their two elementary school-age children, Jonathan and Hilary, live next to Helen, across Lansing Drive. They are active with their children, Little League baseball, and other groups. A stray ball hits our house occasionally, but, for the most part, they are good neighbors.

The same can be said for people living in the duplex across Dawson Road. Jane Martin works at the Farm Bureau and her children shift for themselves after school, but they are sensible children. Newlyweds Bill and Alana Williams live in the other side of the duplex. We talk a lot with the adults but, because of the age difference, are not close friends.

David and Viva Price live across the street on Dawson Road and down a few doors....

Oddly, we're friends but do very little together socially. We took them to the airport today for their five-week trip to Europe.

David is vice-president of the Guilderland Reinsurance Co., a small company that shares insurance risks with the larger companies. Viva is a bright, articulate homemaker with a number of health problems.

Coleen usually watches the Price home when they're away, and they often do little things for us. They picked me up at the hospital a year ago following my prostate operation, took us to the airport in May when we went to Kansas, etc.

It is a helping, rather than a social relationship.

Floyd Brewer, ca. 1983, examining finds from the Nicoll-Sill dig.

Nicoll-Sill Dig
July 12

Members of the Bethlehem Archaeology Group and other volunteers have continued to dig two days a week following the news that we would not have an HVCC class to help us.

The finds are exciting, valuable, and helpful in describing the life-style of the famous occupants of the old 1735 Dutch home.

Today we found clay pipe bowls with initials "JS"; table knives—complete with bone handles; many weapons artifacts, from musket balls to 38 cal. shells; dozens of pieces of pottery, from expensive Chinese (transfer print) porcelain to clunky American stoneware; many hard-to-identify metal artifacts plus old-style keys and glass objects that will take months to fathom the purpose.

We believe the Nicoll-Sill story will be worth a whole chapter in our proposed history of the town of Bethlehem.

Retirement
July 31

I like it. We're more relaxed, better off financially, doing more fun things together, and planning some exciting things for the future.

Coleen seems to be feeling more secure, and willing to spend a little more on luxury things—everything from clothes to furniture.

I'm getting into some reading for my graduate course called "The Power of Rome" and am enjoying it immensely.

Coleen is as wrapped up in church work as ever. Service on the building committee is giving her a policy role.

Digging two days a week is a light but satisfying physical work load for me. Planning for a new lab will soon take a lot of time.

Edward H. Sargent, Jr., ca. 1983.

Edward H. Sargent, Jr.
(March 25, 1916-August 7, 1983)
August 11

Coleen and I attended Ed Sargent's funeral at the Delmar Presbyterian Church today. The sanctuary was overflowing.

Ed worked with me in the School of Education at SUNY Albany and retired a bare three years ago.

He was a many-talented man: professor, county legislator, former Marine lieutenant, friend of prisoners (particularly those at the Albany county jail), father of four children, vocalist in the church choir, board member of many community groups.

Ed would have been pleased with his service if he could have known how it went. His rich life (of service to others) was amply outlined. The attendance was a clear indication of how many lives he touched. If prisoners could have been dismissed for his service, they might have had to move the service to the Palace Theatre...which might have been appropriate.

He was also a showman!

Merrill E. Brewer
(Older Brother)
August 23-24

My sister Janet gave me Merrill's high school diploma when I visited her last Friday. It brought back memories of a favorite brother. We lived together in a small camp near our home in Bridgewater, Maine. With seven children in the family, there was very little room in the house so Merrill and I lived in a camp built earlier by our older brother, Gerald.

I remember well the nights Merrill shared his dreams and problems before we went to sleep: his feelings about school (mostly positive—he graduated from Bridgewater Classical Academy in June 1936); dreams about becoming a nurse—a feat he accomplished against overwhelming odds in a mostly female occupation— he became a male nurse at Gardner [Mass.] State Hospital; anger at his father for wasting his time drinking (oddly, Merrill's death in the Air Force provided an income for his father for the rest of his life); feelings about sex (he was seduced by a forty-year-old woman at age seventeen—it was an exciting experience, he said, but he never had time to marry).

Merrill enlisted in the Air Force early during World War II and later was assigned as a waist gunner aboard a B17 bomber in the 492d Bomb Group (H).

He was killed on his last mission over Germany, on Sept. 16, 1944.

Coleen Brewer (as Mother)
September 5-6

It may be presumptuous of a husband to write about this subject when the perceptions of children would be more real. Even so, I see Coleen as an ideal mother—one who demonstrates that she cares for and loves her children deeply (still does!).

In the early days, she was a "law and order" mother. Jeff and Mark knew when they were doing something wrong almost before they had finished doing it. She would loudly call a halt to the errant behavior. At the same time (often the same day) she would bandage a scraped knee and calm them with soft, reassuring words and a hug.

10

Coleen Brewer with family, ca. 1970. Left to right: Floyd, Jeffrey, Coleen, and Mark.

I might as well not say such things because she'll never change on this point.

She may have erred on the side of over-protection but it is satisfying to see our children living useful, productive lives. I believe there is less chance they would be doing so if she hadn't run a "tight ship." I aided, abetted, and supported but she clearly charted the way for our children's lives partly because she was with them for much longer periods than I.

As the children grew older, she found a balance between "law and order" and advice—always listening before acting. She selected clothes for the children in a sensible fashion, catered to their food whims yet tried to assure them of good nutrition, and often helped them with their schoolwork. She praised good behavior and excellent work in school only when there was a genuine basis for it.

Mothers really never shed those motherly traits. She worries about Mark and Jeff even now; their ups and downs are her ups and downs. I've said several times, "They're grown men now. They can handle their own ups and downs without your help. We taught them to be self-sufficient and they're being just that. Why do you need to worry about them?"

Coleen has often rejected a leadership role in other life settings (church, social activities) but she is a leader by example in her role as mother.

Group Activities
September 30

Americans are joiners and I am no exception; however, I have had a long-standing philosophy: join a group only when you're strongly interested and can make a contribution.

I formed and joined the Bethlehem Archaeology Group after becoming aware that I could make a substantial contribution to the town of Bethlehem. To enhance this membership (and further the group's cause) I registered as a Republican—an unusual step for me. Republican affiliation has opened many doors. I'm glad I did, but in the privacy of the voting booth, I'll continue to vote an independent ticket.

Over the years I've joined only those professional groups that could aid me in my work and permit me to make a contribution. The Association of College Unions International is the best example. I worked my way up from member to president (between 1948 and 1960) and felt good about the quality of my contributions to this group.

Archaeology Lab Complications
October 4

Archaeologists must have a lab to work in in both summer and winter. When lab space is threatened, the problem sometimes assumes calamitous proportions.

There is no heat in the tiny summer lab at Nicoll-Sill so, for all practical purposes, it becomes useless at the end of October.

Ralph Wood, our executive director, reported today that the intended site of our permanent lab, the Walden-meier building on Route 32 South, had been vandalized. Worse, the vandalism caused the town supervisor, Tom Corrigan, to feel that the town shouldn't hook up the electricity or heat the building until matching fed-

eral funds are available to do the job right.

However, Wood and Corrigan agreed to meet there on Thursday afternoon to consider all the possibilities.

I plan to be there and hope to change Tom's mind. We must have a lab.

Changing Telephone Policy
October 11

We're getting close to the wire and either have to buy our current phones from the telephone company or turn them in and buy new phones at a department store.

We're inclined to buy new phones and have to face up to the fact that phones are now like other products in our home. If you want quality, you have to shop and pay for it.

In the process, we're thinking of having jacks put in so we can move phones around if need be.

It is possible that all of us will be paying a $2.00 monthly access fee to connect with the long distance system in January. I feel this is unfair and hope the government stops it. Charges for long distance calls should be made against those making calls (we make very few).

We're expecting higher local phone bills but, as yet, I don't know all the reasons why.

Homo Domesticus Responsibilus
October 14

With all the male enlightenment we read about today, real change is years away for the mainstream. Men still want a wife who will do most of the work around the house; have meals on time; clean, wash and even paint, and mow the lawn (if they can get away with it). All this in return for their work as the breadwinner.

My relationship has changed slowly with Coleen. I always mowed the lawn, did much of the painting and, on occasions, made beds. Also, I helped with the dishes on weekends and on other occasions when she was tired.

In retirement, I do dishes and make beds more often (so she will have the feeling that she's retired too). I also make breakfast regularly and often get my own lunch. Although I still have a busy schedule, I'm trying to do more around the house.

Even so, I still enjoy having meals prepared for me, clean clothes and a clean house (which I still do very little about). Also, as always, we do the shopping together.

We Had Cable TV Installed Today
October 19

We've held out against cable for a number of years partly because we don't watch a lot of TV—maybe two hours a day on average.

However, I miss the news on those occasions when we go out to dinner and, now that Bethlehem Video has CNN (Cable News Network), we can get it anytime after we return. CNN's "Prime News" at eight o'clock is an excellent news program.

Coleen likes movies and we can now get Channels 23 and 38, both good movie channels. Some weeks it's like a wasteland on the three regular channels; now there are more.

Finally, we both like ballet and some opera and we expect to find some good performances on the ARTS channel to supplement what we now get on public television. The charge is $10 per month.

Luncheon Meeting with James Morgan and Ralph Wood
October 20

Ralph and I met at the Hudson River Trading Post restaurant with James Morgan, the new town historian.

We agreed the Bethlehem Archaeology Group should continue as an arm of the town historian's office and he agreed to seek a budget of at least $500 per year for us. Not much, but it's a beginning.

The main item we needed to resolve was Ralph's proposal to renovate two or more rooms in the Waldenmeier Building on Route 32 South for a combined BAG and town historian's office. This will cost the town quite a bit of money, but Morgan will consider the proposal carefully.

Overall, it was a pleasant beginning of a relationship that could last many years.

Morgan seems receptive and flexible, yet cautious—marks of a lawyer, which he is.

The Bethlehem Archaeology Group (a Year Later)
November 15

Originally organized in January 1982, the Bethlehem Archaeology Group didn't really get under way until November of last year. In that short time we've grown to fourteen regular members augmented by an average of ten to twelve Hudson Valley Community College students each semester.

More important, it is a group of people with special skills:

• Ralph Wood, executive director, surveyor, and artifact analyst: clay pipe.

• Floyd Brewer, field director, in charge of educational and excavation programs.

• Benjamin French, assistant field director and photographer and conservation lab associate.

• Ann Jacobs, assistant field director, artifact analyst: bottles, glass.

• Florence Christoph, historian and instructional assistant.

• Jeanne Jacobson, research associate and instructional assistant.

• Linda Luzzi, research associate and office manager.

• Virginia French, laboratory supervisor.

• Jean Adell, artifact analyst: bones.

• Eleanor Norrix, artifact analyst: bottles, glass.

• Carol Wock, artifact analyst: ceramics.

• Gale Derosia, artist/illustrator.

• Claudia St. John, artist/illustrator.

• Matthew Jacobson, computer associate.

We're gaining an average of one new staff member each month.

Shopping (Christmas Style)
November 26

Although Coleen, particularly, is always aware of the deeper meaning of the Christmas season, we both enjoy shopping for gifts.

We think of our grandchildren first since gifts often mean more to children. We drove to a toy store in Altamont where we found furniture for Stephanie's dollhouse. Then we traveled cross-country to the Mohawk Mall in Schenectady looking for a "Lego" set (building materials for a space supply station) for Jonathan. No luck on that, but we did find a sweater for Jeff at the Boston Store and an Exercycle for Mark at Montgomery Ward.

Earlier, we managed to find a sweater for Beth at Peter Harris in Delmar—so, we'll continue looking for Jonathan.

Coleen and I do not usually surprise one another. We get more out of telling each other what we want most. This year she's buying me a desk mounted magnifying lamp and I'm getting her a bathrobe and a nightgown.

Pleasure or Weakness?
November 30

About twice a week I "succumb" to the temptation of having morning coffee and a doughnut at the new Dunkin' Donuts place in Elsmere.

I have to go out for the *New York Times* anyway, so why not relax and read the front page somewhere?

Besides, a retired man has to have some reason for getting out of the house now and then, right? And I sometimes meet people I know, so the sociability factor is important, isn't it?

Occasionally, Coleen needs something at Hilchie's Hardware, right across the street from Dunkin' Donuts', so it saves gasoline to make both stops at the same time, right?

Now that I've run out of reasons/excuses, it seems best to admit that I go to Dunkin' Donuts mostly because I like doughnuts.

Sump Pumps
December 3

The main disadvantage in our home is the sump pump in the basement floor. The town's building code requires them under most circumstances since the water table in this area is high.

Ours is a Zoeller submersible pump and it ran beautifully for five years until last Friday. The first we knew it had failed was when water rose around my feet in the office area downstairs.

D.A. Bennett sent a man out around 3:00 P.M. Friday but he was able only to do patchwork since he went off duty at 4:00 P.M. Additionally, we decided to put in a double pump so if one fails the other will kick in. He can't do that until next week.

We had to call for emergency service twice on the weekend because the pump failed twice.

Live and learn. If we ever buy another house, it will not have a sump pump! We'll buy on high ground.

The Law (the Right to Die)
December 9

I have signed a "Living Will" which states: "If the situation should arise which there is no reasonable expectation of my recovery from physical or mental disability, I request that I be allowed to die and not be kept alive by artificial means or heroic measures. I do not fear death itself as much as the indignities of deterioration, dependence, and hopeless pain. I, therefore, ask that medication be mercifully administered to me to alleviate suffering even though this may hasten the moment of my death. This request is made after careful consideration. I hope you who care for me will feel morally bound to follow its mandate.

I recognize that this appears to place a heavy responsibility upon you, but it is with the intention of relieving you of such responsibility and of placing it upon myself in accordance with my strong convictions that this statement is made. Death is as much a reality as birth, growth, maturity, and old age— it is the one certainty of life. If the time comes when I, Floyd I. Brewer, can no longer take part in decisions for my own future, let this statement stand as an expression of my wishes while I am of sound mind."

End of the Sump Pump Story (I Hope!)
December 15

We know very little about plumbing but it seems some plumbers know even less. Four sumps failed in a row and each time the water seeped into and around the floor downstairs. Finally, the last man ran a power snake through our drainage line outside and still the pump failed.

When he (John Vadney) came back the next day he took off the check valve above the pump and found it defective. We all said hooray! The problem is solved. Why didn't the first man check it?

Prior to the last pump failure, I had been slowly digging up the drain pipe outside looking for a leak and never found one. However, when I went out two days ago to fill in the trench,

16

water spurted up through the ground near the house.

The power snake cutter (end of the snake) had chewed holes in the plastic pipe. We had all of it replaced with heavier pipe so that is unlikely to happen again. So now everything is running smoothly—until the bill comes.

Kid With a New Toy
December 17

We're beginning to record interviews with people who know a lot about the Nicoll-Sill house, and I've been wanting my own equipment to do this job. It's a pain to check out HVCC equipment every time we do an interview.

I sold my Canon AE-1 camera and a wide angle lens ($140) to get money to buy a good quality cassette recorder. With two other cameras, I've been using the AE-1 very little. Also it is expensive to maintain. The last repair bill was $90.

So I bought a Panasonic RX-5030 FM/AM stereo radio cassette recorder at Tehan's, a new catalog showroom store in the Northway Mall. The cost was $123.02 including tax.

I feel like a kid with a new toy.

The sound is excellent. I can play AM and FM radio or tapes. Most important, it has built-in microphones for ease in recording oral interviews. Also, I can tape concerts off the air (through my Fisher 125 stereo receiver). A neat, useful product.

THE HALVE MAEN. REPLICA OF HENRY HUDSON'S
1609 SHIP OF EXPLORATION. MARK L. PECKHAM, 1992.

*N*ow in his first full year of retirement, Floyd threw himself wholeheartedly into his archaeology work. He spread the gospel of
archaeology as a guest speaker at
local functions and watched with
satisfaction as BAG (Bethlehem Archaeology Group) drew in more volunteers, as well as expanded its number of dig sites.

Retirement also gave Floyd the
luxury of time for reflection—on
his life, his death, even his dreams.

Albany Institute of History & Art, ca. 1993.

A Museum Gem
January 12

We visited the Albany Institute of History & Art today, a really attractive,
small museum that prides itself on
quality exhibits.

The exhibit we especially went to see
was a collection of nineteenth-century
lithographs of historic cities and towns
in the United States.

We knew very little about the artists
who did the meticulous work for these
scenes and came away with strong
feelings of appreciation for their skill.

Also, lunch at the institute's tea room
is an experience. Manned (a sexist
word since most of them were women)
mostly by volunteers, a $3.00 lunch
there is worth $5.00 elsewhere. The
volunteers make all the desserts.

Finally, Coleen and I stopped in the
library at the institute to see Charlotte
Wilcoxen, a ceramics expert who has
helped me learn her trade.

New Will
January 15

As I've written before, it is easy to
discuss any subject with Mark—even
one's possible demise. I've been work-

ing on a new will, and the process naturally requires one to prepare information for coexecutors, Mark and Jeff, in case of a common accident in which Coleen and I both die.

We don't dwell on the subject but realists at least prepare for the possibility.

That is the essence behind a will.

What you have is divided between your beneficiaries equally, share and share alike.

If we should die by car tomorrow, it looks as though each beneficiary would get $180,000 to $200,000 or more (less taxes); if we should die by plane, train, or bus, beneficiaries would receive an additional $170,000 or so (less taxes).

...if it happens, why not help those you love the most?

Robert Funk
(Man with the Answers)
January 20

Dr. Funk, current New York state archaeologist, looked over our Nicoll-Sill prehistoric artifacts today and amazed us time and again with his expertise.

We have a heavy concentration of older Indian stone tools, Lamoka, Brewerton, and Normanskill projec-

tile points, some of which could have been made 4,000 to 5,000 years ago. Also, there is a liberal sprinkling of tools made about 3,000 years ago....

Finally, our site was occupied down through the centuries following the birth of Christ, a deduction made possible through a careful analysis of our Indian pottery, some called "dentate" made in A.D. 200 or 300 and some nice looking "chance incised" pottery made as late as A.D. 1350 to 1400.

We've been working on these tools this fall, and following our meetings with Doctors Ritchie and Funk, feel sure that we will add a new page to our local and state history.

Cocaine
(A Serious National Problem)
January 29

One of the most difficult clients I ever tried to help approached me about two years before retirement.

Eileen (not her real name) had a $600-a-week cocaine habit which she financed by sleeping with twelve men each week at a local club. Her boyfriend gave her food and a place to stay. Emotionally, she was a mess: heavy bouts of depression, a high anxiety level regarding any new ventures, increasingly irritable with anyone whose life she touched—including me.

She felt inhaling ("snorting") coke couldn't be harming her all that much,

Indian life in Bethlehem, ca. 3000 B.C. Sketch by Margaret Foster.

but our first session dispelled that myth.

Eventually, after many difficult sessions, a lot of crying, anger, self-understanding, and trial solutions (one step at a time; I encouraged her to sleep with one less man each week, gradually depriving her of money to spend on coke), she stopped using cocaine. She left her boyfriend, got a job as a clerk.

She called today. She now makes $10,500 as a secretary and is engaged to be married. This is reward enough for me.

**Local Personalities
(Flo Christoph, Alice Kenney)
February 10**

Flo Christoph is the historian for our Bethlehem Archaeology Group. She has been coming to our home during the past few Fridays to work on the script for a thirty-minute television documentary we're doing together on the Nicoll-Sill excavation.

It is fun to work with her. We audiotaped a segment of the show this morning and had a good many laughs over our mistakes. We resolved to get more serious next week and run through the entire show in order to be able to share our plan with Dr. Alice Kenney, chief script writer for the library, which administers the new public affairs channel.

When you add up everything she does in any one month, Flo is an amazingly productive person: mother of three, co-author of two recent books, professional genealogist, to mention just a few of her roles. How she finds time to work with us, I'll probably never know. Only her husband, Peter, knows.

Governor Mario Cuomo's First Year
February 16

To me Governor Cuomo is, at once, a bright, hardworking, incisive, complex man who alternately refers to himself as governor and "papa's son."

His inaugural address was brilliant, and he has personalized his administrative role to a point where people realize they are dealing with both an engaging personality and the top dog in the state.

After an initial test of his ability to perform in a crisis (Sing-Sing prison revolt, which ended with eighteen hostages being freed with no bloodshed), he has moved on to handling heavy budget problems and other major issues in the state with both skill and charm. He works long and hard. Will this eventually lead to a national office?

Maybe, but in the meantime, he has to learn how to delegate more artfully, to admit mistakes, and to find a better balance between who he is as a man and what he is capable of becoming as a leader. The potential for greatness is there.

Floyd Brewer (Self-appraisal)
February 21-22

Family background has contributed significantly to my changing feelings and economic status over a period of years.

Born the fifth child in a seven-child family in Bridgewater, Maine, I always had to work hard for everything I wanted: spending money as a child, a chance to go to college, promotions in the world of work.

The pattern became so ingrained that (as I discovered later in life) second best was never good enough for me. I simply had to work hard enough to go as far as I wanted to go in whatever I took on: to a doctorate in education, to the directorship of a large college union, to a full professorship (here I had to compromise and accept an associate professorship)...and to as professional an archaeologist as I can possibly become with limited formal training. Along the way, I had to become president of the Association of College Unions, International, and, with patience, that became reality for me, too.

The point is that the work ethic became so ingrained early in life that it became a major factor in the successes I've had.

In this country, it is possible for a hard-working, persistent person, motivated to reach a goal, to get where he wants to go through careful planning.

I've done a lot of careful planning, building-block style, one step at a time, always willing to accept a small success this or next year if there was promise of greater success three or four years away.

Although test results and other indications of ability show me as well above the average, I see myself as succeeding at whatever I've wanted to do because of careful planning and hard work.

It is possible that all of the above explains why I am always looking for something new to do. Whatever the reason, new things to do at every stage have added a great deal of zest to my life.

Speech to Retiring SUNY Albany Faculty Members
April 3

Sponsors of the "Ready or Not" retirees program asked me to speak about second careers. I was viewed as an ex-faculty member who has successfully negotiated an exciting second career.

That's really the way it came across, judging from the questions before and after the session.

I described my "stumbling" into an archaeological dig twelve years ago (Flower Dew 100 site, Virginia) and how that caused me to develop a careful plan to gain experience in the new field over the ten-year period before retirement. I shared my resume and the Bethlehem Archaeology Group letterhead. Also, it seemed best to show some slides of the Nicoll-Sill site and talk about our new laboratory where we work on artifacts. Finally, I stressed the need for training for a new career and described my teaching at HVCC and work in the master's program in Classical Archaeology at SUNY Albany.

They agreed, I have a very full life.

New Directions in Summer Digging
June 26

The crew is slowly drifting back (school is out, vacations are over), and about nine people are coming to dig on a regular basis.

William Goes, a farmer still working the land adjacent to our Nicoll-Sill site, invited us to dig on the land and look for Indian dwellings. All of us believe there may be some on the land since so many tools have been found there. Since the land is part of the original Nicoll-Sill property, we accepted his invitation.

Ann Jacobs, right, interviewing Mary Elizabeth Van Oostenbrugge at James B. Lyon site.

Additionally, we have begun to explore land on the opposite side of the Vloman Kill where some 1780 Dutch warehouse buildings are alleged to have stood.

Finally, we are examining the land around the oldest home on Van Wie's Point...to see if we should dig there.

Starting a New Archaeology Site at the Lyon Estate
July 26-28

(Letter to Mrs. Mary E. Van Oostenbrugge of Selkirk)

Dear Mary,

We all appreciate your invitation to explore the old Lyon estate and the use of the printed materials you shared with us. We accept your invitation and plan to begin on August 28th. Our usual hours are 9:30 A.M. to 3:30 P.M. and we work on Tuesdays and Thursdays.

During the test exploration period this fall we will

1) search every part of the property for artifacts on the surface—with a special emphasis on the areas you indicated that contain dumps and trash pits. This usually provides a better basis for determining where to concentrate the group's time during the following season.

2) examine all of the papers you loaned us carefully and look for additional sources of information about the Lyon fam-

ily...particularly relationships between the family's life-style and the progress of the printing industry in this area.

3) conduct lengthy interviews with you, Bob (brother), and any relatives who you believe can provide helpful information. We would like to record all such interviews where the person being interviewed is comfortable with such a process.

Original pilings of Winne Dock.

4) share all of the information and conclusions with our executive director, Ralph Wood, and with the town historian, James Morgan. If they agree with our conclusions, we will prepare a "Statement of Intent and Agreement" drawn mainly from ideas on pages 46-47 in Ivor Noel Hume's *Historical Archaeology*, which was designed to protect the landowner's interests and to encourage serious research. We will ask you to examine a rough draft, make any changes you deem necessary, and sign the final version some time early in the spring of 1985.

I will be part of the small exploration team one or two hours every day. I will be working on the Lyon site, but Ann Jacobs will be in charge. If you are unable to reach her on any matter concerning the test exploration, please call me.

We've been wanting to involve ourselves in projects that emphasize the relationships between early Bethlehem residents and industries in the area. A preliminary review of the printed materials you shared underscores James B. Lyon's key role in the advancement of the printing industry in New York and in the nation. His life and that of his family and descendants is an important chapter in Bethlehem's history. We'd like to document it more carefully for possible publication during our bicentennial year.

The Winne Site
July 31

We're looking into new areas for the Bethlehem Archaeology Group and the Winne estate on the Hudson River is another prospect.

1857 home of Barent S. Winne, Sr., on Hudson River, now owned by Ted and Sherry Putney.

National Republican Convention (President Reagan Nominated for Second Term)
August 23

Predictably, President Reagan was nominated (on a single ballot) for a second term last night.

Everything was sweetness and light. He is a guru or king for the Republicans in a very real sense.

John Winne was an assessor on our first town board in 1794.

The Winne family established a dock/warehouse business on the Hudson River in the 1800s. It spurred a lot of trade south to New York City and served as a major outlet for area farmers and manufacturers.

We've decided to do some test exploration work at the former Winne estate, now owned by Ted and Sherry Putney, and a letter similar to the one presented on July 26 in this diary was mailed to the Putneys yesterday.

We're looking forward to new goals in August and September.

He is personally popular with the people, and this could mean millions of switch-over votes by Democrats this November.

He is likely to get my vote, and possibly Coleen's (although she is not happy with some of his actions over the past four years).

Even so, as the nation's founders envisaged, Congress has chosen to limit his options.

He may do as Roosevelt did in the 1930s and 1940s: appeal to the people over the heads of legislators. I hope he does.

Television Program
August 27

Carol King, director of the Bethlehem Channel, asked me to do one of her

"Conversations" programs with her, and we taped for about forty minutes today.

Her questions gave me a chance to explain why our Bethlehem Archaeology Group was organized, something about the specialties various members of the group have, why our local digs are important, and a host of related things.

It was fun to do. This is the second time they have selected me to do a program for our local public access channel.

I sometimes wonder why archaeology is so glamorous in the public eye and my former field is so unglamorous. I was not asked to do a TV program once in eighteen years at SUNY Albany.

First Day at the Lyon Site
August 28

We've been waiting for weeks to begin work at the Lyon site, and Ann Jacobs and I finally broke away for a few hours to prepare the south garden section of the site for some test digging.

My usual manner of narrowing a huge area (or limiting the actual ground we excavate) is to do a careful surface search and follow the search with a representative sampling, using three-foot-square test pits. This usually helps

us determine where to concentrate a large number of staff member hours the following summer.

So we'll do some test squares on Thursday.

The wildlife around the new site is beautiful: deer approached within 150 feet, rabbits scampered about, chipmunks raced through our new paths in the grass, and dozens of squirrels and birds chattered throughout the day.

The Dutch of Albany
September 6

All of us of Dutch origin (including me) wonder where the Dutch went!

The Dutch were among the first to arrive in the early 1600s, followed by the Irish, Germans, and Italians.

Today, the Irish make up about one-fourth of the population of Albany County, with Germans, blacks, Italians, and English almost equally divided at about fifteen percent, and with French and Polish equally divided at about seven percent.

Most statistical listings don't even include the Dutch today, their percentage is so small.

I've often wondered why they drifted away when so much of the rich history (names of streets, buildings, celebrations, etc.) they left with us is still here for all to see.

My name was Brouwer back in those days. Then, we became Browers and now Brewers.

William Kennedy
September 9

The author of *Ironweed* (Pulitzer Prize and National Book Critics Award, 1984) is an Albanian and has lived all of his life in the area. That is not surprising. It is surprising, however, to hear about a well-known author concentrating all of his talent on his hometown (*O Albany!, Legs, Billy Phelan's Greatest Game*).

Two years ago, he was scratching out a living as a part-time teacher of English at SUNY Albany. We sat together at an occasional faculty meeting and few people noticed him in the Campus Center auditorium with a thousand faculty.

Today he is a full professor with tenure, and the MacArthur Foundation has given him $264,000, a five-year, tax-free grant to continue his writing. Also, he was asked to write a movie script, and two of his novels have been purchased for movies.

He has just finished a four-day weekend of honors (by city officials, people in the arts, etc.). He deserves the recognition.

My Recurring Dreams: Reflections of Life's Pressures?
September 12-13

In my twenties (roughly 1944-1950), a frequent dream found me floating in the water in pitch blackness with not the slightest idea of where I was or even what kind of thing I was floating on. The dream was accompanied by feelings of intense fear. Coleen said she would occasionally find me at the window trying to get out — a fact that caused her to be fearful when we lived in a fifth story apartment in New York City in 1946-1947. This dream is probably related to a forced jump out of a training plane into the Gulf of Mexico during my Air Force days.

Another recurring dream has stayed with me most of my working life (1955-1985). The theme is always the same although the setting varies. My home or some familiar figure (often Coleen) is at the top of a steep hill and there is no road, only brush and dense undergrowth. I'm struggling for hours to reach home or Coleen; it seems like every obstacle in the world is in my path: slippery grass, quicksand type soil here and there, prickly, thorny bushes, a huge, fallen tree blocking the only path up the hill, and the like. I often wake up awash with perspiration. It is usually accompanied by intense feelings of frustration. I don't know why I have this dream. The psychologist in me hypothesizes that it may result from unrealistic goals I set for myself but, then, I've achieved most of the goals I've set for myself so why would it continue?

Another regular dream is embarrassingly narcissistic. The president of the United States decides it is in the best interests of our country to reveal the identity of one of our most astute double agents—me—in the hope that Russia will do the same (usually they've pledged to do this in advance). He retires me from years of faithful service simultaneously as the Russian president (chairman of the Presidium) does the same; each touting the number of lives we saved in wars, the daring exploits we engaged in to do our jobs, the number of languages we spoke (seventeen in my case), etc. Why I dreamed this stupid dream so many times between 1960-1975 or so, is beyond me. I can't even guess why. Inadequate recognition for my work? I don't know.

Mrs. Carl Lermann
October 22

Mrs. Lermann is a niece of Barent Staats Winne, a town of Bethlehem pioneer. He lived in the house around which my crew has been digging over the past two months.

She is a seventy-seven-year-old individualist with such a gift for gab that a planned two-hour interview stretched into four hours.

Mrs. Lermann is wealthy, with a residence in Florida along with the home at Chestnut Hill in Loudonville where she granted the interview.

She has dozens of papers, many of them with signatures of famous colonial men and women: Alexander Hamilton, Aaron Burr, and the like. She also has many pieces of furniture that came out of the old Winne house.

We asked permission to microfilm her collection. I hope she grants our wish. We need her papers badly.

New Lab Volunteers
December 4

John Kohl has been a chemist all his working life. Three months ago, he learned about our group's work in the lab and offered his help. He comes two full days a week and is slowly filling the role of conservator. We use the title "conservation specialist" since he doesn't have the formal training; however, he is mending ceramics, planning a system for removing rust from iron artifacts, and doing many of the things I've seen conservators do elsewhere.

William Wasserstrom started with us in an adult education class three years ago and began to work part-time in the field last summer. He now comes to the lab almost every Saturday morning and is gradually working his way

James Engleman with kaolin clay pipe at Bethlehem Archaeology Group laboratory.

into the position of artifact analyst for jewelry, coins, and beads.

James Engleman heard my talk to the Retired Men's Professional Group last spring, came out to dig a half-day a week last summer and now serves as Ralph Wood's assistant clay pipe specialist in the lab.

We lose a person occasionally, but seem to be gaining more than we lose.

**Bethlehem Prehistory
(Goes Farm Site)**
December 17

Dr. Alice Kenney was asked to write a statement on Bethlehem for Albany County's Tricentennial volume. She knows of our work on the Goes farm and asked me to send her something on Bethlehem's prehistoric period.

It wasn't easy.

A review of the literature failed to reveal even one prehistoric excavation in this community, so I offered

Field director, Floyd Brewer, right, showing pictures of Indian stone tools to Pieter Van Derzee, landowner, center, with Pieter's son, Jay, looking on.

some sketchy impressions based on our analysis of about five hundred stone tools which have been turned up by William Goes's plow.

It looks as though the earliest Indians here were Mahicans, an Algonkian speaking tribe that used crude tools as early as 4000 B.C., but later became very proficient agriculturalists. Iroquoian-speaking tribes were here, at times, but it is not possible to pinpoint dates from surface finds. [As page 18 in *Bethlehem Revisited* clearly demonstrates, these early impressions were way off the mark.]

NICOLL - SILL HOUSE, RIVER ELEVATION.
CEDAR HILL. MARK L. PECKHAM, NOVEMBER 8, 1981.

Reality set in. Despite all the volunteer efforts, BAG needed money. The town of Bethlehem came through with $750 and, in the process, Floyd found himself involved to some extent in local politics.

On a personal level, he started to record his own income and expenses and was delighted to find that the quality of life for him and Coleen suffered no adverse effects from his early retirement at age sixty-two.

All in all, this was a year of satisfaction.

Budget For the Bethlehem Archaeology Group at Last
January 2

Our group has received considerable help from the town of Bethlehem: space, lights, heat, and a little cash for plumbing repairs. However, we need a small operating budget for lab and field equipment.

A motion to "Adopt a resolution authorizing the town supervisor to enter into a contract with the Bethlehem Archaeology Group—$750.00" was passed at a meeting of town board today.

Ralph Wood and I attended the meeting in case questions were raised. None were.

At long last we can buy little things without spending our own money.

Local Politics
January 4

My new career in archaeology takes me into politics now and then. It matters a great deal who is elected town supervisor and town historian. One appointment in either of these positions with heavily negative attitudes toward the Bethlehem Archaeology Group's plans and goals could wipe us out.

So I find myself going to town meetings where nominees are being considered and sticking out my hand to meet new faces.

The supervisor for the last seven years, Tom Corrigan, resigned this week. A councilman named Robert Hendrick seemed to be favored for the top job, so Ralph [Wood] and I circulated at the organizational meeting last Wednesday and got a chance to talk with Hendrick at some length. He likes what we're doing. Naturally, we're going to work for his election over the next few months.

Financial Records
January 10

Beginning this month I have begun to keep a record of our income and expenses to see if our spending in retirement has changed substantially from five years ago. At the moment, it seems that we are living about the same as always.

This is very different from our expectations and fears about eighteen months before retirement, when I was struggling through the issue of whether or not to retire at age sixty-two. I wanted to give SUNY Albany at least a year's advance notice.

I remember worrying about whether or not we could have a reasonable quality of life if I retired at sixty-two at a considerably smaller retirement income figure from both Teachers Insurance Annuity of America and Social Security than if I were to continue working until age sixty-five. I am now doubly glad about the decision to retire early.

How We Spend An Average of $300 Every Two Weeks
January 11

We believe in a budget approach to regular biweekly expenses and put the following amounts in budget envelopes every other Wednesday:

Budget envelope for:	Amount
1. Groceries: including paper goods, cleaning and kitchen supplies & cosmetics	$110.00
2. Clothing	25.00
3. Recreation: mostly dinners out, movies	30.00
4. Church	18.00
5. Gasoline	20.00
6. Allowance/Coleen	35.00
7. Allowance/Floyd	35.00
8. Newspapers	14.00
9. Miscellaneous, e.g., stamps, drugs (drugs are a minor expense, since we pay only $1.00 per prescription under the New York State Drug Plan)	5.00
10. Contingencies	8.00
	$300.00

Almost all other items are paid by check.

Charlotte Wilcoxen (Ceramics Specialist and Dutch Historian)
February 9

Charlotte Wilcoxen and I worked together at the Parks Department Archaeology Laboratory on Peebles Island in Waterford. We're good friends, and I greatly admire her as a person (friendly, shares feelings readily, honest) and as a scholar. She knows a lot about pottery.

She came out to our lab this morning to look over the thousands of pottery samples we've recovered from the Nicoll-Sill site. I wanted her to check on my judgment as the group's earthenware specialist, as well as to check on Carol Wock's analysis of porcelain

Charlotte Wilcoxen.

my analysis of the Goes Farm Indian tool collection. [The Goes Farm is in Cedar Hill on the Hudson River.]

Predictably, he was less critical of this draft mostly because I had handled the criticisms he made about draft #2.

Little by little we're moving closer to a prehistory statement on the town of Bethlehem. Prior to six months ago there was nothing.

It is still hard for me to understand a few key points (which I plan to check out with the current state archaeologist, Dr. Robert Funk). Even so, I'm learning fast.

shards, and to look over our stoneware artifacts.

At eighty plus, she is an amazing person. She pointed out numerous errors in our judgment, confirmed some really important facts about the lifestyles of early members of the Nicoll-Sill families, and filled us full of choice pottery stories.

I plan to enroll in her next class on pottery, beginning in April.

The statement should be acceptable to all three of us since we all live in Bethlehem.

Robert Hendrick
March 11

The new Bethlehem town supervisor, Bob Hendrick, took over his duties on February 2. He knows the town well, having been a member of town board for the past three years.

Ralph Wood and I met with him for an hour this morning to:

Dr. William Ritchie
March 3

As mentioned earlier in my diaries, Bill Ritchie deserves the title "Dean of Northeastern Archaeologists." I met with him today to go over draft #3 of

1) bring him up to date on the progress we have made in the Bethlehem Archaeology Group;

2) seek permission to make another presentation to town board

J. Robert Hendrick, Jr.

Second, a little regret that legislators on the national scene don't have the guts to cut the rate of increase in Social Security benefits out of fear that it might hurt their chances for reelection.

Third, a little relief that we will be able to maintain the same quality of life (if good health continues) that we've enjoyed for years. Our combined Social Security income after June 1st, about $830 per month, will mean opportunities to travel, to buy a new car or piece of furniture when we need to, and generally, to have those little luxuries that make life something to look forward to.

Overall, the system is good, but too generous for many, including us.

in May, when we hope to gain the board's approval for a series of motions or actions that would launch us into a bicentennial publication firmly and officially.

He likes our ideas.

How I Feel About Social Security Benefits
March 17

First, a little guilty that young working people are going to have to pay a higher percentage of their salary to support my generation; far more than I had to pay, percentage-wise, to support my father's generation.

How Are the Elderly "Fixed" in 1985?
March 18

From talks with Mark and sources such as the American Association of Retired Persons, newspapers, and magazines, it seems that only a small percentage live below the poverty line today. The AARP's figures are more negative than other sources, but my impression is that only about 3 or 4 percent of the elderly fall below the poverty line compared to 10 percent or so of the rest of the population.

This is a tremendous change from the 1960s, when I heard horror stories about elderly poverty that encouraged

Left to right: James Engleman, Ann Jacobs, Floyd Brewer, Ralph Wood.

me to make conservative decisions with regard to our security in old age. So my impression is that most elderly today are pretty well fixed.

If so, why shouldn't their income be taxed like any other income? It would certainly help reduce the deficit, which is the overriding concern in my view.

First Regular Meeting
Bethlehem Archaeology Group
April 16

Ralph Wood convened the first regular meeting under the new constitution today at 3:45 P.M.

We've had meetings in the past, but it feels more like an official group when you begin to meet the requirements of a constitution, making its way through the state Education Department, for the status of incorporation.

Seven officers and trustees attended: Jean Adell, Ben and Virginia French, Ann Jacobs, William Wasserstrom, Ralph Wood, and I.

The nominating committee chairman (Wasserstrom) gave a report, Ralph Wood provided an updated report on our negotiations for a contract with the town [Bethlehem] and more information on the status of our incorporation application. I discussed the importance of keeping up with archaeology literature and the process of writing drafts regarding the meaning of our artifacts.

My Memories of Vietnam
April 28

In a few days, it will be ten years since the end of the Vietnam War; newspapers, magazines, and television programs are full of references to the war.

How did I feel about it ten years ago? It is not difficult to recall my main impressions.

First, disillusioned undergraduates milled around my office/classroom building every day planning this or that confrontation with administrative officials. I often wondered why they didn't go to Washington where all of the decisions were being made instead of spinning their wheels on campus. Even graduate students in my classes were harder to work with. The only time I ever walked out of a class was in May 1970 when my students became unruly and overbearing. I said as I left the classroom, "Come and get me when you decide you want to learn what I have to offer." Three days later, a delegation of my students asked me to come back to class.

Horrible Pictures

No war is ever pretty but this one came into our living room on television every night. More than fifty-eight thousand Americans died and many were shown dead on the television screen.

Who can ever forget pictures of the Vietnamese villagers at My Lai, massacred by American troops (1968) or those children on fire from an American napalm bomb, running down Route 1 near Trang Bang (1972), the use of awesome firepower on flimsy little huts, the American soldiers who called themselves "Tunnel Rats" as they went after "Charlie" (the enemy) in underground tunnels, and dozens upon dozens of pictures of American efforts to stamp out an implacable foe—only to find him reappearing again. It must have seemed like a reincarnation of the Alamo for President Lyndon Johnson.

I wondered early on, if Vietnam was that important to us, why didn't we send air support to the French at Dien Bien Phu? It might have turned the tide for the French, and they would still be a bulwark for the West in that part of the world. (A dream, maybe, but now we'll never know.)

And For What?

On many occasions, I found myself in agreement with the students: President Johnson and, to a lesser extent, the Congress got us into a long, bloody war without sufficient public support. But how does a president determine whether or not he has such support in a democracy (which airs its dirty linen in public, thereby offering the enemy a great advantage)?

My answer at the time—really a hope —was that he was talking—or should be talking—with key congressional leaders about a formal declaration of war. Why not?

Did we just want to *slow* the expansion of communism in the area or did we want to *firmly limit* such expansion? A formal declaration of war— with appropriate assurances to China and the Soviets that we were content to confine the conflict to Vietnam— would have cleared the air and untied the hands of our generals. Johnson had a chance to win such approval from the Congress at the height of the Vietnamese Tet offensive in February (or early in 1968), but he muffed the ball. "He didn't want to win; he only wanted not to lose," as President Nixon so aptly put it in his book, *No More Vietnams.*

My First Political Meeting
May 13

Ralph Wood's son, Bruce, bought a fistful of tickets to the Town of Bethlehem Republican Party's annual fund-raiser and gave us two of them.

It was a $15 per person cocktail party to help finance Bob Hendrick's campaign for town supervisor this fall.

To use the word campaign is a bit of a joke here because no Democrat has ever been elected to a town office [in recent years]. Anyway, they go through the motions, swap a few charges, and the citizens vote. Sometimes the school board elections are more exciting. At least these positions are seriously contested.

Anyhow, I drank a little wine, had some fancy hors d'oeuvres, and talked with many town officials and members of the board.

By 6:30 P.M., a full hour into the affair, it was so packed with people that I decided to leave—no easy task because of the numbers. By 6:45, I made it to the door and squeezed by the town supervisor and two board members. Free at last!

Women at the Military Academies
May 22

Our neighbor's daughter, Maura O'Brien, entered West Point three years ago, and we've followed her progress ever since. I've been curious: will the average woman stay in the service after graduation?

We'll have to wait and see what Maura does after her five years of obligatory service in the army.

Maura O'Brien.

Overall, women have been in the academies since 1976, and stories about them say their attrition rate (40 percent) is only slightly higher than the rate for men (37 percent).

It seems to me that women face a tougher uphill fight to profit from service academy training. Family conflicts and the combat-exclusion rule would be near the top of the list as reasons for not remaining in the service after graduation.

Maura has also learned that executive recruiters from the corporate world want academy graduates badly. Many corporations are willing to match or improve upon their estimated annual salaries as officers, about $30,000.

The Detoxification of America
May 23

Some ten years ago I began to emphasize the importance for student personnel administrators to offer an alternative to alcoholic beverages at college parties. I was convinced that a nationwide grass roots campaign to de-emphasize alcohol was in the beginning stage and would eventually become the "in thing." All of us endured a lot of ridicule from undergraduate students at the time. For most, to get "bombed" at a party was a right and a privilege. But we kept after it.

As it turned out, the changing attitudes on campuses toward encouraging alternatives to alcoholic beverages is but one small part of a national movement that is succeeding beyond our wildest dreams. Now *water*, yes *water*, has for many replaced liquor, beer, or wine at many a business luncheon, and is creeping into parties everywhere at all age levels. It must have some "fizz" and a pleasant taste (such as Perrier, Saratoga, or Canada Dry). I can only say hooray! At last!

Allison Bennett
(History Writer, Par Excellence)
June 5

Former town historian Allison Bennett stopped by the lab today to discuss a possible writing role with the soon-to-be-formed Bethlehem Bicentennial Publication Committee, the writing arm of our group.

She was very impressed with everything we had done to gear up for a factual history and said she would consider the matter and give me an answer within a few weeks.

Allison writes the local history stories for our newspaper, *The Spotlight*. Most people feel she has found a good balance between good journalism (to create reader interest) and historical detail (to help readers recall the key aspects of any historical subject).

If a member of town board asks me, "Who's going to write this volume?" I'd like to say, "Allison Bennett will be one of the writers!"

Early Finds at the Winne Site
June 13

We worked all day at the Winne site on the Hudson River in Cedar Hill, a hamlet in the Town of Bethlehem.

Members of the group uncovered a trash pit some one hundred feet away from the rear entrance to the present 1857 home. Creamware, pearlware, and porcelain fragments date the pit to the late 1700s and early 1800s. The pearlware has a green edge, indicating a color preference of Adam Winne and his wife (since they had access to the same kind of table pottery with a blue edge). A late 1700s redware bowl was also unearthed.

Even more helpful in describing the Winne life-style of this period was the iron pot "crane" used to swing pots into the fire for cooking food. Also, a large piece of an iron pot was found with the crane. When we started the excavation, we knew absolutely nothing about the family during this time period except land transfer information. Now we at least have a start.

On Father's Day...
and Changing Values
June 17

Father's Day has come and gone about thirty-five times for me, and my feelings about it have changed over the years.

I still like the attention and would never call for eliminating the focus on fathers [for] at least one day each year, if for no other reason than to reinforce the importance of families in our society.

But the role of fathers has changed subtly over the past thirty-five years. In a sense, descriptions of modern fathers come closer to what I've always thought they should be—just the opposite of the stern, macho, boss-like figure of the past—to a partner in the child-nurturing process, a help-mate for mothers, a planner and problem-solver, yes, but in consultation with wives and children when they reach the age of reason.

Why shouldn't dads be there when a knee is scraped (the same as moms)? Why shouldn't dads worry about whether or not junior should play football (as well as moms), and change diapers, get a meal now and then, support the children by attending school functions, supervise a Boy Scout troop—and all those things that only (mainly) moms used to do?

There is absolutely no good reason why dads can't be in control of their own destiny, do the things that give them pleasure in life, *as well as* help mom raise the children—especially if mom is working. Today, so many moms are working that a new philosophy is almost a must.

My son Jeffrey comes close to the ideal; he works hard but he also helps out at home. The job interferes now and then (as mine did); however, he has found a good balance.

I thoroughly approve of the modern roles society is shaping for dads. Children will have a healthier role model and are more likely to be successful in *all* the roles they take on in life.

Ann Jacobs (Assistant Field Director)
June 20

It was good to see Ann Jacobs back at the Lyon site [in Cedar Hill] today. She missed several months of lab work and the opening of the digging season because of pressures at home.

Ann Jacobs.

Her mother, age eighty-eight, passed away last week, just a week or so after Ann's son was married in Iowa....

She is in charge of the Lyon site, by means of which an effort will be made to re-create the life-style of a well-known Albany printer (1858-1929) who used Bethlehem as a bedroom community.

With Ann back in charge, things will go smoothly. She's bright, well organized, and a loyal, hardworking member of the Bethlehem Archaeology Group.

Changing Sexual Patterns
(Healthy or Unhealthy?)
June 27

In my final ten years of teaching at SUNY Albany, the sexual revolution unfolded in American society and ignited many hot discussions in my classes. How to help counselors in training learn better ways of helping undergraduate students, particularly those in residence halls, deal with the underlying tensions was a major goal in my counselor/training classes.

Years ago we used to joke with the rhyme:

Hogamus, higamus,
Men are polygamous;
Higamus, hogamus,
Women monogamous.

Or something close to this. I may have spelled the words incorrectly.

No longer is such a joke appropriate.

Women clearly feel more free to have sex outside marriage, and premarital experience is the rule rather than the exception. Women have, in part at least, been freed from the "tyranny of their reproductive biology," a demand voiced and recorded by an author of one of the books I used in class in the early 1970s. Women are now looking at a range of options available to them as opposed to getting married and having children right away. Indeed, it seems feasible now to consider hav-

ing fertilization take place outside the body—an extreme option but likely to be adopted by many women when the technical problems and moral issues are resolved. Also, women can foreseeably reduce or eliminate the long-held preference for a male as a first child.

On the surface, it appears that the "free ride" many of my male students were joking about in the 1970s may not become such a funny situation for males in our society. Their response to the female challenge for a major shift in the issue of sexual dominance—how and when children should be started—could well become the major issue betwen the sexes in the 1990s.

Clearly, sterilization has evolved as a popular form of contraception. Many men in my circle of acquaintances twenty to thirty years ago considered a vasectomy, but few followed through, including me.

Today, hundreds of thousands of men in their forties are having vasectomies. In part, at least, this is their way of achieving the sexual freedom enjoyed by their children. And women are having tubal ligations in great numbers.

Newer films, books, and stimulation from the changing sexual mores we so often hear, see, or read about have encouraged wider experimentation

43

coming ingrained in the psyches of older Americans who, in turn, are making it easier for their children and grandchildren to live the life-style they choose for themselves. This is tension-relieving in character and [promotes a] more constructive sexual dialogue among the generations.

Mary Celia Estey Brewer (1893-1945)
August 1

My mother died on this date forty years ago. It was a difficult period for all of us in the family because we loved her very much.

Why? Well, all of her children knew she cared for us, that she would be at home when we needed her, that she would see we had good meals and get off to school on time, that she would help us out if we got into trouble with the neighbors, and that she would mend our clothes when we tore them. But, most of all, that we could count on her for love and affection.

I've often wondered how all of us would have fared if we had had a working mother who was away from home a lot. I notice lonely, latchkey children in the neighborhood who come home from school every day to an empty home. Will they make a good adjustment in life?

Possibly, but if I had the privilege of choosing, I would choose my mother who was always home when we needed her.

Mary Estey Brewer.

with and enjoyment of sex. We're more likely to tell one another how what the other does makes us feel— unheard of in the 1940s and 1950s.

We no longer feel it is "unhealthy" for young people to have sex before marriage (I never did) and we are far more tolerant of different sexual life-styles— such as homosexuality—than we were previously.

I doubt seriously that the sexual revolution will make sex redundant and males irrelevant.

Rather, I believe a healthy transformation is under way, and a more constructive attitude toward sex is be-

Our Life in 1945
August 3

The trip to Maine for Mom's illness and funeral was by train. Coleen and I were living at 701 Centerville Avenue in Belleville, Ill., where I served as an instructor at Scott Field. I taught pilots, navigators, and bombardiers how to use navigation and radio equipment aboard B-24s and B-17s.

Coleen got $50 a month as a serviceman's wife and managed to put every single allotment check in the bank. We drew on this account to finance a week in a motel in Houlton, Maine, as well as meals and the train fare.

We lived on her salary of $25 a week (at Swift & Company): $3 of her weekly salary was deducted for Blue Cross, she spent an average of $4 to $5 a week for groceries, and paid our landlords, Mr. and Mrs. Herman Ulrich, $9 a week for a single room, shared kitchen and bathroom privileges, and Coleen's busfare to East St. Louis was $1 every day she worked, or about $5 a week. There was very little left for recreation; however, my pay as a serviceman increased from $50 a month to $75 when we left in 1946 and we were able to eat out occasionally and take short trips out of town on my salary.

**My Feelings About the Bomb
Forty Years Ago**
August 5

Coleen, my brother Gerald, and I were on the train on this day forty years ago

when news of the first atomic bomb, dropped on Hiroshima, Japan, was spread by the conductor and trainman.

There was jubilation in the aisles: shouting, loud talk, exclamations like, "Now, we'll win!" and general anxiety release. I joined in some of this—happy that it might save thousands of American lives, relieved that many of us would be released from the service sooner than expected—all the while unaware how much damage had been inflicted on the Japanese and their city, but feeling a little like, "Well, they started it; now, by God, we're going to end it."

As we got off the train in St. Louis (and Gerald continued on to Texas), my thoughts turned to deeper issues. I was young (twenty-four) but capable of feeling the horror of the act and concerned that the power balance among nations that eventually acquire "the bomb" might radically alter all future conflict—even prevent it, I hoped.

We thought a lot about the atomic bomb in the months that followed August 5, 1945. Was it excessively cruel? Were the estimates that a million lives were saved by dropping the bomb realistic? Would we, our children, and grandchildren always live in fear that a similar bomb might be dropped on us some year hence?

Soon after discharge from the Air Force in 1946 and sometime after I began

Ben French excavating Mahican hearth.

master's degree study at Teachers College, Columbia University, I read John Hersey's *Hiroshima*. It was an eye opener. For the first time, the U.S. public got a down-to-earth picture of the impact of the bomb on several Japanese families. It was a living hell. Worse, there were early signs that survivors would be rejected like lepers by their fellow citizens. Some 200,000 died within a few weeks; a total of 340,000 died within five years at both Hiroshima and Nagasaki.

Was it worth it? Maybe it was. At the very least, fear of the bomb has prevented a major superpower conflict for forty years.

First Hearth at the Goes Site
August 24

Ben French and John Gold uncovered the beginning of an Indian hearth last Tuesday and continued excavating the area today.

All of the earmarks of an ancient hearth appeared this morning as they moved down below the plow zone about five or six inches.

Rim pieces of very old Indian pottery appeared along with a lot of charcoal and, later, some large pieces of animal bone—some of it burned.

I grew more and more elated as the morning wore on. Enough organic material, especially bone, was uncovered to obtain a radio carbon 14 date on the hearth. Dating labs ask for twenty-five to thirty grams and, as nearly as we could tell in the field, we collected almost that amount today.

Now, if some stone tools are found around the hearth an inch or two further down, we can date them. The hearth should be finished by next Tuesday P.M.

The Job I Left in 1983
August 25

It was easy for me to retire in May 1983. Working at the college level, particularly in a university setting, had taken on a number of tension-producing aspects. It was no longer fun. Too much pressure to write. Too little recognition of quality teaching. Declining budgets resulted in less service to students—fewer social programs which brought students and faculty together, fewer phone calls to students interning in other cities (because of a declining budget for phones).

Higher education is changing for professors. Yes, there will be more jobs for young people in the 1990s but there will be much less security—many fewer tenured positions. Our faculty was "organized" in my last five years of teaching, and faculty unions are likely to grow in militancy and power.

The decline of tenure (which has a positive side) and the increasing influence of faculty unions are likely to alter radically the traditional relationships between faculty and college administrations...mostly for the worse in my judgment.

Death of Thomas "Ed" Mulligan, Jr. (Former Town Historian)
December 16

Over the past few weeks I have been visiting the home of Ed Mulligan on Monday evenings to go through his papers with his children.

He died last April 22, and I offered to help his children examine his voluminous files. My hope is to include brief biographical information on all former town historians in the bicentennial history.

My Long-standing Aversion to Neckties and Tight Clothing
December 17

We often see Chinese on television and I usually think, how *plain but comfortable* their clothes look. Obviously, Chinese clothing styles wouldn't go over well in America, but why can't we meet them halfway?

Getting rid of neckties for men would be a good beginning. I can tolerate a necktie in December through February, but even then, I often wonder why someone invented them. So many men wear atrocious, garish-looking ties. In many instances, they don't even enhance one's appearance.

Why give people the feeling of being cinched (or corseted for that matter)? Some types and brands of underwear leave me feeling bound and strangled in the wrong places as I try to sit comfortably.

Long ago, I decided to wear a tie as little as possible, and I've been buying thin, knit (absorbent) pajamas and wearing them under my trousers in place of the usual cotton underwear. I cut off the legs in March.

So much for style in America. The designers and other influencers of fashion ought to ask more often what the people want.

Division of Labor
Between Husband and Wife
in Retirement
December 21-23

It seems to me that the division of labor between husband and wife should change in retirement (at the point both are retired).

During the first six months of my retirement Coleen joked a lot about this matter— things like, "Well you're retired but I can't retire," or "You're still busy; things haven't really changed all that much."

I *was* very busy that fall. It wasn't possible for me to extricate myself completely from commitments made before retirement. It took a few months for me to learn how to relax and still work at meaningful tasks.

Even so, I began to say to Coleen, "You should feel retired as well...not work as hard...expect more help from me around the house."

She agreed, but how could we find just the right balance so I wouldn't be underfoot too much, so she could continue to have private times alone and with her friends?

Just talking about it seems to help, and, gradually, over a period of two and a half years, we've settled into a different routine. She seems to like it and so do I.

Coleen has continued her heavy involvement in the life of the church, has her friends over and visits them, enjoys her monthly gourmet group luncheons and attends an occasional women's event, e.g., teas at other churches. Also, she arranges time away from home, and sometimes has lunch at the Delaware Plaza shopping center when she gets her hair fixed.

I have established regular days away from home for archaeology: Tuesday, Thursday, and Saturday A.M. Sometimes I leave for the same purpose on other days but usually only for a few hours and only when I'm not needed at home. I try to be around when the car is needed.

Together we attend Bethlehem Historical Association and related program meetings, and we are doing more things than in the past. It was unheard of in the past to shop on a Monday or Wednesday afternoon. I either had classes or was preparing for them. Now we go out for an occasional lunch during the week and to a program or movie immediately after. We shop at odd times. In a sense, there is no routine. We do as the spirit desires whenever the mood strikes. That's nice.

Coleen has continued to wash the windows and keep the house clean. She makes her own bed and always prepares dinner. She is still the cook because she is good at it. She usually washes the dishes except on weekends and when I notice she's tired. She takes care of the shrubbery and flower beds and occasionally rakes leaves or grass. She makes her own breakfast. She pays all of the bills, and she also does all the laundry.

I have continued to wash the car and have begun to make my own bed regularly.... I always mow the lawn and rake most of the leaves and grass. I always make my own breakfast, sometimes lunch. I do all that is needed to keep the car well maintained. Also, I shovel most of the snow.

FREIGHT HOUSE, DELAWARE & HUDSON RR.
SLINGERLANDS. MARK L. PECKHAM, AUGUST 10, 1994.

4 *Nineteen Hundred Eighty-Six*

The consummate organizer and planner, Floyd shepherded some of the archaeology lab's history room volunteers into a research committee. Their annotated bibliography of records and materials germane to local history would back up the work of yet-to-be-identified writers for the town of Bethlehem's bicentennial history. Consequently, Floyd was gratified to see his groundwork paying off when, in late February, the town approved the formation of a Bicentennial Commission, with a publication sub-committee.

Meanwhile, Floyd was also striving to bring order to BAG—with a constitution, regular meetings, a budget, and a strong leader.

His meticulous planning also spilled over into his personal life, as he and Coleen honed their shopping skills—browsing for bargains in the huge discount stores, comparing insurance and health care providers, and taking an interest in electronics technology.

Discount Stores
January 25

It seems that discount stores are popping up everywhere peddling everything from groceries to clothes. I don't know how big the movement is nationally, but it is likely that sales run in the billions of dollars.

Coleen and I visited BJ's, supposedly the largest discount store under one roof, selling everything from groceries to garbage cans and tools to television sets. They require you to become a member of BJ's Wholesale Club. You have two options: fill out a lengthy form giving them your bank account numbers and amounts or pay by cash.

We chose cash. Coleen was turned off by the store. Many things we wanted to buy come in lots of a dozen or several pounds.

We often would have bought an item if smaller quantities had been available. A sharp eye can spot bargains, however, and I spotted some decent padded stacking chairs and bought three of them for about $11.50 each, plus 5 percent and plus tax. Perhaps the 5 percent is their profit.

Education   Department

Extension of Provisional Charter

BETHLEHEM ARCHAEOLOGY GROUP

THIS INSTRUMENT WITNESSETH That the Regents of The University of the State of New York have amended the

    <u>**Voted**</u>, That the provisional charter of **Bethlehem Archaeology Group**, located at Delmar, county of Albany, state of New York, which was granted by the Board of Regents on September 20, 1985, be and the same hereby is extended to July 27, 1995; and that prior to that date an application for the further extension of this provisional charter or for an absolute charter will be entertained by the Regents, but, in the event that such application is not made, then after July 27, 1995 and upon notice by the Regents, this provisional charter shall terminate and become void and shall be surrendered to the Regents.

Granted July 27, 1990, by the Board of Regents of The University of the State of New York, for and on behalf of the State Education department, and executed under the seal of said University, and recorded as **Number 20,711.**

Marlin C Barell
Chancellor

Thomas Sobol
President of The University and Commissioner of Education

We have bought a number of items at Tehan's, a discount catalog store at the Northway Mall. We bought a table lamp there last evening ($70 plus tax). It is a very good quality lamp. I bought a Botany 500 coat, with a zip-in lining for winter wear, for $70 plus tax. The same coat has been advertised in the *New York Times* for $135. SK Fashions at the mall normally sells it for $80 but they were getting rid of the few they have left as the season for selling this type of coat nears an end. So...it pays to look at the discount stores.

Working With Volunteers
January 28

Most of the thirty-six years I worked for pay, the people I supervised either got paid in money or college degrees. In short, they had tangible reasons for staying on the job.

Now they work with me only because they want to do the work. The rewards are slim but they do exist.

Like me, many want to do something in return for Bethlehem, where they have enjoyed living for twenty to thirty years.

Like me, many want to dabble in meaningful, hands-on work which is personally satisfying.

Like me, many enjoy history—particularly writing new pages of history.

But some flit in and out. If they have slight doubts about whether or not they are welcome or needed, they come infrequently. Some want to work mainly with their hands, not their brain; if the work taxes the brain too much, they quit. Some don't want to work and pay dues at the same time ...and so on....

In a nutshell, a supervisor of volunteers has to find ways around all these individual whims in order to keep a good organization going.

In the early months of forming an all-volunteer organization (in 1982) it seemed as though it would be all fun and few, if any, problems.

It was a naive expectation. In forming the Bethlehem Archaeology Group, we encountered all of the typical problems: (1) need for a strong, definitive leader, (2) need for a constitution, (3) need for regular meetings, and (4) need for a regular budget and system for spending funds and accounting to the group for such expenditures.

Even after we solved all of those problems, we discovered that some people didn't work well together, some came for work irregularly, some needed a lot of supervision—others very little, some wanted leadership roles, others didn't, and much more.

Well, we're coping and the organization is running smoothly, but it requires a lot of fine-tuning, and individual egos need a lot of nurturing.

The Bicentennial Publication Research Committee (Organizing)
February 5

It's fun to organize something new. The thrill probably grows out of years of work in student activities and college student unions. Even so, the fun doesn't diminish when the development area changes.

Musty-book specialists. Left to right: Jean Lyon and Eleanor Turner.

Getting a history room going at the lab last year was the beginning step toward the formation of a bicentennial publication committee.

As more and more people volunteered for work in the history room, a small Bicentennial Publication Research Committee formed to get a head start on meeting the needs of writers who will join the committee's work in a few months.

The research committee currently has four members: myself, Adrienne Gordon, Jean Lyon, and Eleanor Turner. All of us enjoy prowling through boxes of musty old papers and such things as deeds, ledgers, old resource books, maps, and photographs.

In many small ways, I reinforce the need for the committee's work, go over goals, and seek their ideas for doing the job right. So far, so good.

We like one another, and everyone is working earnestly and regularly.

The Bicentennial Publication Research Committee (First Major Project)
February 6

We meet at town hall once each week—Friday afternoons, 1:00 to 4:00. There are lots of jokes and good-natured kidding, but we have begun to do an annotated bibliography of all major records and materials pertinent to town history.

Should We Buy a Compact Disc Player?
February 13

Our old Fisher stereo player broke down once too often two years ago so

I had it repaired again and sold it with all of our long playing records.

What to do?

I miss all the beautiful classical music, but it seems unwise to buy another regular stereo when the new CD players offer much better sound. Some of my friends who own one wouldn't ever go back to LP records.

But is the CD player just another boom technology that will fade (or at least diminish) soon when the market becomes saturated or something better comes along?

The price of players has come down to $150 but you still have to shell out $500 or so for good quality equipment. The price of compact disks has settled down to $15 or so—about twice the cost of an LP record.

I don't know. I'm still sitting on the matter (and deriving a reasonable level of enjoyment from classical music on WMHT radio).

It is easy to see that CD sales are on a roller coaster ride. In another two or three years, compact disks may account for as much as fifty percent of the business in record stores.

Still, there are only about five thousand titles on compact disks now versus fifty thousand or so on LP records.

Is it better to watch and wait? I've been doing that for almost two years and will probably continue to do it for some time to come. I am rarely this indecisive about anything, but it is hard to make up my mind about CDs. In short, I'm not sold on CD players as yet.

Summary of my Feelings about TV Evangelists
February 23

I'm not happy with the empires some of them are building with money from mostly elderly and poor people. Robert Schuller's huge Crystal Cathedral in Garden Grove, Calif., Jim Bakker's Heritage USA theme park in Fort Mill, S. C., Oral Roberts's university and his unnecessary City of Faith hospital, and the Christian Broadcasting Network's extravaganza (three large buildings, 4,000 employees) in Virginia Beach, Va., masterminded by Pat Robertson, are all monuments to large egos, however well-intentioned. These are not jealous feelings about successful men; they are sad feelings about the bilking of so many elderly and poor.

Even so, I will concede that these flamboyant egos do some good. Many shut-in elderly can get their religion at home, and many of them want and need an anchor in life. For millions of people, Jesus is such an anchor— whether they hear about him on TV or in a church.

On balance, despite the good they do, the evangelical movements have gotten out of hand.

Town Board Approves
Our Major Bicentennial Goals
March 1

Last Wednesday evening, the town board approved the formation of a Bicentennial Commission and our sub-committee, the Bethlehem Bicentennial Publication Committee. Further, the board authorized the use of the town seal in conjunction with our seal on our letterhead. Finally, the board authorized the town supervisor, in consultation with the town historian, to appoint an editor for the proposed town history volume.

All of this means seven more years of pleasant retirement activity for me. It took four years (1982-1986) of persistent energizing, organizing, and research activity to convince a few key people that the Bethlehem Archaeology Group had serious, scholarly goals, but, in the end, some board members were very outspoken in their support of our activities.

This was my first brush with local politics. It won't be the last; I'm going to see this project through to a successful conclusion.

The Liability Insurance Dilemma—
Scandal or Real?
March 24

Last week we received our annual bill for a million-dollar liability insurance policy the town requires of us. It protects the town from liability for accidents that might occur at the lab and for accidents that might occur when an animal or human wanders onto our dig sites. It does not cover accidents to the diggers, which, the Rose & Kiernan Company advises, should be covered by the individual excavator's home insurance policy.

The bill was increased from $167 in 1985 to $250 for 1986—an $83 increase. This is a lot of money for a small, non-profit group. But, we have no choice. We must pay the bill.

Towns, cities, and just about everything involving life in America are being socked with higher liability insurance bills today. It has reached a point where many are "going bare," as the saying goes. They can't afford any degree of liability insurance. This is one area that government must step into with both feet.

My Feelings About Terrorism
(Qadaffi)
April 12

First it makes me angry. When a state-supported group encourages attacks against innocent civilians on commercial airplanes (where they are defenseless), the action is not only immoral but outrageous, from any point of view.

Second it makes me impatient with our leaders in Washington for (seemingly) doing very little about them. In recent days we have learned that some kinds of action are under consideration but, so far, nothing. Sometimes, democracies are slow to act.

Third, it leaves me feeling frustrated when friendly governments seem unwilling to apply economic sanctions; yet, they seem to hate what Qadaffi stands for as much as we do.

Second building of the First Reformed Church of Bethlehem, ca. 1890.

Fourth, I am perplexed at why European governments friendly to the West can't see that doing nothing about terrorism is really a means of encouraging it. Even worse, preventing our military from using our bases in their countries to strike back at Libya is a disguised form of support for Qadaffi's crimes against humanity — including their citizens as well as ours.

The time has come for action. Talking diplomatically and economic sanctions haven't worked.

We need to do what Israel has been doing for ten years: make such terrorist acts costly for the offending governments.

After hearing CBS TV news tonight reviewing American air strikes against Libyan terrorist training installations,

I am feeling encouraged. At last we are fighting back.

My Impressions of the History of the First Dutch Reformed Church of Bethlehem—1763
April 26

This is a very special church. We may do some archaeology work around the grounds soon—a surface search to see if further research (in 1987-1988) might add some significant knowledge to the church's history.

Two books are already in print: the first written by their pastor and key members of the church in 1913, the second written by members connected with their bicentennial celebration in 1963.

Ralph Wood, our Bethlehem Archaeology Group president, is vice president of the church's consistory, the governing organization. The pastor is normally president of the consistory.

I've browsed heavily in both books. One intriguing question is, was the first church building the "little red church" in church legend? Was it really built on the site of the present church? No one knows for sure. It would seem more logical to me that it might have been built nearer the main road (now Route 9W) in Selkirk.

It is easy to see that the church farm is an important part of the long history of Bethlehem's oldest church. The land was deeded to the congregation on December 24, 1795, by Stephen Van Rensselaer for the sum of ten shillings, "for and as long as the said congregation shall perform divine worship and for no other use, intent or purposes whatsoever."

It was used by the first recorded minister, The Rev. George Christian Frederick Bork, for whom the church constructed "a convenient dwelling house and barn." He served from 1798 to 1803. Also, it was rented in later times and brought considerable income to the church.

Another intriguing question (since the church farm building is no longer there) is whether or not archaeology would be able to recover significant information about Rev. Bork and his life-style. It would really be a challenge to reconstruct his life—if the consistory would allow us to cut down a few trees in the area in which the church farm was located. I'm curious about him.

"Crack"— The New Cocaine Menace
June 4

Thank God I'm out of the counseling business. Working with crack addicts today must be frustrating.

This highly addictive form of cocaine is sold in pellet-size "rocks" in small plastic vials. The price can be as little as $10.

Users are probably attracted to it in the first instance because it gives them an instant high. They may also prefer to smoke their drug, and crack is designed to be smoked.

The worst feature of this new form of cocaine is that almost anyone can make it in their own kitchen. Ordinary cocaine is mixed with baking soda and water into a solution that is then heated in a pot. The resulting material, somewhat purer and more concentrated, is then dried and cut into tiny chunks. That probably means that its use will spread like wildfire.

Another Look at President Reagan
June 29

Millions of Americans are thinking about things like freedom and liberty this week as we celebrate the centennial of the Statue of Liberty. Many are feeling proud about being Americans despite the attacks on our citizens by terrorists and our huge fiscal deficit.

It seems to me that at least part of the credit goes to President Reagan—for restoring the faith of the people in the office of President, for projecting the White House as an institution in this nation and abroad, and for swinging the pendulum back toward conservative values that so many Americans cherish.

It is easy for the average citizen to see the negatives that, paradoxically, seem to have developed with all the positives over the last six years. Thousands are leaving their farms, rural banks are failing at an alarming rate, taxes were cut but defense spending went up and the national debt is now a record $2 trillion, the poor have borne a disproportionate share of the burden as less money was made available for social spending...yet..the economy is booming, housing starts are way up over a few years ago, strikes are way down (due, in part, to Reagan's handling of the air traffic controllers' strike), the role of the federal government in our daily life has been lessened (a reduction was badly needed), and, most important of all, Reagan has helped the U.S. project confidence and authority abroad— so badly needed to keep the lid on war and terrorist activity.

I don't like some of Reagan's values— his anti-abortion position, his efforts to share power and influence with the religious right, his seeming unwillingness to train his big guns on the national deficit...but I do like his efforts to build self-confidence into the American spirit, to project an almost visionary zeal in conveying his conservative values to the nation, to solve sticky problems with grace, dignity, and respect for the rights and feelings of his opponents, and to build a more conservative judiciary—badly needed to counteract some of the excesses of the 1960s and 1970s.

Finally, he really is a good role model for millions of middle-agers. If he can do that well at age seventy-five, I ought to be performing miracles at age sixty-five. At the very least he gives us courage to try.

Major Changes in Health Care: Better or Worse?
July 30

We visited Coleen's sister, Joan, in Southington, Conn., last Saturday and Sunday and couldn't help but notice a new walk-in medical building open 24 hours every day, the sign proclaimed. We have a similar facility in Clifton Park.

Impressive support for candidate Kaplowitz. Left to right: James Hogan, Frederick C. Webster, Bernard Kaplowitz, and Stephen R. Wright.

If I were really sick, would I use one of those facilities rather than a hospital emergency room? Probably not, but I can see where people without health plans might be willing to take any doctor available to them in such places for a wide variety of non-serious problems. Trouble is, how can you judge whether or not a problem is really serious? Would the average uneducated person be able to make sensible judgments? I have doubts.

Even so, walk-in medical clinics will inevitably reduce the pressure on medical emergency rooms in hospitals. The long-range benefit to society is likely to be helpful.

The Bethlehem GOP Steak Roast
August 21

Last evening I went to the local Republican party's annual fund-raiser at Picard's Grove. It was attended by about 750 party faithfuls who talked up a storm, drank hundreds of gallons of beer, played horseshoes and volleyball, and finally settled around the tables for Picard's well-known steak dinner.

Bernard Kaplowitz, the town's attorney, is running for a seat in the New York State Assembly being vacated by Larry Lane. He tried to speak to the group (and to introduce his competitors, Gary Swan and John Faso) but, alas, few stopped talking. They didn't even stop when Kaplowitz introduced Andy O'Rourke as a candidate for governor. It was absolute bedlam most of the time. You couldn't have a decent conversation with your dinner partners on either side without shouting.

Even so, I met a good many people who are important in our town history work, and I'm glad I went. The cost was $30. After all expenses are paid, the local party netted about $4,500.

**County Records
(A Valuable Resource)**
September 8

The former town historian, Ed Mulligan, accepted a gift of several dozen county record volumes about ten years ago and stored them in an outbuilding behind his home. Each one is large and heavy. There are thirty-six vol-

Charles E. and Evelyn Alford.

umes in a complete set.

The volumes include land transactions from 1630-1895 and carry titles such as Grantors, Grantees, Mortgagors, Lis Pendens, Maps, and Land Transfers.

A genealogist in the Bethlehem Historical Association, Ed Alford, helped me do an inventory of the entire collection and remove two complete sets: one for our lab library, one for the town historian's office.

Ed Mulligan is gone now, but I know it would please him to know that his county record volumes are being put to good use.

My Fantastic Breakfast Cereal Mix
September 20

If it became widely known, it is likely that my special dry cereal mix would be regarded as eccentric, to say the least. But I like it. My mix includes:

1) Kellogg's Crispix, a corn/rice product;
2) General Mills' Cheerios, a toasted oat mix;
3) Nabisco's Shredded Wheat, whole wheat and bran;
4) Kellogg's Product 19, a multi-vitamin supplement cereal containing corn/oats/wheat/rice;
5) Pet Co. Dairy Crisp, a high calcium rolled oat cereal;
6) Post Grape Nuts, made from natural wheat and barley;
7) Nabisco's 100 Percent BRAN; and
8) Raisins.

I like about a cup of this mix every morning topped with mandarin orange sections and sliced banana.

It tastes good, and it's high in fiber, crunchy, and chewy and, when eaten with about one cup of 2 percent milk, it is good for you. It may contain a little too much sugar but the amount is acceptable if one eats few sweets throughout the day. I always supplement my cereal with an egg or something with protein.

A Good Library's Contribution to the Community
October 27

Does a good library depend only on an excellent collection of books, mono-graphs, films, and magazines to serve the needs of an active intellectual community?

Many do, but ours does not. The Bethlehem Public Library involves the community by sponsoring dozens of programs throughout the year: (1) a series of travel-oriented programs, a number of piano/voice recitals, some science lectures and films, numerous movies, dozens of children's programs, (2) dozens of good films through its own television studio, (3) many "Evening on the Green" programs of a more popular variety on the back lawn in the summer, and (4) dozens of programs sponsored by community groups that use the library's meeting room facilities.

Growth in Typewriter Technology
November 26

Coleen helped me buy a Smith Corona XD6500 electronic typewriter last week. I had saved much of my allowance for several months, and she added $50 as my Christmas gift from her.

The publicity never tells you how or why they choose the fancy designations. XD6500 must mean something. At any rate, the cost was $390. No tax in this case since it was purchased for a tax-exempt group. The writing function is cranking up with archaeology group reports, and I have been concerned about being left with something to type with in case the computer breaks down.

Tri-County Banjo Band performing on the Village Green stage, June 1985.

It is easy to see that typewriter manufacturers have been forced to adjust to a computer-conscious world. The XD6500 has a 7K (7,000 characters) memory along with a display screen that enables the operator to do many things:

1) look up words in a 50,000 word dictionary;
2) type in bold print;
3) use it with a computer printer.

Also, it has many other automatic features I'm learning about as I practice using the machine: (1) automatic half space, (2) auto carriage return, (3) auto centering, (4) auto underscore, and (5) auto indentation.

Moreover, it has a spelling correction system that (1) finds errors, (2) corrects (literally removes) one letter or a whole word at a time, and (3) relocates misspelled words. Also, it uses changeable daisy printwheels and features many programmable items such as stop codes, your own commonly used jargon (archaeology), and an advanced search capability.

It is obvious that typewriter manufacturers are striving to compete in a computer-centered world.

Adrienne Gordon sorting ceramics at the laboratory.

**Article for Local Newspaper
Sums Up Five Years of Work**
December 16

"Translating Artifacts Into History"
by Floyd Brewer

Can people who dig in the dirt also write? That perplexing question is being faced by some thirty members of the Bethlehem Archaeology Group who have been uncovering evidence of Bethlehem's history over the past five years. About a dozen members of the group have begun to analyze and write about their finds; however, they realize that more help is needed from people in the community with practical knowledge in specific areas.

For most members of the group, it is a mixture of fun, adventure, and meaningful work. During the winter months, the group washes, labels and identifies thousands of artifacts recovered the previous summer. This is done in a laboratory provided by the town in the former Waldenmaier building on Route 32 South. Although all members of the group are non-professionals, every effort is made to follow procedures that are standard in archaeology laboratories everywhere. The main goal is to interpret information derived from archaeology, interviews, and original documents and work it into meaningful written drafts. Such drafts are already emerging from years of work on the Nicoll-Sill estate, the Slingerlands family vault, and the Goes farm, where Indians lived for thousands of years before the Europeans arrived.

The group's publication committee has met five times and is now seeking assistance from others in the community who enjoy historical research, writing, or both. A committee of twelve members is envisioned. The author of this article serves as editor, Peter Christoph and Adrienne Gordon are associate editors, and Eleanor Turner is secretary-treasurer. A number of assistant editors will be appointed when all the membership positions are filled.

Edward Homiller, metal restoration specialist, applies his knowledge of chemistry and metals.

THE FREDERICK BRITT HOUSE, ROUTE 32 NEAR
FEURA BUSH. MARK L. PECKHAM, AUGUST 27, 1976.

5 Nineteen Hundred Eighty-Seven

Floyd devoted many of his 1987 diary entries to reminiscing about everything from ice harvesting to hankies. His most personal remembrances, of course, are of his youth and family—his older, boy-crazy sister Maxine, his brother and buddy Merrill, his influential mother—and the life they shared during the Great Depression.

His reveries end, however, in October, when Floyd—and all of Bethlehem, for that matter—were rudely returned to the present by Mother Nature. An unusually early snowstorm, when the leaves were still on the trees, shut down the town without power for several days. Like many other residents, the Brewers tried (unsuccessfully) to compensate for a now non-working sump pump by bailing out their basement, turned to some unconventional methods for cooking, endured long lines, and rediscovered the pleasures of candlelight and good friends.

Holiday With Friends
January 1

We spent a quiet New Year's Eve at home last night watching a film on public TV recapping the events of Albany's tricentennial year. It was richly historical in nature and a joy to watch.

Our friends Ralph and Muriel Wood came over this afternoon for tea and talk. We always swap family stories. I also shared my excitement about a review of an audiocassette tape I did this morning. (The tape covered the visit of doctors William Ritchie and Robert Funk to our lab to go over our prehistoric artifacts.) At long last, I know when the large stone tools we have were made. Funk and Ritchie agreed they are typical of life during the so-called Vosburg (archaic) times —about 3000 B.C.

So, little by little, I am piecing together Bethlehem's prehistory—an exciting process because it has never been done before. We will clearly add some pages to history.

Bethlehem's Prehistory:
A Mind-Numbing Experience
January 24

We are in a rough draft stage in preparing Bethlehem prehistory copy for the bicentennial history.

There are almost 1,000 stone tools from our Goes farm prehistoric site, and one would think you could just organize the tools and easily describe the Indians who lived here over the centuries.

Not so. It is frustratingly difficult. Every sentence is painfully formulated around evidence that is hard to interpret.

Example: does the mere presence of two bifurcate (and one Kirk) projectile points in the Goes farm collection mean that our earliest visitors came around 6500 B.C.? Such points are typical of the southwestern Indian cultures in the 5000 to 8000 B.C. range.

How My Opinions Are Formed
January 28

It seems fitting to write on the subject of politics following President Reagan's State of the Union speech last night. I watched all of it on television as well as the Democratic response immediately after.

First, it should be mentioned that I have not contributed to the National Republican Fund even though I am an enrolled Republican on the local voting lists and a member of the Bethlehem Men's Republican Club. Lack of making a contribution to the national organization, however, doesn't mean I don't follow national political life closely. I do, and I fume and fuss over the big issues, as much as the average citizen in our town.

The Romance of Household Glass
February 17

Dorothy Zdgiebloski and I drove to Troy this afternoon to meet with early glass specialist, Ann Haughmaster.

We took many of our Nicoll-Sill glass fragments with us and sought her help in identifying them.

To our surprise, Mrs. Haughmaster explained that most of our 110 fragments were 1900 through 1940 or so. It was a particularly good record of household glass used by Harry Dinmore, Sr., and his wife Marion, the last occupants of the house (1927-1960), but almost nothing owned by families before 1900.

Why? We are particularly perplexed because there is so much pottery from the earlier families.

We do have some nice pieces: Spanish lace glass from the 1880s, pattern glass from the turn of this century, and more.

Even so, Mrs. Haughmaster spent some of the time going over several great (scholarly) glass books with us, and we will probably buy some of them eventually. The trip opened our eyes to the myriad forms of glass used in America in the 1800s.

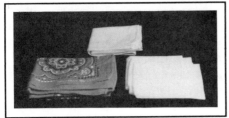

Handkerchiefs over the ages. Left to right: red bandanna, white cotton, Kleenex.

The Evolution of Handkerchiefs in My Time
February 18

I used to cringe when my Dad and I went into a restaurant, to watch him haul out a bright red, large figured bandanna-type handkerchief and honk his nose into it. He gave me one shortly before he died in 1976. It measured twenty by twenty-three inches. It has an intricate black design filled with touches of white and numerous black and white dots. Mine has the words "washfast" and "color" on the bottom with a small elephant symbol in between.

For years I have used a standard white cotton handkerchief—plain 15" by 15", no design of any kind, and I try to use it discreetly (quietly) in public. Even so, I notice few men using handkerchiefs like this today. Most use paper Kleenex-type tissue, probably because they or their wives don't see any point in ironing handkerchiefs when a disposable product is so cheap and easy to carry.

Perhaps I haven't changed because I like the feel of a cotton handkerchief

Stephen F. Bub.

and because you can't always find a place to throw a used paper tissue. Anyhow, as in my Dad's time, the winds of time have swept by me but I'm not ready to change as yet.

Electricians in Short Supply
February 19

Steve Bub and Paul Ammerman of LeGallez Electric in Delmar came to our house today to install a ceiling track fixture, an extra outlet, and three ceiling spotlights. It took them about two hours. We have been waiting for them for over two months. I could have tried another company, but they do quality work, and I didn't want to take a chance on someone else.

A lot of people in this area say electricians are in short supply. If so, you wonder why the schools don't turn out more? It's a good, clean living and, if they play their cards right, they can work indoors during cold, inclement weather and out of doors during warmer, better weather.

The spots should ease the pressure on my eyes, which have been bothering me because of the extra volume of reading for an increased writing role. Soon, I will be reading a lot of copy written by members of the Bicentennial Publications Committee. The spots arrived in the nick of time.

Ice Harvesting
March 20

Ice harvesting, long a thing of the past, was brought to life last evening by Henry Meyer and Lois Dillon at a meeting of the Bethlehem Historical Association.

They were still using iceboxes in the 1920s and 1930s as I grew up; however, there were some differences between ice harvesting in New York and Maine, judging from ninety-two-year-old Henry Meyer's remarks.

In Maine, blocks of ice were stored in well-insulated ice houses and covered with sawdust. Here, according to Meyer, they were covered with hay.

In New York, ice harvesting was big business, and they went about it with horses, special snow (or sludge) removal equipment, and a variety of saws. In Maine, it was mostly individual families cutting for themselves.

It was an interesting era with furniture-like boxes in the home. We didn't own one. My dad was old-fashioned about such things.

Another Look at Diet
April 2

A lot has been written about fat and cholesterol consumption in the 1980s, and the public (as well as Coleen and I) have made many changes in diet. I sometimes wonder if all the changes are necessary, yet the changes I have made were ever so gradual and were based on a careful reading of major research results—particularly longitudinal studies.

For example, we bought the saturated fat story and gradually reduced our intake of foods such as red meat, butter, and all foods containing saturated fats (I have hung onto a donut a day because coffee and donuts have been such a pleasurable part of my diet since my teen years). Complete elimination of all foods with saturated fats in my diet would so alter the quality of life that there would be few pleasures to look forward to. Why be grim about it?

Indian exhibit at town hall.

Educational Exhibitions
April 22

Our Own Prehistory Exhibit

Adrienne Gordon, Eleanor Turner, and I went to town hall today to put up our first prehistory exhibit. It was difficult.

How could we create interest in a bunch of dull, gray stones? How could we get across all the names and time periods covering all the cultures discovered on our Goes farm site?

We finally settled on a greatly enlarged diagram depicting projectile points that were used in Bethlehem from 6500 B.C. down to A.D. 1600. We put dates only on the major cultures: 3000 B.C., 2500 B.C., and 1800 B.C. in the archaic period, for example.

Also, we installed "Mugwa," an Indian head done by a museum north of here, and two small bulletin boards full of pictures of the crew in action at the site.

Finally, I included a framed poem about Indians done by Dorothy Hosey, a retired fourth-grade teacher in Bethlehem. It's good. I hope people take the time to read it.

Dorothy Hosey, poet and teacher.

Florence Christoph.

Altogether, this one exhibit required about twenty hours of my time (and seven hours each of the time of my two assistants). Is it worth it? Probably, yes. At least a few hundred people using the auditorium will get to see it. Some, particularly town employees and the members of the town board, may become interested enough to support our town history book project.

Flo Christoph
May 4

All of us are pleased that Flo Christoph has returned to dig with us this summer. She is a professional genealogist and the wife of Peter Christoph, associate editor of our bicentennial history.

Flo took a class in archaeology with me at Hudson Valley Community College in 1982. Subsequently, she worked for two summers at the Nicoll-Sill site and for one summer as assistant field director at the Winne site. Paying jobs came her way, and we lost her in the spring of 1985.

She was back today working on a square around the front porch of the First Reformed Church farmhouse. As always, the artifacts seemed to gravitate toward her—or, possibly, she misses very little. Further, she adds a great deal to our lunch hour conversations. She knows so much local history. I am looking forward to swapping stories with her about the families that lived in the church farmhouse.

My 66th Birthday
May 16

A sixty-sixth birthday doesn't feel too different from a fifty-sixth birthday ... except, maybe a few more aches and pains; reading glasses are a must now, not just a convenience; children and grandchildren are much more appreciated now that I have more time to think about their part in my life; my marriage is more vital than ever in that companionship is really vital in retirement; work is more meaningful now that I am doing what I really want to do and don't have to worry about paychecks and supervisors; luxuries in life are more available now that I don't have to worry about how I spend every dollar; and service to the community, a contribution I always wanted to make but couldn't find enough time for, is a reality.

So, while I don't feel too differently about the birthday itself, life is much better than ten years ago. Funny, I always thought things would grow worse as one got older. Not so in my case.

Sister Maxine
May 23

My earliest memories of Maxine go back to 1925 or so. She was ten, I was four. She helped me dress—particularly to tie my shoelaces which were so frustrating. She sewed up tears in my clothes, got breakfast for me when Mom was busy, and, as I grew older and began attending school, she got me off to school in the morning.

Maxine always joked about my "snail-like" pace in the morning. "You're worse than Fred Snow," she'd say. Fred Snow was a storekeeper in town who shuffled around his store slowly, half whistling as he walked.

She helped Mom with meal preparation and, in particular, made some really great donuts. This is probably why a donut and coffee are still favorite breakfast foods today.

As I approached eight or nine years of age, Maxine told me all about the birds and bees and illustrated her remarks by describing her own exploits with boys. Some would call her boy-crazy.

To me it was exciting new knowledge that I was too young to use.

Brother Merrill
May 26

My earliest memories of Merrill involve both support and conflict. He tolerated me as a spunky kid. I was continually testing the waters to see how far I could go. I was once so angry with him around age four (and he about eight) that I threw a pair of scissors at him which stuck on either side of his nose. The enormity of that

Merrill E. Brewer, killed in action, WWII, September 16, 1944.

act engulfed even me at such a tender age. What if the points had stuck in his eyes? Of course, Mom paddled me and it was the worst paddling I ever got. Merrill never did try to get back at me for that incident. Instead, we became the best of friends and years later, he let me move into the camp with him.

I loved Merrill—probably because he was the closest brother in age. He helped me in fights with other kids. He told me what to expect in school and he was usually right. He gave me some of his best clothes when he outgrew them. He took me fishing and taught me how to clean rainbow trout soon after we caught them, and how

to cook them by the stream. Merrill was a favorite brother—not just of mine, but of most children in the family.

Small Town Life in 1921-1930
May 29

Dad brought home a funny looking box with knobs on it sometime in 1928. He twisted the knobs and out came music.

I'd seen a radio at Clara and Sam Hartley's home a couple of years before but didn't get to run it myself. Soon we were listening to the radio every night. One program began with a squeaking door, and we heard the phrase "the Shadow knows" many times. It was a first-rate thriller. Also, the whole family gathered around the radio every Saturday night for "Uncle Ezra's National Barn Dance," if memory serves.

Mom complained when all of us heard on the radio that Calvin Coolidge would not run for president again in early 1928. Dad thought Herbert Hoover would do a good job though. He was raised on a farm somewhere out West, and he had done such a wonderful job feeding the hungry in Europe during World War I. We cheered when he was elected although I was too young to appreciate the serious side of politics.

No one I met in town had any good things to say about Al Smith, the man who ran against Hoover. Some called him a "city slicker from New York."

Franklin D. Roosevelt
1931-1940
June 10

A certain desperation developed among the farmers in Bridgewater around 1932-1933. They cursed a lot. Some lost their farms because they owed too much. Everyone I knew voted for Franklin D. Roosevelt from New York. They clearly felt he would help the farmer, if anyone could.

Roosevelt's speeches on radio were stirring. He talked about a war on poverty. He left everyone I knew in town with the feeling that something would be done about the Depression. Even so, it seemed to me that things didn't change all that much in our town. My brothers and sisters had to scratch for themselves. Finally Dad began to accept painting and construction jobs, and we worked for him. If memory serves, he paid me forty-five cents an hour for painting the schoolhouse in 1936. I was fifteen by then.

Part-Time Work Scarce
1931-1940
June 12

I scavenged the dumps for old medicine bottles and sold them back to Tom Nickerson at the drugstore for an average of two cents each. Also, when in season, I picked raspberries and sold them to townspeople for twenty-five cents a quart. A lot of kids, along with me, picked mustard in the potato fields for twenty-five cents an hour. In the field we would sing a kind of chant that came over the radio.

June 13

We often substituted the word "mustard" for "cotton" and other things that related more to our own work and home environment, as in the following verse. Sometimes I would make up a completely new line or two. It was a game played with sweaty brows and yellow mustard hands:

Seven-cent cotton and forty-cent meat,
How in the world can a poor boy eat?
Mules in the barn, no crop laid by,
Corn crib empty and the cow's gone dry.
Well water low, nearly out of sight,
Can't take a bath on a Saturday night.
No use talking, any boy is beat,
With seven-cent cotton and forty-cent meat.

My Mother
June 17

My mother was the single greatest influence on me to walk the straight and narrow, or to do things right. I always found her home. She was always willing to listen to me and she often helped me patch up a neighborhood quarrel (fights among the kids). Usually, her approach was even-handed and she was unfailingly courteous with other parents. I noticed that others liked her because of her courteous manner and resolved to emulate her style of relating to others as well as solving problems.

This "listen before you talk, courtesy before aggression" style of relating to others has served me well to this very day. It is one major reason why I am successful at most things I do. I have the same angry rough-and-tough impulses as others do in my psychological makeup but I've learned many times over to unleash them quietly and constructively. This invariably preserves my mental health, yet wins friends and influences people. I shall be in my mother's debt until the end of my days. This philosophy lapses occasionally but it guides me most of the time.

How I Feel Today
About the Constitution
July 9

The Bill of Rights is inadequate for a few isolated issues today and a further amendment to the Constitution is clearly in order.

An Equal Rights Amendment seems to be the only vehicle that will put women and other minority groups on equal footing with men and whites generally. Despite all the statutes, they still get less pay than men for comparable jobs, they still get stuck in poverty after failed marriages, and they are still underrepresented in government and on executive levels in our society.

This is the only area where I feel an amendment to the Constitution is warranted today. The issue has been festering too long. Let's have it out and commit our decision to print. One more try and the necessary thirty-eight states might ratify the amendment this time around.

Other than this, the Constitution is a truly amazing document for maintaining checks and balances in our country.

St. Thomas Continuing Education
July 15

St. Thomas Church sponsors an excellent summer program on a wide variety of subjects from history to cooking. This week five people enrolled in their program, "Digging up Bethlehem's Past," came out to work: John Barker and John Davitt, high school sophomores; Marian Choppy, a second grade teacher; Helen Ortali, a homemaker; and Jeanne Schrempf, a staff assistant at St. Thomas in charge of continuing education.

As always, it is fun to work with new people. They ask questions, they of-

Thomas V. Corrigan, supervisor, 1978-1984.

ten want to read about archaeology, they are excited when they find something special (like a clay pipe bowl). Regulars would say, "Ho-hum, another piece of clay pipe," but a new person wants to know all about it.

John Davitt, especially, seems interested in the field. I urged him to read Ivor Noel Hume's *Martin's Hundred* today. It reads like a novel, yet it is all about archaeological problems in recreating the first settlement in Virginia.

The General Electric Foundation: Friend of the Community
August 25

Tom Corrigan, former town supervisor, arranged an appointment today for the two of us with James Conheady. He is director of community relations for General Electric. Tom introduced me, and we exchanged pleasantries for ten minutes. He is young, maybe thirty-eight or forty, and very personable. I told him about our project, ending with the hope that the GE Foundation would help us finance the

Kenneth P. Hahn.

**Growing Political Involvement
in Town Affairs**
September 15-16

This was the day for all registered Republicans to vote in the primary (noon to 9:00 P.M. at the library). The only contest is between Kenneth Hahn (incumbent) and Charles Fritts for the position of receiver of taxes.

I believe the town of Bethlehem is well managed and that there is sufficient involvement of the citizens in the decision-making process—through a system of districts with a committeeman or woman in each. Committee personnel are always asked how they feel when conflict arises or a new member of the town board is needed to replace a retiring member.

publication of our town history. He said the request would be considered when we had some specific figures to share. I agreed to provide some over the next few months. Conheady asked if we needed short range help and I said, yes, particularly for library and field equipment, also for a part-time secretary eventually. He said a few hundred dollars might be advanced soon. When the check arrived, it was for $1,000.

Such was the case when a number of key Republican party officials and committee personnel grew dissatisfied with Kenneth Hahn , receiver of taxes, who refused to support the party's designate (Bernard Kaplowitz) in a contest for a New York State Assembly seat last year. His support of Gary Swan, an independent candidate, effectively split the vote and Kaplowitz lost the election to a Columbia-Greene County candidate.

Although Hahn has been in the job twenty-four years and is about fifty-nine years old, the Republican committee decided to run Charles Fritts as its candidate for receiver of taxes in yesterday's primary. Both men appear to be well qualified to do the job.

Hahn and his friends in North Bethlehem were angry, and they mounted an aggressive campaign to put Hahn on the ballot. They got twelve hundred signatures on a petition to secure his place.

My job to help elect Charles Fritts has been pretty minor—mostly phone calls to get out the vote, particularly those who are known to favor Fritts. Additionally, I have attended a strategy meeting in the home of Sue Ann Ritchko, a member of the town board.

Hahn won the election—2,286 to 1,050. He put up a good fight, and it paid off for him.

Power Emergency
October 5

A freakish, seven-inch, very wet snow fell yesterday with most leaves still on the trees. I watched from my kitchen window as a huge branch of our ash tree in the front yard fell across the road with a resounding crash. Traffic was blocked immediately. An eerie situation confronted me as I took a tree limb saw and began to remove some branches so traffic could pass. It began to snow more heavily, and more branches began to fall: crack, crack, thud as whole trees fell in the woods

nearby. It was scary. Could a branch from my neighbor's tall poplar trees across the street fall on me? I decided it could and got out of there fast as the cracks and thuds grew louder. A minute or two later (about 8:30 A.M.), one of my neighbor's huge poplar branches did come down where I had been standing. Lucky again.

October 6

Although these notes are being written on the third day of the emergency, last Sunday was the worst.

As my neighbor's huge branch fell across the street, so did another neighbor's up the ravine where the power line runs. This tree cut off the power to our home and many around us. It was 8:33 A.M.

This is a town with a high water table level, and many homes have sump pumps. So the countdown began. Could we bail fast enough and long enough to keep the floor from flooding downstairs?

We decided that the severity of the storm and the probable damage throughout the area meant that we would be without power for at least a couple of days more, so we hired two high school boys to help us bail water. By 1:00 A.M. Monday on day two, we decided it was hopeless and let the floor flood.

October 7

Still no power. The damage in the area is staggering. Although there are lines everywhere, I've managed to buy hot coffee and rolls or donuts every morning at Stewart's on Delaware Avenue. We usually go to the Grand Union deli counter or Friendly's for lunch. Sometimes we go out for dinner—Helen Nickel invited us for dinner one night—and sometimes we just warm up leftovers in Coleen's chafing dish, a sort of domestic Bunsen burner. So we're getting by.

It is amazing how little you can do without electric power. No warm water for showers, no lights for reading or simply getting around the house at night, no effective (simple) hot food preparation—and the list goes on....

John Vadney, an area plumber, came over to pump out our basement today. The water rose seven inches on the wall, threatening to submerge the motor in the furnace and other expensive pieces of equipment. It will take at least forty-eight hours for the water to subside.

October 9

Our friends, Ralph and Muriel Wood, came over for dinner tonight. They still don't have power and are clearly upset about it. They were soothed with a hot meal [our electric power was turned on today] but the under-

current of unhappiness persisted. They have a 3,500 watt Honda generator going in their garage and they have some heat and enough juice to keep the refrigerator freezer cold and substandard light in the living room for reading. They also keep their sump pump going with a feed line off the generator.

In retrospect, such a generator would have solved some of our problems. The water in our basement was the worst problem. We could stand reading by candlelight and dressing more warmly for indoor living, but we were really unhappy about the water problem.

We will soon buy a Coleman stove and lantern—both run by little canisters of gas. Also, we will buy a Honda generator.

Power Emergency: Back to Normal
October 11

Coleen went to church, and I went to the lab this morning as usual.

I moved my typewriter back downstairs and did some copy for the December issue of the *Bethlehem Report*—a town publication that goes into twelve thousand area homes.

The phone company representative pinned down our problem, and phone service was restored. Three calls came in within the hour.

Coleen prepared our usual Sunday meals, and we watched the news, "60 Minutes," and our favorite Sunday evening TV programs.

It's nice to be back to normal. We take all these electrically powered luxuries for granted and have grown so dependent on them that it is both shocking and uncomfortable to be without them for almost a week. I vowed today to be far better prepared for the next emergency.

Cars in the Dunkin' Donuts Parking Lot at 9 this Morning
November 16

Evidence that trade patterns have changed over the past few years can easily be seen in Dunkin' Donuts parking lot on any day.

At 9 this morning, I looked out the window and saw

- A Saab sedan—Sweden.
- A Chrysler Fifth Avenue luxury sedan—America.
- Two Isuzu 1/2 ton trucks—Japan.
- A Mitsubishi 1/2 ton truck—Japan.
- A Buick sedan—America.
- A Ford Mustang sedan—America.
- A Volkswagon camper—Germany.
- A Chrysler Voyager minivan (mine)—America.
- A Citroen sedan—France.
- A Yugo sedan—Yugoslavia.

It is a source of continual amazement to me that our country has assimilated so many foreign products so rapidly.

Is it mainly due to Reagan administration policy? Or, is it due to pressure from millions of Americans for such goods?

THE BETHLEHEM HISTORICAL ASSOCIATION
MUSEUM, FORMER CEDAR HILL SCHOOL.
CEDAR HILL. MARK L. PECKHAM, SEPTEMBER 7, 1985.

[6] *Nineteen Hundred Eighty-Eight*

This was the year of the first meeting of the Bethlehem Bicentennial Commission. Floyd's main interest was seeing that a history of the town be published in commemoration of Bethlehem's 200th birthday. He eased off his archaeology work in favor of devoting most of his energies to assembling a writers' group—volunteers all—to produce copy for the history. An equally daunting task was the spectre of somehow raising $25,000 to meet the book's publishing costs.

This work was set against a backdrop of maintenance chores in Floyd's personal life—everything from retaining his health to fixing the furnace to sealing his driveway!

Walking: Good Exercise for People in Their Sixties
January 25

I have switched to walking as a main form of exercise—on average two to three brisk miles a day. My feet are extra warm when I return from a walk —even on a cold day.

Is this sufficient exercise in an exercise-happy world?

My family physician thinks it is and so do I.

When it is impossible to walk because of the weather, I use an Exercycle in my office downstairs.

Most important of all, my walks are relaxing, the neighborhood is a pleasant place to walk, and I often do my best thinking on a walk.

Some men my age run in this neighborhood. During the warm months, they often appear ready to fall down. To me, this is unwise for people in their sixties. Time will tell which method is best.

The High Cost of Health Care
February 6

My brother-in-law, Albert "Bucky" Wellington, retired a few weeks ago. He learned that it would cost him $230 a month to maintain his family health insurance policy. Imagine! This is more than many people pay for mortgage and taxes on their home each month. Our average payment on our three bedroom ranch home is only $323 a month, right now.

Bucky really has no choice. He must keep on working to pay bills like that.

When will health insurance premiums stop their upward spiral? The answer is hard to come by.

I notice in the current issue of *Time* magazine that General Motors spent more than $2 billion on medical care coverage for its 2.3 million employees during the first nine months of last year. This is especially striking when you look at GM's profits for the same period: $2.7 billion.

All of this is bound to force radical change in the next few years.

The Winter Olympics Opens
February 13

Coleen and I watched two-and-one-half-hours of the opening ceremony at Calgary, Alberta, this afternoon.

In a few words, the pageantry was colorful, beautiful, highly organized, and informative. It was very entertaining.

We particularly enjoyed ABC television's flashbacks to earlier Olympic winter games and the use of a twelve-year-old girl to light the torch.

Surprisingly, the musical selections by groups numbering in the hundreds were especially stirring. All were amateurs.

We watch very few sports programs throughout the year, but we watch many hours of the Olympics.

So, why would non-sports fans enjoy so many hours of Olympic sports?

Part of the answer is the colorful manner in which Olympic competition is presented on television and in other media. There is a barrage of information about the lives of the contestants. It may be hype, but it is interesting hype.

Also, one is keenly aware that you are seeing the most highly skilled athletes in the world. That is exciting.

Third, you get caught up in the trials and tribulations of athletes from your own country; you see them struggling against seemingly insuperable odds, and you want them to win for themselves as well as for our country. It is a great feeling when they get a medal.

Finally, in some sports (such as the seventy-meter downhill and the luge races) the risks are high, and you simply can't take your eyes off the screen.

The New Hampshire Primary
February 16

Vice President George Bush must have had some sleepless nights since the Iowa caucuses. One late poll showed him in a dead heat with Senator Bob Dole in New Hampshire, and a second place finish for Bush would certainly start a downhill slide.

I don't have any strong leanings toward one candidate as yet.

Vincent Donnelly, Main-Care furnace veteran since 1962.

Furnace Malfunction at 3:00 A.M.
March 6

Coleen woke up this morning about 3:00 A.M. and noticed that it was unusually cold in our bedroom. She turned the heat up on the thermostat in the living room: the motor ran but the burner would not ignite the gas heat. I woke up a few minutes later and decided to call Main-Care, the furnace maintenance company that has served us for twenty-two years. Within five minutes Vincent Donnelly called me from his present location. They offer twenty-four hour service. He promised to be here "within thirty to forty-five minutes."

Sure enough, he arrived about 4:30 A.M. and discovered that the pilot relay switch was sticking. He had it fixed within a half hour.

What to do? Go back to bed at 5:00 A.M. or stay up?

I chose to stay up. Coleen took a Valium and went back to bed.

We are thankful that we have had a competent furnace maintenance service for many years. We really needed them this morning.

First Meeting:
Bethlehem Bicentennial Commission
March 12

At long last the Bethlehem Bicentennial Commission was organized today to plan events that are five years away. Sue Ann Ritchko, a member of the town board, and Cynthia Wilson are co-chairpersons.

Other members are Floyd Brewer, James Conheady, Dominick DeCecco, Verne Kenney, Bernard Kaplowitz, Robert Kerker, Peter Kermani, Ann Patton, Claire Ruslander, and Sue Zick.

I spoke about ten minutes, ending with a description of our main problem: raising $25,000 to publish the history.

The Annual Physical Exam (Floyd)
April 7

My annual physical began at 5:00 A.M. when I filled a small (4 ounce) plastic container with urine, a routine with all of my exams over the past forty years.

The Bicentennial Commission. Seated: Cynthia Wilson, left, and Sue Ann Ritchko, Co-chairs. Standing, left to right: Valerie Restifo, Robert Kerker, Sue Zick, Floyd Brewer, Ann Patton, J. Robert Hendrick, Claire Ruslander, Bernard Kaplowitz, Dominick DeCecco. Missing: Marty Cornelius, Barbara Muhlfelder, and Pieter Van Derzee.

My appointment with James C. Leyhane, M.D., was for 9:00 A.M., but before I got to see him it was necessary to check in with the receptionist (at about 8:55 A.M.), be weighed in by the nurse (162 pounds at 9:10 A.M.), and relax in a waiting room (until about 9:15 A.M.).

Dr. Leyhane is an excellent physician. He began his usual thorough check of my physical condition with a twenty- to twenty-five minute medical check-list: e.g. any special problems? Last eye exam? Problems after a recent hernia operation? All the way to small things like, how much alcohol do you drink? (one small glass of wine daily).

Most important of all, he is always willing to respond to my questions.

How do you feel about the "living will" I placed in my file in your office? He liked the spirit of the terms of my will but pointed out a problem with the New York state law that went into effect April 1. The lawyers who drafted the law specified that doctors must base their actions on current patient wishes—but they didn't define what they meant by "current": two days? two years? two months?

Also, I wondered if he would arrange a consultation for me with a magnetic resonance imaging specialist for a

James C. Leyhane, M.D.

double check on my stomach complaints. I have dodged an endoscopy for three years and an MRI test is the only viable alternative. He said he would.

He then gave me the usual tests in a physical: prostate, heart (with stethoscope), blood test, etc., and he could find nothing wrong.

I thoroughly enjoy my annual exam and discussion with Dr. Leyhane. He is careful to point out the pros and cons of almost everything we talk about—leaving considerable room for

me to take responsibility for my own health care. I like that.

Hope for Non-Smokers
April 28

About 25 or 26 percent of Americans now smoke, but that is down from 38 or 40 percent about thirty years ago. Progress is slow because the habit (addiction to nicotine) is so difficult for people to overcome.

Even so, New York City's new anti-smoking law for virtually all public places is a boon to non-smokers' rights as is the tendency for the average smoker to ask, "Do you mind if I smoke?" in many settings today. More and more non-smokers are saying, "Yes, I do mind."

We have a strict rule against smoking at the lab. Coleen and I remove all ashtrays when we entertain or have an overnight guest. We leave two or three out for use as coasters for our own glasses of water, milk, etc., but we try to remember who might smoke among the visitors to our home and remove them when they come.

And now people can't smoke on airplanes during flights of less than two hours, and more and more restaurants are establishing non-smoking sections. Little by little, non-smokers are being subjected to less smoke. Thank God for the gradual change that is taking place in society.

The Pressure on Physicians to Avoid Prescribing Expensive Tests
May 18

During my annual physical exam almost six weeks ago, Dr. Leyhane pledged to arrange a magnetic resonance imaging test of my stomach and related vital organs. He knows of my long-standing complaints about feelings of discomfort in the stomach, yet an unwillingness on my part to have an endoscopy (in which a tube is forced down the throat).

No word from him caused me to follow up with a phone call last week and again today. He is clearly dragging his feet. He is not convinced there is anything wrong and neither am I. However, I feel it is best to err on the side of prevention—expensive test or not (the cost is around $800).

He may be waiting for a 700-page directory called the "Medical Technology Assessment Directory," which physicians around the country have been receiving over the past two weeks. It supposedly represents a beginning toward holding down health care costs. But, what if a patient is willing and able to pay the cost of the test? Should patients like me get caught in a red tape snarl created by government controls on cost? I think not. I'm going to insist on the test, and soon!

Town of Bethlehem Survey
June 13

Last Saturday, I attended a meeting sponsored by Republican town leaders at which 125 to 150 citizens were asked to distribute a questionnaire in selected areas of Bethlehem. Town board member Sue Ann Ritchko explained the objectives with clarity and enthusiasm.

The mission is to find out how our citizens feel about twenty issues ranging from building a new community center for young people to the effectiveness of most town departments.

I filled one out today, and there is space for two voters to record their feelings on each form. Coleen made it clear that her response on the community center issue will be different from mine (I strongly disagree). I am not happy paying an additional $20 a month in taxes for a community center, but I feel the town needs a place for our young people to gather and socialize.

So, I need to deliver the questionnaire and an attractive flyer to about thirty-five homes sometime this week. It is my way of helping a town in which life has been good to us for twenty-two years.

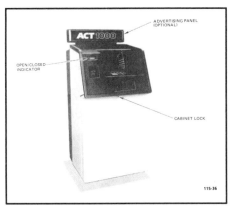

Key Bank ATM.

Would I Want My Bank to Convert to Cash Machines?
July 15

In a word, no. I much prefer to deal with a person behind the counter. There is usually a little small talk and it is our best opportunity to meet new members of the bank staff. Also, I've heard a few horror stories about people having trouble with the machines and having to wait an hour or more to straighten things out.

Deliver me from a completely automated bank!

Even so, I fear automation's ugly head is creeping out our way.

Citibank ads proclaim the glories of their "success machines" through which you can conduct "fifty-five different transactions just by touching the full-color screen." Soon, they will have over 1,000 new machines in New York City, some 70 percent more than they had before.

I prefer to get my cash and make deposits with a living, breathing man or woman—even if I have to wait in line to do it. There is usually someone I know in the line who wants to exchange some town gossip. That's part of the fun in banking.

The Democratic Convention in Atlanta
July 20

We watched several of the key speeches at the Democratic National Convention and a few choice phrases sum up our feelings:

Ann Richards of Texas, keynoter: humorous, a lot of enthusiasm for the Michael Dukakis/Lloyd Bentsen ticket, a lot of George Bush bashing.

Senator Ted Kennedy of Massachusetts: hard-hitting, a lot of George Bush bashing, some rich philosophy.

Rev. Jesse Jackson of North Carolina: electrifying, emotional, and a lot of emphasis on "common ground" and planks in the Democratic platform.

It is nice to see a lower level of conflict at the convention. You get the impression that the Dukakis team is doing some clever managing behind the scenes. They don't want to repeat the fracas of 1968 and similar conventions that created the impression that Democrats couldn't manage their way out of a paper bag. The harmony reigning at this convention could help them win back Democrats they lost to President Reagan at earlier conventions.

The Republican National Convention in New Orleans (President Reagan Revisited)
August 15-16

President Reagan's speech to the convention provided an occasion to think through his administration's accomplishments over the past seven and one-half years. You have to take some of his statements with a grain of salt. His achievements aren't quite as sweeping as he implies; yet, there has been considerable progress [in areas such as]:

- Peace and prosperity.
- Taxes.
- Inflation.
- Unemployment.
- U.S./Soviet competition and tension.

There are some negatives: we may have a social safety net but it seems to me that both blacks and the poor are worse off than they were in 1980.

—The budget deficit went from bad to worse.
—Africa, Central America, and the Middle East are still problem areas.

I'm glad the Reagan administration didn't win its battles on abortion and school prayer. The laws are OK as they are now.

On balance, it seems to me President Reagan will go down in history as a great executive. His positive achievements far outweigh his failures.

Republican National Convention—The Quayle Factor
August 17

Whadya mean he's an unknown? I've been reading about him for years, yet so many delegates at the convention seemed to know very little about Senator Dan Quayle of Indiana.

It was a politically bold decision by George Bush when he named Quayle his vice-presidential nominee. I hope he sticks to his guns and follows through with his first big decision.

Those Pesky Annual Chores (Sealing the Driveway)
September 11

Among the jobs that must be done annually is one I do not enjoy.

Sealing the driveway with a coal tar emulsion requires a lot of preparatory work:

1) I cut the lawn back along the edges of the driveway today since good weather is projected for tomorrow.

2) Additionally, I examined every square inch for tiny cracks—and sure enough, there are many of them. Also, I noticed that the

area where the driveway meets the road is starting to break up. Visions of having to pay for a new driveway one of these years soon popped in my head.

3) So, what to do? Obviously, I must buy a five-gallon can of sealer/filler ($9.29 plus 7 percent tax) as well as the usual coal tar emulsion sealer ($8.25 plus 7 percent tax).

Left to right: Martha Shattuck, Floyd Brewer, Peter Christoph.

There is really no choice about this matter. If you let it go, you often pay a higher price another year.

Driveway Sealing (an Onerous Job)
September 12

It took about five hours to clean the dirt out of the cracks in the driveway and to apply a coat of sealer/filler to these areas (about a third of the driveway).

I could have used rubber gloves but find that they are more of a nuisance than a help—so, my fingernails get filled with the coal tar product.

I could have bought a bag of patching material for the big holes but decided to use the sealer/filler in ample quantities instead. Results: unsatisfactory.

I've had troubles using the road patching mixture (containing small stones coated with a coal tar emulsion). Without a heavy roller, it is hard to pack it into the holes firmly.

So, I scraped up a bucket of small stones—less than a half inch in diameter—and, when the weather improves, I'll try mixing my own patching concoction with the fine gravel and some of the sealer/filler.

Organizing a Writers Group for the Bicentennial History
October 1

As my laboratory duties wind down, my work with writers is cranking up. Surprisingly, it is difficult to interest people in a research/writing role for the bicentennial history. I have learned over and over that many people doubt their ability to write. Several people have turned down an invitation to work with a particular section of the book.

I am in very good shape on the editorial/writer level (with Peter Christoph and Martha Shattuck as associate editors) but need several assistant editor/writers to handle basic areas such as churches, farms, schools, etc.

So, I am trying once more to organize a meeting of prospective assistant editors/writers and hope to be more successful this time.

The superintendent of schools, Les Loomis, is trying to help me find someone to write the libraries and schools story.

Organizing to Write Part II of the Bicentennial History
October 4

Much of my organizational energy and time over the past month has been spent getting ready for an October 17th meeting of the Bicentennial History Committee.

My plan for the meeting is to (1) help the group get acquainted, (2) provide a background statement on the progress thus far, (3) suggest a modest writing project for each assistant editor with a copy due date of January 15, 1989, (4) discuss ideas for further projects in each area with copy due dates of May 15 and September 15.

In a sentence, we're off the ground, but a way needs to be found to channel the energies of sixteen people toward producing copy on a regular basis. I am hopeful most members of the group will accept this concept of gradualism for one big reason: I don't want to contract an ulcer—and that's what could happen if they keep me hanging for a year or two without any tangible signs of progress.

Bush/Quayle/Moynihan/McNulty/ Nolan/Faso
November 8

This is one of the few elections in memory in which all of the candidates I voted for won. However, the Bond Issue for Road Repairs was approved. I thought it should be defeated.

Bush, Quayle, and Faso are Republicans. Moynihan, McNulty, and Nolan are Democrats.

I am well aware of the pitfalls of ticket-splitting (e.g., Republican president, Democratic Congress, etc.) but I want to get the best men and women in key jobs and am willing to trust in their ability to get together and negotiate when the chips are down.

New Grocery Shopping Pattern (Shop 'N Save)
November 10

Coleen and I make an "occasion" out of the weekly shopping trip when we can—as we did this morning.

We leave the house about 9:15 A.M., have a bagel and a cup of coffee out, and spend an hour and a half picking up our groceries for the week.

We enjoyed shopping at the new Shop 'N Save chain grocery so much over the past two weeks that we went back again today. It is owned and operated by the Hannaford Brothers of Maine and is located opposite the Westgate Shopping Center on Central Avenue. It is a beautiful store with wide aisles, excellent service, and a wide variety of brands. I like their bakery and meat/fish departments best, but they have just about every standard grocery department you can name plus a few more. You can buy flower arrangements for your table, have a film developed, sample new products at "tasting" spots around the store, and even pick up a small appliance if you wish.

Everything is so clean and fresh-looking. Our local Grand Union manager would do well to check out his competition.

How I Feel About the Medicare Catastrophic Coverage Act of 1988
November 11

For once a government program may become cost effective!

Except for the poor (making less than $10,000 per year), everyone enrolled in Medicare will pay an additional monthly premium for Part B catastrophic coverage. That is, physicians' fees, out patient and ambulance services, blood and blood products, and, in 1991, drugs.

We're not happy about it, because I worked for over thirty-five years to earn good health care (including catastrophic) through a private company and now am being required by law to pay for the same coverage twice. The major medical coverage we've had for years is quite good, although, like the newest catastrophic coverage under Medicare, it does not provide indefinite nursing home care for as long as we may need it.

Even so, I believe the country needs this kind of health care coverage. Millions of people less fortunate than we are will sleep better at night knowing they have improved catastrophic protection—the single biggest worry of most of the older people I talk to.

My guess is that the government will now get into the health education business in a bigger way.

Entire Family Together
November 24

This is an unusual event in America's mobile society: an entire family together for a long weekend.

Someone wrote that the average American consumes 7,000 calories on

Front, left to right: Floyd Brewer, Stephanie Brewer, Jeffrey Brewer. Rear, left to right: Jonathan Brewer, Coleen Brewer, Mark Brewer.

Thanksgiving Day. I can believe it. We were eating or nibbling from 1:00 to 4:00 P.M.

Jeff and I did a lot of leaf-raking on the lawn to work off our dinner, but mostly the day was good food, conversation, football on television, and dozing—a great way to spend Thanksgiving.

Social Security Payment Adjustment
December 21

The long awaited Social Security payment adjustment (to pay for the new catastrophic coverage described on November 11-12 in this diary) was received in the mail today. As always,

the government increased our payment—by 4.0 percent—before taking away a much larger figure to cover the insurance.

The notice says:

<u>For Floyd Brewer</u>-
a. Gross benefit amount: $643.90
b. Medicare insurance
   monthly premium: <u>31.90</u>
c. New monthly payment: $612.00

<u>For Coleen Brewer</u>-
a. Gross benefit amount: $299.90
b. Medicare insurance
   monthly premium: <u>31.90</u>
c. New monthly payment: $268.00

We didn't need it, but I don't mind doing my bit to help those less fortunate than we are.

Those Marvelous, Stick-on, Removable Labels
December 30

About fifteen, five-by-seven black and white photographs will be mailed with an article next week to an editor for publication. The photographs have to be accompanied by caption information.

I have discovered that the identifying caption data can be typed on stick-on, removable labels and placed along the one and one-half inch end of each photograph that the photo developing company leaves for notes and handling.

Several mistakes were made in the typing and I simply peeled off the copy and replaced it with a newly typed version.

If what I have done gets in the way of the editor's makeup person (who must figure out where and how to use the photos with the article), she can simply peel them off after she puts the numbers and other identifying information around the pictures in her computer.

Removable, stick-on labels are a marvelous invention!

New Year's Eve in Recent Years at Our Home
December 31

We just haven't had the urge or need to do something exciting on New Year's eve in recent years. Is it because we are getting older? Maybe.

In reality, it seems like any other evening to me. Our neighbor and friend, Helen Nickel, plans to do the First Night bus rides (from various recreation sites in Albany) this evening. She is going with her nurse friend, Joan Ching. The idea is to reduce the risk of accidents by using the bus. They will buy a button for eight or ten dollars and it entitles them to get in eight or ten places at the bus stops. They will end the evening at midnight by going to the riverfront for fireworks.

We stayed home. Coleen prepared a special dinner. She lit candles and generally made it different from our usual dinners.

Then we watched "Live from Lincoln Center" on TV—a marvelous performance by the New York Philharmonic (conducted by Zubin Mehta) and Placido Domingo, tenor. It was a comfortable evening followed by bed at 11:30 P.M. We let the new year arrive without ceremony.

SLINGERLANDS COMMUNITY METHODIST CHURCH
MARK L. PECKHAM.   AUGUST 6, 1994.

7 Nineteen Hundred Eighty-Nine

*T*his marks the seventh year that Floyd has been keeping a diary, and early in the year, he notes what he sees as the purpose of his daily record:

I want a diary that is at once both therapeutic for me and as broad as my huge study; something all-embracing yet focused on specific goals; a collection of odds and ends that concerned me at one point in time; a summary of my joys and tribulations; my frustrations and tensions; a reflection of my thoughts as I look at local, state, national, and international events and personalities; a review of my struggles to make a difference in the lives of others; and an analysis of the roles I and others play in the great game of life.

This is something of a departure from his original goal for keeping the diary—namely, to determine if retirement is treating him as well financially as his working years did. Perhaps this shift is a reflection of his dual association with the Bethlehem Archaeology Group and the bicentennial history committee. It most certainly connotes his contemplation of his own mortality. He appears to work harder to reconstruct the lives of the people whose artifacts are unearthed at local dig sites, ever more appreciative of what we leave behind. He also begins to sharpen the focus on yet another major project, his own family history.

Gearing Up For a Report on James B. Lyon
January 17

My crew completed the Lyon site in 1987, but we are just now getting around to handling the artifacts.

How much do we really know about the home life of the well-known turn-of-the-century printer whose business eventually became Williams Press in Albany?

The answer is—very little; however, we hope to change that through a careful analysis of hundreds of artifacts retrieved from the grounds of his old estate in Cedar Hill.

He was a well-known confidant of political leaders and a quality printer, particularly during the heyday of his company from 1890-1915. From time to time, I will record my impressions of our research. My lab staff will begin sorting the artifacts next month.

Question: Who built the old house he purchased in Cedar Hill around 1890? We'll have to wait and see.

George Bush Takes Office (How We Feel)
January 20

Coleen and I watched quite a bit of the inaugural activities last night and today.

Billing himself as a "new breeze" with a "will over wallet," Bush probably used just the right words for the times. These are good times: peace is on the rise around the world; the cold war between the United States and Soviet Russia is fading. Unlike 1961 when John F. Kennedy came to power, the times don't require grand visions and hyperbole.

We feel a twinge of regret for Ronald and Nancy Reagan. They seemed a little sad about leaving the White House and we commiserated with them.

But the mood among hundreds of George Bush admirers was upbeat, and we liked the frivolity. Barbara Bush will bring a different (more homey) feeling to the White House, and George Bush is likely to work hard to achieve bipartisan consensus on the big problems facing the country.

Thomas Knight, 1994.

We wish him well. The first one hundred days should give us a good idea of his probable success or not.

Tom Knight Joins the Lab Photographic Staff
January 21

I am overjoyed that Tom Knight has joined the lab staff as a photographer. He has worked in photography at the Library of Congress and has considerable skill in the field. Tom and his partner, Don Simpson, own and operate The Third Eye, a photography business at the Four Corners in Delmar.

Tom already does all of our developing work and has made many suggestions for improving our pictures.

They specialize in reproducing old photographs, in black and white developing and printing, and in educating the area's amateurs and professionals in the art of photography.

Am I relieved! Chuck McKinney and I have been doing reasonably good work, but we're just getting into the really difficult problems: tiny features on stone and clay pipe objects, bulky, dark metal artifacts, really, everything from huge two-hundred-pound metal scales to a tiny silver 1852 three-cent coin. Tom's offer of help comes in the nick of time.

What Sort of Diary Am I Writing?
(My Philosophy)
January 22

Some diaries I have read concentrate on routine subjects: trips to places around the town where the writer lives, the weather, an occasional car or train wreck.... Some are more interesting to read, particularly those by writers who reflect the pressures on themselves to turn out great literary works.

I want a diary that is at once both therapeutic for me and as broad as my huge study; something all-embracing yet focused on specific goals; a collection of odds and ends that concerned me at one point in time; a summary of my joys and tribulations; my frustrations and tensions; a reflection of my thoughts as I look at local, state, na-tional, and international events and personalities; a review of my struggles to make a difference in the lives of others; and an analysis of the roles I and others play in the great game of life.

We're here for such a short time. Why not make the most of it? Live within our means but live zestfully and fully. A diary should be all of the above plus a legible record for historians of the future.

AT&T Versus MCI
(Telephone Service)
February 4

We decided to retain AT&T service soon after the federal government broke up this huge company a few years ago and allowed some competition in the industry.

We're glad we did. If the competition that developed is healthy, it doesn't seem that way to us. Coleen's sister, Joan, tried MCI (Telecommunications Corporation) but switched back to AT&T because of dissatisfaction with MCI's billing procedures. Our friends, Ralph and Muriel Wood, considered MCI but stayed with AT&T because they couldn't reach friends in Maine and relatives in the state of Washington through MCI. (Their service may cover these states now.)

Still, I notice that MCI is growing: profits of $346 million last year, acquired a large number of large business customers last year with their toll-free 800 numbers, now has 11 percent of the $50 billion long-distance market—compared to AT&T's 68 percent and US Sprint's 7 percent.

Our son, Jeff, has Sprint's service and seems to like it. No matter. We're happy with an old shoe. We'll stay with AT&T.

A Look at State Politics
February 22

I used to tell my male students that money and women are the main reasons new employees in the labor market run into trouble. Misuse either one and you're out on your ear.

Mario Cuomo, New York's governor, is okay with women (with his stable marriage to Matilda), but he is running into trouble with money. He is having to make hard choices to compensate for the loss of funds to New York caused by federal tax cuts. He has slashed the budgets of the state university system and numerous human services programs that affect the lives of thousands of citizens.

He is still a highly charismatic, intelligent leader but, to make it with the people over the long haul, he must now make firm, clear decisions on sensitive matters (e.g., Shoreham nuclear reactor, discrimination in Yonkers housing and schools, crime due

to drug use, and whether or not he will run for president in 1992).

After two terms in office he gets a B+ but he will have to work hard to maintain it.

Betty Sewell,
Professional Genealogist in Canada,
Accepts Estey Contract
March 14

I talked with Betty Sewell in Fredericton, New Brunswick, this morning and she agreed to work on my mother's family line. This is terrific news! She is the author of several books on Canadian genealogical source material and is considered very competent in her work. Her book on the 1851 Census in Canada is widely used.

I often say women are underrepresented in history to the lab personnel and writers working with me on our Bethlehem bicentennial history... and I always follow this remark with the question: Why don't we do something about it?

In this vein, I am determined that my mother, sisters, and other female relatives shall occupy a prominent place in our family history. This especially applies to my wife, Coleen, whose efforts and judgments have influenced so many people in our family and friendship circles. Without her, I would be much less effective in so many of my endeavors in life.

Nicoll-Sill ceramics display, town hall.

The collective effort within the Bethlehem Archaeology Group to reach this point was enormous—literally thousands of volunteer staff hours. Adrienne Gordon and Carol Wock did most of the identification work with the artifacts. Nanci Page, Trudy Pert, and Chuck McKinney helped to put the exhibit together.

Proof of Scholarship
March 24

Three large display cases at town hall were filled with "700 years of ceramics on the Nicoll-Sill estate" today.

The exhibit follows submission of a thirty-page article on Nicoll-Sill ceramic finds to the *New York State Archaeology Bulletin*. It is another form of proof of good scholarship with over 13,000 ceramic fragments from the town's oldest extant building (1735).

It contains twenty 12" x 8" Riker mount display cases full of our best samples and covers Indian occupation (A.D. 1200-1500) as well as all of the families that lived in the building from 1735 through 1960.

Never before have I been so proud of the quality of the group's output. It is indeed proof of serious scholarship. We have created some new pages for the history books.

My Favorite Recreation: Walking
April 19

We once owned bicycles, a mechanical rower, an Exercycle and other gadgets for exercise. Now they're all gone. Why? I really prefer walking for exercise. I like the smell of the cool, crisp air during the colder months, and I love the sounds of birds and other aspects of nature during the warmer months.

Sometimes I stop and talk with a neighbor or pet someone's dog.

Yes, I am aware that it might improve my cholesterol count, but I don't walk because of that. Yes, I know it helps my cardiovascular system, and I do walk partly for that. But, deep down, I walk for pure enjoyment.

It is a lot more fun than doing push-ups or chopping wood. It is a lot easier to do than going to Nautilus or some exercise place for a workout.

Come to think of it, I've enjoyed walking wherever I've been, both in this country and abroad.

Coleen as a Mother
May 14

Coleen Brewer, ca. 1983.

We celebrated Mother's Day by taking Coleen to the Tom Sawyer Motor Inn Restaurant (her choice), and Mark brought her a beautiful desert plant with delicate green leaves filled with a network of white veins. Darker all-green leaves provided a backdrop, and the plant was growing in sandy soil with several colors (layers) showing on the bottom. It requires very little water.

Coleen is still a mother even though her children are thirty-nine and forty-one. She is keenly interested in their welfare, putting their interests ahead of hers.

She loves to hear news of Jeff's family, and they must know this. Jeff called this afternoon and she talked at length with both Jeff and Beth.

Further, she loves her grandchildren—seeing them as an extension of herself. She asks very little for herself and, as always, she is very frugal with money. She was more interested in learning what Mark wanted for his birthday (May 26) than in receiving something for her birthday on May 29.

To me this is the essence of motherhood in one's older years. It is one reason why I am still deeply in love with my wife. I share her family-centered values.

Vital Role of the Board of Appeals
May 18

I appeared before the Board of Appeals twice this month in support of an application for a variance by The Third Eye, a photographic studio and the owner of the building at 559 Delaware Avenue. The first session with the board was May 3.... The second session was last evening.

The Upper Delaware Avenue Neighborhood Association was more muted in its opposition last evening and those favoring the variance (including the former town supervisor, Tom Corrigan) gave spirited support.

But existing ordinances are clearly on the side of those opposing the variance and the seven-member board had arranged for its attorney, Donald DeAngelis, to cite chapter and verse. The situation doesn't look good for The Third Eye—whose photographer, Tom Knight, is vital to turning out a quality bicentennial history.

Even so, the board chairman (the late Charles Fritts) conducted the hearing in a fair, even, sensitive manner. It is clearly a good means for resolving zoning disputes among the citizens.

**Getting Off the Ground
with Bicentennial History Chapter
Community Organizations**
May 26

At last night's meeting, Kathleen Noonan, historian for the Bethlehem Women's Republican Club, turned over two large notebooks to me. They are filled with all manner of papers and photographs on the club, which was founded in 1926.

It was a bit overwhelming for me and, today I asked my assistant, Lisa Gray, to read the contents carefully and prepare a two-page summary for my use. I asked her to look especially for personal stories of the founders, colorful incidents in the life of the group, and black and white pictures suitable for publication.

This is the first test of our ability to synthesize a huge amount of data on a community organization and turn it into an appealing story.

If it works well, we will follow this same procedure on more than seventy organizations in Bethlehem's past and present.

Local Politics (Support for Sue Ann Ritchko)
June 4

After driving back from Ludlow, Vt., today, I attended a meeting at Sue Ann Ritchko's home with about twenty people. All of us will begin collecting signatures on "Designating Petitions" next Tuesday to place Sue Ann on the ballot for the Republican Party primary election on September 12, 1989.

All of us support her mainly because she has had a lot of experience in government: four years as a county legislator and four years on Bethlehem's town board. Further, I find her a stimulating, provocative leader

Bethlehem Women's Republican Club. Standing, left to right: Mary Prothers, Mildred Albright, Kathleen Becker, Marion Camp, Jeanne Vogel, Billie Dye. Seated, left to right: Helen Smith, Sue Ann Ritchko, Mary Bardwell, and Marjory O'Brien.

with good ideas and a winning manner of presenting them to the public.

We are not kidding ourselves. It will not be an easy campaign. The local Republican Party's committee system has endorsed Kenneth Ringler, a local businessman. He is well-liked and is currently serving as chairman of the powerful planning board. I will try to get forty signatures; six hundred are needed to get Sue Ann on the ballot.

The Annual Garage Sale: An Experience in Social Solidarity
June 24

Earlier this week, my neighbor, Sally Young, invited me to join in a multi-family garage sale which was advertised by her neighbors, Yale Sussman and Sherry Goldstein, across Dawson Road. Sussman and Goldstein are married and have two children but prefer to keep their original surnames. I couldn't help wondering (but didn't ask) what last name the children use.

We all did something to help. I borrowed signs from a local real estate firm and put them up; Sally made additional posters. The sale was to start at 9:00 A.M. today.

By 7:45 A.M., as all of us were setting out our sale items, four "early birds" arrived to see what we had...and were told we weren't ready. Sally had spent at least twenty hours in advanced planning and she was well organized for the sale. I spent a couple of hours last night—boxing small items, pricing them, putting up directional signs, and a dozen little things. Part of the fun for Coleen and me is agreeing on what should be sold and how much should be charged for each item.

Should the Oliver House be Preserved?
July 4

A few weeks ago Edward Kleinke, architect and former town planner, came to me for comment on an old building at Orchard Street and Fisher Boulevard in Delmar. He is preparing an evaluation of a developer's plan to build houses on the property—for use by the planning board. Coleen and I looked over the outside of the building and noticed the ancient (1830s) features but could easily see that it is about to fall down. Later, Kleinke gave me a copy of Dr. Robert Kuhn's remarks at an appeal board hearing and I read at length about his impassioned plea to save the house. He works for the historic preservation office downtown but lives near the site.

I asked Kleinke if he would arrange a meeting inside the house with the developers, his office, a historic preservation official, and the Bethlehem Archaeology Group represented. The meeting is scheduled for tomorrow.

Town Board Community Involvement Policy
July 27

I attended a meeting of town board last night to hear Bruce Secor, commissioner of public works, present a plan for expanding the town's recycling program to include bottles and plastics. A citizen task force has been studying the problem for more than a year. About fifteen people have been meeting regularly to address a serious landfill problem in our town. Space to dump waste is running out fast.

In brief, the proposal is to distribute plastic collection boxes and to encourage citizens to subdivide them with bags filled with the large categories of trash: newspapers, bottles and glass, and plastics. Cans will not be included now.

Town board has a regular habit of taking problems to the people and, as a result, the board has fewer problems in implementing new policies. The members seem genuinely glad to see people attend board meetings to raise questions from the audience. It is one big reason why Bethlehem is regarded as a nice place to live.

Kenneth Ringler Wins Bethlehem Republican Primary for Town Supervisor Post
September 12

My phone call to Ritchko election headquarters at 9:20 P.M. this evening from my poll-watching position at the Bethlehem Public Library turned out to be representative of all twenty-two election districts in Bethlehem:

District #2:
Kenneth Ringler: 105
Sue Ritchko: 89

I went to Sue Ann's home for the final party from 9:30 to 11:00 P.M. and all of us commiserated over the loss. One conclusion: it is an uphill battle to fight a well-organized party with a loyal, hard-working committee system. The final totals were:

Ringler: 2,503
Ritchko: 1,621

However, as Sue Ann told the press, "It was a good clean race that raised a lot of issues."

Now we'll pick up and move on. Ken Ringler deserves our cooperation and support in the months ahead.

Father William E. McConville.

Siena College Installs a New President
October 4

This seems to be education week. Coleen and I attended the inauguration of Dr. William McConville at Siena College today. I was representing the University of Maine at Presque Isle, my alma mater. I borrowed a robe from Ralph Tibbetts, a friend from SUNY Albany days.

It was a delightful affair—short speeches of welcome by several key officials, an inspiring address by Father McConville, some good choir music, chance meetings with graduates of my former SUNY Albany graduate program, and a picnic-style lunch on the lawn after the program.

Father McConville appears to be a catch for Siena College. He is only forty-three yet he is already a well-published scholar and a lecturer of some note. Most important of all, he appears to have adapted quickly to Siena's family-style campus and is already on a first-name basis with key members of the alumni, students, and faculty. I will follow his progress occasionally in subsequent volumes of this diary.

Chapter on Hamlets, Bicentennial History
October 6

Mrs. Ritchko is looking around for things to do since she lost the primary election for town supervisor...and, I believe she will do an excellent job of writing the chapter on hamlets. She said yes this week, and I organized a meeting of people (research assistants) who can help her. We will concentrate mainly on uncovering original records where any of the eighteen hamlets are mentioned. Joe Allgaier and I will lend a hand.

In my travels around Bethlehem, I have often encountered strong feelings of pride in particular sections of town—Slingerlands residents are fiercely proud of their small town residential character; Cedar Hill people dote on their history; if you live in Delmar, you are close to the action,

the seat of power; and Normansville residents are proud of their heritage and the Normansville Church is the center of their drumbeating. The list is endless. Therefore, it is crystal clear to me that a chapter on the hamlets is an absolute necessity.

My Mother
October 10

My mother, Mary Celia Estey Brewer, was a gentle, caring person who saw her primary role in life as helping her children achieve success in school and in keeping the home fires burning (literally) as her husband provided for the family. She was a good listener, and often a tactful trouble-shooter when problems arose among her seven children. She was a great cook with a number of specialties enjoyed by the whole family: baked beans and brown bread, cakes, pies, donuts, roast beef, and numerous nicely-prepared vegetables right out of the garden. Often required to economize on her slim household budget, she could fix potatoes a dozen different ways. Further, she repaired her children's clothing and helped us to feel that we were just as good as anyone in town when we set off for school.

I loved my mother and am now writing a family history in which I plan to feature her unique role in our family. Regretfully, she died at a very young age (fifty-two) in 1945 and we didn't get many chances to demonstrate our love for her or share our grandchildren with her.

Why We Give Annually to the Delmar Volunteer Fire Department
October 15

This was the day that Delmar volunteer firemen came around to all the neighborhoods in their shiny fire engine and slick-looking uniforms—the annual "support your fire company" day.

We gave them twenty dollars, and we always give. Where would we be without these self-appointed angels of mercy? Two of them drove me back to the hospital in the fire department ambulance at the height of a bad winter storm in 1982. I was in pain after premature release following a transurethal resection. It was wonderful to have them come so quickly. And I've heard stories about them risking their lives to save an elderly person or a young child at a fire. They must do it out of a sense of mission. Lord knows, they don't do it for money.

At times, I get the feeling that the three most appreciated organizations in our town are the volunteer fire departments, the library, and the senior citizens office at town hall—in that order.

Smoking Again
October 18

Smokers in public places annoy me. I am aware that many people have a difficult time kicking the habit, but the least they can do for others is to wait an hour until they leave a public restaurant...or the few minutes they are in the post office or other public building.

However, it is nice to see small changes in the behavior of smokers. I've noticed that some of them are taking the most remote seats possible in restaurants. One confirmed smoker is now trying to avoid smoking during her meal at the Four Corners Luncheonette in Delmar—and lights up as she is paying her bill. We're looking forward to the day when she can wait until she gets outside. And, in meetings I've been attending, smokers often sit at the end of (even a little away from) the table and often ask, "Do you mind if I smoke?" Many non-smokers are now responding, "Can you wait awhile?" or, "I'd rather you didn't."

The Most Exciting Events in September and October
October 22

Hurricane Hugo (September 21) and the California earthquake (October 17) created a great deal of excitement and concern in this area over the past month. So many people have relatives in South Carolina, where Hugo hit with a fury, and in Oakland-San Francisco, where the loss of life from the collapse of a two-decker highway approached an estimated 270.

The overall damage of Hugo is estimated at $5 billion but the human cost far overshadows broken sticks and stones. The phrases "enormous deprivation" and "astonishing generosity" best describe the overall picture. Cleanup crews from many states descended on South Carolina to help the residents restore power and get their homes back in shape. The government's Federal Emergency Management Agency was slow to act but thorough when it did. Inspectors must review the damage before approving claims. Only about two thousand claims have been approved thus far out of more than 23,000 filed. About fifty people died in the hurricane.

October 23

For a few days I was tempted to record the 190-point drop in the market on October 13 but then came the 6.9 earthquake in the bay area on October 17. It was nothing like the quake in Soviet Armenia but tell that to any of the people in the Marina section of San Francisco and they will say, "We suffered too!" And the businessmen in Santa Cruz where most of them lost everything—it will take years to re-

cover. Most of all, the horrifying spectacle of a double-deck freeway collapsing in Oakland squashing dozens of motorists with tons of concrete...led to scene after scene of dead bodies being pulled from flattened cars.

Living along the San Andreas fault must leave the residents in a continual state of psychic tension. Do they ever get used to it? Historians and psychologists say they do but, given a choice, I would prefer not to live along the fault. We love to visit San Francisco but have often said..."Ten days is enough!" Even so, if we are to judge from history, Californians will pick themselves up, rebuild, and wait for the next quake.

Preoccupation with Animal Control
October 24

Ruth Bickel and I began a careful reading of the minutes of town of Bethlehem government today at the town clerk's office. I was struck by the stringent problems with the control of domestic and wild animals:

1803—Bounty for a wolf's head-$60, raised to $100 in 1805. (It must have been a terrific problem since a hundred dollars for one wolf's head must have been a fortune in those days.)

1804—$2.50 fine for cattle found wandering on the highways.

1806—Hogs and geese to be kept fast (not allowed to roam).

1814—Rams to be kept fast from first day of September until the tenth day of November.

Additionally, I noticed that the bounty for a wolf's head had dropped to $10 by 1814.

The Local Vote
November 7

As a registered Republican, I usually vote for Republican candidates partly because I know them better. Once in awhile, I do not support the local party's choice (as per notes in this diary on September 10-12) and go my own way as I did with the Ritchko-Ringler race in the primary for the position of town supervisor.

A Democrat, John Smolinsky, is running for a town board seat against Sheila Galvin and Charles Gunner. Two positions are open; one candidate will have to lose.

Deep down, I want an environmentalist (like Smolinsky) on the board, but he would be a gadfly on the back of one of our strongest town officials, Bruce Secor, commissioner of public works, and I don't want to do anything that might cause Bruce to resign. So, reluctantly, Coleen and I voted for Gunner and Galvin today along with Ringler, Lyons, Cross, and Fritts—a straight Republican ticket. Late results tonight show that the entire Republican ticket won. Smolinsky lost by more than one thousand votes.

18th Annual Albany Festival of Nations
November 13

Coleen and I attended the Festival of Nations yesterday at the Empire State Plaza. It was fun mingling with thousands of people who came to nibble on Scandinavian pastry, Armenian baklava (we had both), and dozens of other ethnic foods.

This year, the chairman, Manoj Ajmera, hails from India, and two Russians, Cecelia Soloviev and Taisia Fedorov, vice-chairman and secretary, respectively, handled the details, while a Ukrainian, Luba Kushnir, took care of the money in her role as treasurer.

Most of all, we liked the dances and songs of other countries performed by dozens of local representatives of these local groups. Some were dull (like the French Canadian singer) but others were lively and colorful (like the Polish dancers from Schenectady).

The festival makes you much more conscious of the huge number of people from other countries living in the Albany area—a feeling of one world and a feeling that I like very much.

Too Many Fast Food Restaurants Destroy a Town's Character
November 20

We have a McDonald's restaurant and a Dunkin' Donuts coffee shop, and I like the doughnut place. Any town needs two or three such quick-stop places. But then a Ponderosa steak house moved in last year, and we've been there a couple of times. Also a Wacky Wings restaurant took over a spot up at the Delaware Plaza. In addition, we have a Ben & Jerry's ice cream parlor and The Country's Best Yogurt, two places Coleen and I visit occasionally.

Now I hear that Burger King wants a place out this way, and there are rumors of two additional places of the fast food type.

I don't want any more growth in this direction. Soon we will lose the rich variety of locally-owned places like Tool's Restaurant and the Toll Gate ice cream parlor and restaurant if there is much more competition from the chains. That would be a tragedy for Bethlehem. I plan to speak loudly at planning and appeal board hearings against further development like this. Enough is enough!

Generational Differences with Computer Skills
November 27

My grandson, Jonathan, age fourteen, sat down with me at my computer last Saturday, and he asked a number of questions about how my new Panasonic printer works. I explained the limited ways I was using the machine and he proceeded to "hack" away with the buttons to show me how I can get more out of it.

I hadn't bothered to use the variety of type possible. He demonstrated how easy it is to change the type. I hadn't bothered to put the computer on continuous print for longer papers and Jonathan asked, why not? Further, he demonstrated how it is done. I could easily have found that one in the manual but was content to tear off one page at a time.

The experience demonstrates what I have known for a long time—young people who grow up with computers in the schools find those thick instruction manuals less formidable than us older folks.

Phrases Others Use That Annoy Me
December 2

"To be really honest with you..." some people begin, in response to my question; and I always think, aren't you always honest with me? Don't they ever consider the impact of this phrase on others?

And some people I have known keep saying "you know" in their conversations with me...to a point where I sometimes tell them that I am so distracted

Last day at the office for Supervisor Hendrick.

Retirement party for Town Supervisor J. Robert Hendrick. Left to right: Gloria Johnson, Kay Hendrick, J. Robert Hendrick.

by all of their "you knows" that I miss the point they're making.

Waitresses who greet us cheerily as we enter a motel coffee shop early in the mornings...with "And how are we this morning?" I think, how sickening. And people who say "you're kidding" when they know I'm not, annoy me to no end as do people who keep saying, "that's interesting." I often think, What do they mean by that? I would rather have them evaluate what I say.

Town Supervisor, Robert Hendrick, Retires
December 7

Coleen and I, along with Ralph and Muriel Wood, bought tickets to Bob Hendrick's farewell party. About 160 packed two rooms at the [Normanside Country Club]. A "cocktail buffet" means three portable (heated) carts with pasta, meatballs, hot ham and rolls with raisin gravy, and several hot hors d'oeuvres brought around by waitresses periodically. We talked with a great many people from all walks of Bethlehem life.

It was clear that many in the group thought Bob Hendrick had done a great job as supervisor over the past five years. He thanked Ruth Bickel (who presented him with a $300 gift certificate) and everyone there for coming—particularly town employees whom he singled out for special praise.

THE FOUR CORNERS DRUG STORE
DELMAR. MARK L. PECKHAM, AUGUST 28, 1975.

18TH C. DUTCH BARN. TROUBADOUR FARM
GLENMONT. MARK L. PECKHAM, AUGUST 24, 1991.

8 *Nineteen Hundred Ninety*

For Floyd, this was a year filled with setbacks.

As editor of the town's bicentennial history book, he was feeling increasing pressure as deadlines loomed. Worried he might omit some group, individual, or contribution from the book, he scurried to gather even more information for his chapter on town organizations.

His hard work, however, could not stem other obstacles—declining attendance at the Bethlehem Bicentennial Commission meetings, loss of other editors and writers for the bicentennial history, and a flap over the methods Floyd was using to drum up funds to buy desktop publishing equip-

ment for the history book's production.

Even his niche in his adopted field of archaeology came under scrutiny when he was called to task for failing to credit others adequately in an article he submitted to an archaeological magazine.

All this was during a year when Floyd, normally a healthy man, found himself uncharacteristically enmeshed in a world of doctors, medicines, and hospitals.

Still, as the year ended, his optimism rebounded, and he brushed aside many of 1990's dark clouds, vowing in a late December diary entry his intention to move on to "Plan B."

Organizational Meeting:
Town of Bethlehem
January 2

Kenneth Ringler was sworn in as the new town supervisor today at noon, along with Charles Gunner (former high school principal), councilman; M. Sheila Galvin (an attorney), councilwoman; Roger Fritts, town justice; Martin Cross, highway superinten-

dent; and Carolyn M. Lyons, town clerk.

It was a speedy meeting with Ringler reading page after page of names of salaried town employees and calling for a vote after each department's list was read.

The only controversy in the entire meeting was the lone Democrat's (Bob

Kenneth Ringler, town supervisor.

Comment on Town Salaries
January 5

Top officials in Bethlehem receive a little over $50,000 and chief administrative officers—in basic areas as police and finance—earn salaries in the $40,000 plus range. There are numerous clerk/typists and account clerks earning $15,000 to $20,000; public works and highway technical personnel making $20,000 to $35,000; and numerous part-timers earning $4.75 (switchboard operators) to $8.03 per hour (police radio dispatchers).

In short, running a town this size costs a lot of money. The total annual budget is $16 million or so.

Having watched the growth process and ever-accelerating taxes for twenty-four years, my feeling is that it is time to level off. We need to stop the tax spiral so the over-sixty residents can continue to live here. This is especially important in that the over-sixty group is the fastest growing segment of Bethlehem's population. Bring in light (smoke-free) industry to increase the tax base, but don't raise taxes for the average citizen.

Burns) challenge to the town attorney's (Bernard Kaplowitz) continuation as both head of the local Republican Party and town attorney. He sees a conflict of interest in this arrangement—but wisely did not try to bring the matter to a vote.

Once again, the board voted a $500 contract for the Bethlehem Archaeology Group—badly needed this year. I enjoyed the meeting and feel more in touch with town affairs than I have felt in years past.

Financial Records
January 26

It is useful to me to look at the changes in our spending habits today compared to five years ago. Frankly, it is a much brighter picture than I expected when we were at the point of retirement in 1983.

The old axiom "nothing ever goes down" seems to apply. ...groceries have gone up about $25 every other week, recreation has almost doubled, and I am putting $20 in a special family history account every other week. Otherwise, our expenses are similar to 1985.

There are some prophets of doom out there who say the economy is headed for a recession but I don't see enough evidence of it at this point to make any changes in our spending.

The market value of our house has gone down to about $125,000 or so, but in most ways, life is just as rosy as it was five years ago.

Facing Up to Reality
March 13

Our lab equipment, furnishings, and numerous boxes of artifacts must be compressed into three rooms (and another three rooms of storage downstairs). The lab crew packed dozens of items yesterday, and a highway department maintenance crew moved the heavy things downstairs. Dozens of banana boxes full of objects recovered from area archaeological sites were moved off of shelving in the lab so the shelving can be dismantled and re-erected downstairs.

And so we've accepted the fact that we'll have only half as much space in which to do our work, and we're trying to cooperate with the highway maintenance crew in charge of revamping the Waldenmaier building and turning it into a first class recycling center.

From the town's point of view, recycling waste material has become a major priority in town government in 1990. The state has put on a lot of pressure with a new law, and the town must comply or be fined.

Allison Chesbro Bennett
March 25

Coleen and I attended a Friends of the Bethlehem Public Library luncheon yesterday at which Allison Bennett was the main speaker. We went mainly to hear her, and agree with many others in Bethlehem that Allison Bennett is a pretty special person. She talked about writing *The People's Choice*, a history about Albany County art and architecture, and painted a picture of a woman determined to make a difference in our community. It was a "you can make it happen" kind of philosophy I very much admire. We share many of the same values.

Allison married into a well-known family in Bethlehem. Her husband, William D. Bennett, was president of the Selkirk Security Supply Corporation, a wholesaler and distributor of

117

Allison Bennett, historian.

and gradually spread throughout the area.

Beyond *The People's Choice*, Allison has published *Times Remembered* (1984) and *More Times Remembered* (1987), collections of her articles in *The Spotlight*, a weekly paper. I know a lot of people who enjoy Allison's *Spotlight* articles. I read them word for word, sometimes twice. No doubt she will publish *"Many More Times Remembered"* when she has sufficient articles accumulated.

Allison Bennett's contribution to Bethlehem's history will live on many years after her death.

quality plumbing and heating supplies. His father, William M. Bennett, established the business soon after World War I and Bill joined him in the business following his discharge from the Navy in 1945. Their son, Keith, is now vice president of the company.

The Bennett Family in Bethlehem
March 26

William M. Bennett's family line can be traced back to Daniel Bennett (1777-1813), who came to this area from Fairfield Green, Gloucestershire, England, in 1802. Later generations of the family prospered at the family farm on Bennett Hill in Clarksville,

Jennifer Coon—High School Junior
April 6

Jennifer came to see me at the lab yesterday to learn about the field of archaeology. She is enrolled in the guidance department's Shadow Program which brings young people together with specialists in various fields to help them discover if it really interests them. A *Spotlight* photographer arrived about 2:00 P.M. to take pictures.

It seemed to me that our meeting was helpful to Jennifer. I gave her a tour of the lab, explained how dozens of things around the lab relate to the process of conducting an archaeological investigation and writing about the results. Additionally, we talked

Jennifer Coon learning about archaeology from Floyd Brewer.

"Turbo Pascal 5.5 Objects." Greek to me, but to them it was a system for teaching young people how to write their own programs. We agreed it would be a good birthday gift for Jonathan. The cost is $149.95. Because of the expense, Mark and I will share equally with Jeff and Beth in buying it next fall. Beth bought a software package to "create your own stationery," which she plans to do on the family's Radio Shack Tandy 1000.

about training programs, mainly anthropology.

I enjoy sessions like this immensely and feel they are often important for students and volunteers. Jennifer said it was helpful.

I couldn't help but think—such a store didn't exist fifteen years ago.

Babbage's—The Computer Software "Package" Store
April 14

Mark and I went shopping with Jeff's family this afternoon, and spent a lot of time at Babbage's software store at the Crossgates Mall. Amazingly, there is little else in the store except row after row of shiny little cellophane-wrapped packages of computer software in myriad forms.

Jeff and Jonathan showed considerable interest in something marked

Senior Citizens Health Prevention Programs
April 18

Working at town hall every Tuesday afternoon makes it easy for me to stop by the community room to have my blood pressure checked. This helpful program for senior citizens is sponsored by town board and administered by two former board members, Ruth Oliver Bickel and Marion Camp. My blood pressure yesterday was 138/78. The ideal is anything under 140/90, so mine is good.

The local Association for the Blind was also represented in the commu-

Ruth Oliver Bickel.

nity room, and I listened to their message. I was amazed to learn that nearly blind or blind citizens of this area can get a free radio over which there are daily broadcasts. The Albany *Times Union* is read in the morning, the Schenectady *Gazette* in the afternoon. Additionally, they demonstrated a new "talking clock" and several other convenient gadgets designed to help people who see poorly or cannot see at all.

The Issue of Blood Type
May 10

During a recent transurethral operation at St. Peter's Hospital I learned

that I had received two units of A-negative blood during the second operation from the nurse attending me this morning. She was exchanging information about my record with another nurse.

I said immediately, "But I'm not A-negative." I've had O-positive assessments all of my life, beginning with my work as an air cadet in 1944.

This was the day that my eyes looked a little yellow, a condition also noticed by the nurse. She reported the condition to doctors Oberheim and Nebro (a bladder/kidney specialist). Both said it was common following a traumatic operation; yet, they seemed to redouble their efforts to double-check the reason for it with extra tests. I appreciated this.

Glad to Get Out But...
May 16

It was great coming home with Coleen and our nurse/neighbor/friend, Helen Nickel, this morning. I feel weak, but immensely relieved to leave the hospital. Even so, I am troubled that the errors made in the operating room during my two operations could easily be made with one or more future patients, and I am having a difficult time living with this possibility. Finally, I made a firm decision today to request an administrative hearing of procedures followed in the operating room during my May 8 operations

Bethlehem report

and let the chips fall where they may. I can do no less.

Bethlehem Report:
Another Vital Newsletter
May 30

There are several good sources of information about the changing scene in our town, and *Bethlehem Report* is one of the best. It is issued by Lynn Corrigan in the town supervisor's office, and naturally contains a lot of information about town government. However, I find it to be high on facts and short on personal opinion, two qualities I admire in publications like this.

The current issue contains an article by the town's new recycling coordinator, Sharon Fisher, with helpful graphics, explaining how citizens will soon be asked to sort trash.

Also, our new supervisor, Ken Ringler, reviewed his first three months in office. We particularly appreciate his Bethlehem beautification ideas. For starters, the town recently planted a tree in a small island in the street at the Four Corners, and paved the rest of the island with historic bricks removed from the "Old Yellow Brick Road," located in Normansville.

The newsletter is must reading for us.

Sony Compact Disk
Radio Cassette Player
June 12

The family got me started toward purchasing this equipment for $267 through generous birthday gifts on May 6, and I've been playing it for over a month.

First, compact disks do everything claimed for them: flawless, beautiful music for fifty to seventy minutes, depending on the selection.

When a disk is inserted, the length of time required to play it appears in a little window on the front of the set. Then you simply push the "play" button.

I have yet to learn how the laser principle picks up the sound from the record but it is sufficient to say that the sound far outweighs the long-playing records in my former collection. Further, this equipment has a five band graphic equalizer enabling me to adjust the sound to my taste: almost always low background music emphasizing the bass speakers.

Dr. Richard A. Atkins
June 30

Our neighbor, Dick Atkins, eighty-two, passed away last Sunday at the Albany Medical Center. I attended a memorial service in his honor at the Methodist Church in Delmar yesterday. We believe he died of complications due to emphysema, a disease in which the alveoli (tiny air sacs) in the lungs become damaged. His respiratory illness has been obvious to neighbors for more than ten years. He often read the paper leaning over the back of his car—obviously a comfortable position for him.

Dick was first deputy commissioner for local government for New York state from 1969 to 1972 when he joined the State Senate Task Force on Critical Problems, a position he held until 1981, when he retired.

He earned a B.A. from Hamilton College (1929), an M.S. from Syracuse University, and a Ph.D. from Harvard. Dick and his wife, Helen, had three daughters. Other than the minister, only his daughter, Virginia, spoke at the memorial service. He lived a quiet, unassuming life, and his final ceremony was quiet and uneventful, possibly just as he wanted it to be.

**Hospital Responds
to My Letter of May 26**
July 15-16

It is obvious that the hospital staff did not want to deal with the life-threatening aspects of my May 26 inquiry in print; however, my sense is that a good faith effort was made to examine hospital procedures regarding the potential for giving the wrong blood type to a patient.

Even so, if I hear of another instance of this problem, I will quickly ask for a hearing before the hospital's Quality Assurance Committee and relate my experience as they examine the new case. One way or another, the wrong blood type problem has to be stopped.

July 6, 1990

Dear Mr. Brewer:

Thank you for recently affording me the opportunity to speak with you. As requested during our discussion, the following is a brief summary of the information that I provided to you in response to the questions that you raised in your letter:

There were no operational or procedural problems within the

transfusion service. An error had been made by a phlebotomist (who drew your blood) in identifying and labeling the specimen which was submitted to the transfusion service. The phlebotomist was placed on suspension for three weeks and later resigned.

A search of Transfusion Service records from 1983-May of 1990 conducted when your May 7 specimen was received showed no previous records for you with respect to the typing or cross matching of your blood. Therefore you were not known by Transfusion Services to be O Positive.

Compatibility testing between donor and recipient is required by New York State Public Health Law. Such compatibility testing was performed. However, since the specimen submitted to Transfusion Service as yours was that of a different patient due to a phlebotomy error, the crossmatch was compatible with that specimen.

I would defer any response to the question that you raised concerning whether or not you were subjected to a potentially life-threatening situation when given the wrong blood to your attending physician.

Transfusion Services may not use any records other than those in their own files in determining the patient's blood type. Those filed may only be used for comparison with the results of the current testing.

You were admitted to the Recovery Room at 9:40 A.M. and remained there until 5:30 P.M. at which time you returned to the Operating Room. During that time Dr. Oberheim was aware of your condition and was monitoring same. He saw you during that time period on three occasions.

In order to avoid recurrence and the potential for a mislabeled specimen we have implemented the following procedure: If a patient has an order requiring a specimen for the Transfusion Service, the phlebotomist may draw only that patient and must return to the laboratory with the blood specimens immediately.

Should you have any questions concerning this matter, or require any additional information please do not hesitate to call upon me.

I was happy to learn that you are feeling well and continue to hold St. Peter's Hospital in high regard. We regret the difficulties that you encountered but feel confident that we have

The Village Stage presents *Pajama Game*, March 27, 1994. Left to right: Helen Scott, Muriel Nevens, Cheryl Karam, Lee Ryan, Carol Butler, and Linda Panzer.

undertaken the appropriate action to assure that our patients are provided with quality care.

Very truly yours,

Judith M. Phaff
Director of Risk
Management

Bethlehem's Village Stage
August 6-7

Coleen and I have enjoyed Village Stage performances for several years, most recently their performance of *The Bells Are Ringing*. Mrs. Dominick (Patricia) DeCecco organized a group to put on a variety show in honor of the Bethlehem School District's fiftieth anniversary in the spring of 1983. It was such a resounding success that the group stayed together.

It was Pat DeCecco who suggested that the variety show troupe stay together, who invited attorney William Schoonmaker to work with her in acquiring incorporated, tax-free status for the group (he suggested the name); who struggled through the development of a constitution for the group; and who developed a budget ($6,240) for the first play, *The Fantastiks*, presented on March 1-2, 1985. Every group has a prime mover, often the first president, as in this instance.

Patricia DeCecco has been an anchor for the group's many performances since 1985, including *Ballroom* (1986), *Little Mary Sunshine* (1987), *An Evening of Three One Acts* (*I'm Herbert, Public Eye* and *From Five to Five Thirty*) (1988), *Pajama Game* (1989), and *The Bells are Ringing* (1990). All of these were spring musicals. The group has also presented a number of free plays throughout the area in the fall as well.

Most Village Stage troupers are employed full time and many have a family. You wonder how they find the time for rehearsals and all the performances and, ultimately, you conclude that it is a labor of love. They love the stage, and the many members who work on tickets, publicity, backstage, etc., just want to be part of exciting events.

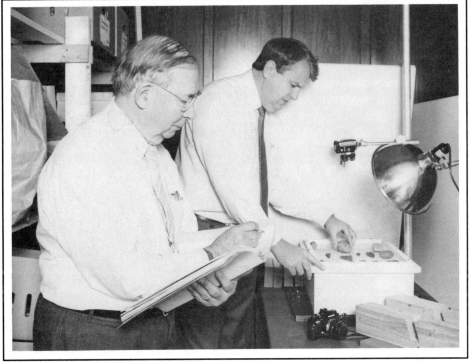

Benjamin French, left, working on photographs at Archaeology Laboratory with Chuck McKinney.

The group often says its primary purpose is to "entertain, enrich and educate." I can testify that it does all three very well.

Benjamin French
August 12

The Bethlehem Archaeology Group's field photographer, Ben French, died last Wednesday, at the age of seventy-five....he underwent two operations to remove blood clots from the cranium the first week in May and gradually lost ground until his death. Other references to Ben in this diary over the

last few years show that he probably suffered the brain injury several years ago. Despite suggestions from his wife and others, Ben would not ask physicians for a thorough biomedical workup. He might have lived a much longer life if he had sought expert medical assistance sooner.

Ben French's funeral at 2:00 P.M. today in the Delmar Reformed Church was attended by about seventy-five people. He had directed that he should be buried at the National Cemetery because he was especially proud of his status as a lieutenant colonel in the U.S. Signal Corps in World War II.

Bethlehem Tomboys
August 16-17

As I write the community organizations chapter for the bicentennial history, a number of unusual groups have surfaced. The meteoric rise of the Bethlehem Tomboys, a girls' softball team, is a good case in point. Neither Coleen nor I follows sports, but one can hardly miss noticing a group with a name like that.

Dr. Irving VanWoert, a local radiologist, first coach of the team, and manager Susan Singer inspired the first team of fifteen young girls to win an Albany area championship in the summer of 1972 and third place in Miss Softball American playoffs in Anaheim, Calif., the same year.

These victories attracted 200 girls to the team in 1973 and membership peaked at a little more than 300 in the late 1970s. This is phenomenal growth in a clean, healthy sport.

I try to dig beneath the surface as I write the history of a group. How did they finance all of the Tomboy teams? Apparently local businesses footed the bill. Who handled all of the organizational details, contact with parents, uniforms, etc.? I've learned that John Castiglione and his wife, Sally, did this in the beginning in their capacities as president and vice president of the first board of directors. They were assisted by Sally Abele, secretary, Fred and Jean Frattura, Rex Hornibrook, Nan Richter and Bob Ruckerstuhl, all

board members and undoubtedly parents with daughters on a Tomboy team.

Things picked up considerably around 1975 when the teams started playing on the beautifully maintained town recreation department's fields on Elm Avenue.

Now the teams use professional umpires and are involved in divisional playoffs at the end of each year. The town is fortunate in having such a great opportunity for young girls (ages ten to seventeen) to compete and in having men of Irving VanWoert's caliber to work with them.

The Men Married to the Women in Coleen's Gourmet Club
August 19

May Blackmore and Helen Nickel put on a gourmet picnic dinner today at Helen's home for the club members and their husbands. It was attended by Floyd and Coleen Brewer, May and William Blackmore, Doris Gold (widow), Mary and Alan Davitt, Elaine and Martin Smith, Helen Nickel, Dorothy and Darwin Hinsdale, and Peggy and Joseph Zimmerman. Corn curls were served with guacomole and jalapeno dips as a first course along with wine, a non-alcoholic beverage, and other drinks. After forty-five minutes or so, Helen and May served grilled lemon chicken, refried rice, jellied gazpacho, bean salad—all topped off with a delicious flan and tea or coffee.

I enjoyed long conversations with Bill Blackmore, a retired research physician full of stories; Alan Davitt, a Catholic liaison official with state government; Martin Smith, a retired man who enjoys his postage stamp hobby; Darwin Hinsdale, who saves up jokes; and Joe Zimmerman, a political science professor at SUNY Albany who seemed a little ill at ease socially. However, his work with doctoral students turns him on. I tried to learn more about them than to tell of my own retirement activities. It was a fun picnic and an interesting collection of people.

Kenneth Ringler, Town Supervisor
September 7

Ken Ringler saw me for a half hour this morning to review my need for $6,742 worth of desktop publishing equipment for the Bethlehem Archaeology Group's second book.

I found him a good listener who is supportive of helpful town projects, but also one who doesn't make snap decisions. I gave him several typewritten pages outlining income and expense estimates and left feeling that my request would get a fair hearing.

Ringler has numerous serious budget problems, and I was a little surprised that he would give an officer of a group that has only a loose connection with the town such a cordial hearing.

I liked his manner, his penetrating questions, and his willingness to take a proactive stance toward helping me get the funds needed.

My Role Model in Archaeology
September 12

We arrived at the Hampton Inn in Williamsburg last evening, and after dinner at the Cracker Barrel, we settled in for the evening. I visited Norman Barka, professor of anthropology at the College of William and Mary, at 10:00 A.M. today. Dr. Barka is responsible for starting me in archaeology.

He has remarried since I saw him last to one of his archaeology students, and she occasionally digs with him on St. Eustasius, the Dutch West Indies. He invited me to dig with him there any summer I can. It was a nostalgic visit for me with a man I very much admire, a key figure in historical archaeology in this country and abroad. He offered some hints for my second book and urged me to read Dr. Kathleen Deegan's story of St. Augustine.

Coleen Brewer, ca. 1941.

and, I thought, she probably comes from a ritzy home and I wouldn't stand a chance with her. Despite my doubts, I resolved to find a way to meet her on Saturday and ask her to go to a movie with me. This picture [at left] was taken in April 1944, a few years after we met, but it is very much like she looked when I first saw her. This explains why I carried the picture in my wallet for forty years.

**Dutch Barns
in the Town of Bethlehem**
September 21

Coleen and I attended a lecture on Dutch barns in upper New York state at the Cedar Hill museum last evening. The speaker, Mark Hessler, stressed the architectural aspects of Dutch barns.

**Working Up the Nerve
to Meet Coleen Hamilton
Fifty Years Ago This Week**
September 14

We drove from Williamsburg to Colonial Beach, Va., today and swapped stories about how we met fifty years ago tomorrow noon. Coleen said she first saw me walking on the lawn at the Aroostook State Normal School (now the University of Maine) at Presque Isle earlier this week fifty years ago, and I said I first saw her on Wednesday and made up my mind that I just had to meet her. She was beautiful, she had a pleasant smile,

His remarks recalled the Dutch barns I've driven by in our own town. As Allison Bennett has noted on page forty in *Times Remembered*, there are at least six in Bethlehem: (1) Elm Avenue south of Feura Bush Road, (2) corner of Route 53 and Elm Avenue, (3) Van Dyke Road off Route 443 (now demolished), (4) Route 9W opposite the First Reformed Church of Bethlehem, (5) Jericho Road in Selkirk, and (6) Feura Bush Road in Glenmont.

The features are similar in all of these barns: strong H-frame construction inside; steep, slanted, high-peaked roof; low side walls; small air holes in the upper portion of the end walls;

wide clapboard siding; and a small shed-like roof extending out a few feet over the barn door.

These barns are sturdy. Although most of them are in poor repair right now, they have stood the test of time for more than two hundred years.

Bethlehem Community Christmas Festival, Since 1942
September 23-24

As I write about groups for the community organizations chapter in the bicentennial history, it has become clear that our history is full of inspiring examples of community cooperation and initiative to solve a variety of problems. The Bethlehem Community Christmas Festival was celebrating its twenty-fifth year when we arrived in 1966.

Mrs. Warren C. (Joanne) Kimmey was chairman of the festival that year and, as *The Spotlight* reporter noted, "the festival originated as a community involvement to keep alive the true spirit of Christmas, that of caring and sharing for those in the area who need help."

Our impression then was that the festival was indeed a huge community undertaking. A central committee included Mrs. Perry Dunn in charge of community relations, Miss Marjorie Reid as secretary, and John Haker as treasurer. Mr. and Mrs. Arthur Dill from the Bethlehem Lutheran Church

were in charge of the White Christmas program, Mr. and Mrs. Robert Denny were in charge of the clothes closet, Col. and Mrs.. J. Marotta, representing St. Thomas's Church, handled hospitality, Mr. and Mrs. Everett Watson took care of decorations, Mrs. Joseph Stella was in charge of wardrobe, Mr. and Mrs. Millard Larkin from the Methodist Church published the program, Mrs. Pasquale Pugliese of St. Stephen's Church was in charge of remembrance, William Bub, a popular electrician in town, handled staging and scenery, and Mrs. Everett Parry was the committee's publicity chairman.

I mention all of these names only to show how many parts of the community were working together for a good cause.

But why was the name changed? No one seems to remember for sure, but I suspect some group complained that the public schools (middle school and later the high school) shouldn't be used for sectarian purposes. Too bad that such constraints are downgrading some really inspiring examples of community cooperation and initiative.

Bethlehem Dentists
September 25-26

No fewer than twenty-one dentists are listed in the 1990-1991 Tri-Village Directory. I drove my neighbor Ruth Weir to Dr. Virginia Plaisted's office at 74 Delaware Avenue yesterday. She pulled three of Ruth's teeth. Ruth said, "To save my teeth it would have cost about $3,000; so, I decided to have some of them removed—cutting my cost for the total job to about $1,000." Dr. Plaisted's wall files were bulging with patient records, and I assume this means she is both a popular and a busy dentist.

Coleen and I have been going to Dr. John E. Manne's office at 64 Delmar Place for almost twenty years. He cleaned our teeth last week, something we have done twice each year, and I returned this morning for an apicoectomy on a lower front tooth and a gingivectomy on a lower right wisdom tooth. I was somewhat surprised to have him discover both of these problems since I use a Water Pik regularly and do everything possible to keep my teeth free of food particles after meals.

We have stayed with Dr. Manne all these years because he is a very competent dentist who does everything we need. He has not referred either of us to another specialist in almost two decades of visits to his office.

Joe Allgaier Accepts Writing Role for the Government Chapter in the Bicentennial History
October 1

Joe Allgaier, associate editor, agreed to fill a vacancy created by the withdrawal of Valerie Thompson as writer of the government chapter.

I had breakfast with Allgaier at Tool's restaurant this morning. We went over the objectives for the chapter, and I shared a number of documents with him.

He will begin with some research on Phillip Van Rensselaer, Bethlehem's first supervisor in 1794, but will quickly expand his work by looking over the numerous volumes of minutes of town board meetings and road expansion records.

Joe is an excellent researcher and a skilled writer. The government chapter is in good hands and a lot of people in and out of government will help him do a quality chapter.

Music Over the Ages in Bethlehem
October 17

Most people I meet in my travels have never heard of the Delmar Concert Orchestra and Delmar Choral Society, but we musn't forget that Bethlehem citizens were exposed to beautiful music provided by these two groups in the 1930s. They presented complete works such as *The Mikado* under the direction of Donald W. Dewire, conductor, and his wife, Ethel, accompanist.

I talked with orchestra member George A. Lansing (violin) the other day and he recalls with enthusiasm the privilege of playing a Stradivarius on loan from the Smithsonian Institution. Claude White (trombone) loved his instrument so much that he organized a dance band on the side, all of this along with working full time.

Mrs. Lucille Palmer remembers singing the role of Pitti-Sing in *The Mikado* and the feeling of satisfaction she got from the applause of appreciative citizens. Undoubtedly, similar groups existed in the nineteenth century, but I have yet to find a record of their existence.

Ralph B. Wood in his workshop.

Martha Dickinson Shattuck Speaks at Bethlehem Historical Association Program
October 18

Martha spoke on the subject of "Mother, Wife, and Tavern Keeper: Women and the Law in Seventeenth Century Albany, NY. " Unlike most speakers at BHA programs, she did not use slides; instead, she painted pictures with words about the lives of women in early Albany.

It was a life of hard work—a lot of cooking and cleaning at home, often work in brawling taverns, yet freedom to speak their minds in court (many did) and freedom to seek divorce (few did).

I asked if infidelity on the part of wives was a problem aired in the courts and Martha replied no—her research uncovered no such cases.

This was a rare opportunity to hear some results of the excellent work being done in the New Netherland Project at the State Library in Albany. Researchers there have published several books on early Dutch life that are especially valuable to historians, librarians, and related fields.

Ralph Wood's Love of Tools
October 19

I visited Ralph Wood's workshop in the basement of his home at 43 Longwood Drive in Delmar today. My purpose was to take black and white pictures of him using a few of the hundreds of tools he owns. In particular, I wanted him to demonstrate how he uses the old wooden planes, drills, and other antique tools. The pictures are needed for an exhibit in town hall next month.

Ralph explained the uses of a number of tools as he demonstrated how they are used. He seems to have a natural feeling for the tool designer's plan for each tool he discussed. Although I had been in his workshop before, I took special notice of his ability to fix just about anything, whether it requires a metal part manufactured on one of his machines or a piece of wood in any shape or size. A visit to Ralph Wood's workshop inspires a feeling of awe for his skills. It is a tool lover's paradise.

**John E. Manne, Dentist
and Sportsman**
October 21-22

I wrote about Dr. Manne's work as a dentist in this diary on September 25-26 and October 2; however, his leisure time as a sportsman deserves mention as well.

John has been a member of the Bethlehem Sportsmen's Club for more than thirty years. He is such a fixture at the club's lodge on Dunbar Hollow Road in Clarksville that he can tell the long story of the club without stopping. In fact, his stories about a wide variety of subjects are one big reason Coleen and I enjoy our visits to his office.

He said the first meeting of the club was held at the Delmar Tavern in 1946. Harry Ochner was elected president; Edward Kuhl, vice president; Charles Quay, treasurer; and Edward Hehre, secretary. The club bought ten acres (with an option for more) on Dunbar Hollow Road on June 11, 1947. In October 1947, the group formed a Junior Rifle Club to promote safe gun handling and responsible behavior. He said the rifle club was largely the work of committee members: Mr. Prue, Dr. Maxon, and Charles Palmer.

In the same year (1947) John Souk, Frank Burke, and Frank DeNough served on another committee to purchase the entire farm and erect a clubhouse. Now, forty-four years later, the club has a sumptuous log house on 230 acres, a picnic pavilion; trap, pistol, and rifle ranges; a pond; and a field archery range. Membership grew from the initial 20 members to a peak of 200 and now stands at 160. Dues were $12 per year in 1946, now $40.

John waxes enthusiastic as he talks about the "beautiful and convenient club grounds and lodge. My family can picnic, swim, hike, shoot, and compete in matches." He knows guns and is chairman of the special gunhandling committee. Against a backdrop of angry editorials and citizen complaints against gun ownership today, John Manne is a voice of reason in a sea of citizen discontent. In his view, guns are as American as apple pie and will be with us forever.

Speech to Slingerlands Methodist Church Men's Club
October 29

About fifteen or twenty men gathered in the church library last night to hear me tell the story of "Gems from Bethlehem's Past," a theme I've used before with other community groups. A friend of twenty-four years, Harry Howes introduced me to others and helped me set up the slide equipment. Our lab chemist, Dr. Edward Homiller, is a member of the club and was present last night.

I find it easy to speak without notes, recalling a hundred or more facts about Indian life and the early pioneers we are in the process of documenting for *Bethlehem Revisited: A Bicentennial Story.* I never get tired of telling the stories that are so intricately interwoven with my life and happiness in retirement.

There were a lot of questions, some difficult to answer. I felt the group got really absorbed in the subject. They gave me an apple pie to bring home, and a strong round of applause.

The Slingerlands Community Players
November 2-3

Coleen and I arrived in Bethlehem in 1966 and became immediately aware of the Slingerlands Community Players, a dramatic group that got big headlines in both *The Spotlight* and the *Times*

Union and *Knickerbocker News.* I was so busy getting adjusted to a new position at SUNY Albany that we didn't buy tickets until the 1968-1969 season (*Dear Friends*). We weren't all that keen about the first play we attended (can't remember why), but we loved their performance of *The Fantastiks* a short time later, and several plays after that.

We learned that Ruth Wilbur organized the Players in 1952. The first officers were Morris Schaeffer, president; Sylvester J. Bower, vice president; Mary F. Nugent, secretary; Ruth Oliver Bickel, correspondence secretary; Mrs. Sylvester Bower, treasurer; and William E. Zimmerman, business manager. There were eighteen charter members.

We heard a lot about the Quarto Players after we arrived but did not see them perform. I learned that Joanne Kimmey, Zaida Johnson, Betty Taylor, and Ruth Wilbur performed in New Jersey, New York, and Massachusetts to rave reviews. *The Literary Tea Party* was one of their big successes. We read that they often performed without a stage. Once they played in a sanctuary where their main props were beer cans.

Often directed by Ruth Wilbur, Katherine DePorte, Zaida Johnson, Paul B. Pettit, among others, the Players put on many plays in the 1950s and 1960s: *Amid the Alien Corn, Death of a Salesman, My Three Angels, Harvey, All*

My Sons, Years Ago, Suspect, and *The Remarkable Mr. Pennypacker,* to mention just a few. Some really innovative programs were created by Katherine and David DePorte, and dozens of Bethlehem citizens listed in the programs show that the Slingerlands Community Players were a major cultural tour de force in their time.

Bethlehem Soccer Club
November 20-21

Editors of *The Spotlight* registered surprise in their November 14 edition that the Bethlehem Soccer Club had grown large enough to require its own playing fields. The editorial said, "The club is now buying a 19-acre pasture...for about $100,000...[to provide] playing space for seven fields... and parking for 300...."

I am not a bit surprised. Coleen and I have watched our grandchildren, Jonathan and Stephanie Brewer, play in community leagues in Lawrence, Kan., Hawthorne Woods, Ill., and now Macungie, Pa. One could sense the growing interest in the sport nationwide.

The Bethlehem Soccer Club is clearly part of the trend. Organized by George and Connie Tilroe in 1978, a small group of fourteen began the sport in our town. George Tilroe served as president that year; Charles Guinn, vice president; Janet Morris, secretary; and Arthur Guarino, treasurer.

I called William Silverman and William Cushing tonight to check on current membership figures for the club and learned that the 1990 membership is 1,500. This is phenomenal growth from the initial fourteen members in 1978.

Most important of all is the group's emphasis on non-competitive play, a feature of other programs throughout the country. They say their basic purpose is to "promote the game of soccer through an intra-club program and through the Capital District Youth Soccer League."

Also, they say a later phase of their land acquisition plan will add a refreshment stand and toilets. This seems reasonable to me when one considers the number of young people they serve.

I will do my part by calling attention to their programs in my speeches and by donating some money now and then. It is certainly a wholesome program for local youth that deserves encouragement.

Setbacks for the Bicentennial History
December 29

Our well-known Dutch church scholar, Dr. Howard Hageman, is at the Albany Medical Center recovering from the removal of a brain tumor. It was benign and he has a good chance to recover. Surgeons believe they have protected his short-term memory. I will check in with him in a few months to see if he is able to work on the chapter on religious life in Bethlehem. It did not surprise me yesterday when Sue Ann Ritchko stopped by my home to say she couldn't continue with the task of writing the chapter on hamlets for the bicentennial history. She ac-cepted a national leadership role in the field of nutrition in Washington last year and is too bogged down with "crisis management" responsibilities to finish the job here.

Now it will be necessary to activate Plan B with the hamlet chapter. I will do this next week.

THE OLIVER HOUSE , DEMOLISHED OCTOBER 5, 1990.
ORCHARD RD., SLINGERLANDS. MARK L. PECKHAM , 1985.

9 *Nineteen Hundred Ninety-One*

Combining business with pleasure, Floyd took to his bicycle, visiting local personalities and businesses as he earnestly endeavored to chronicle as many aspects of Bethlehem life as humanly possible.

With Bethlehem's bicentennial now only two years off, those who would finally write, photograph, and edit the local history book were emerging. What was once only Floyd's vision was really beginning to be a tangible product—fund-raising was under way, renowned local artist Len Tantillo had agreed to paint the Nicoll-Sill house for the book's cover, and a copy of the Chicago Manual of Style, which the history book's editors would use as a standard, became Floyd's constant companion.

Looking for a Better Shave
January 2

I want the new Gillette Sensor Razor but have been unable to find one, to date. *USA Today's* analysis fits everything I have read about the Sensor. It provides a smooth, effective shaving experience. I'll try again during our weekly shopping trip tomorrow morning.

My first razor during my college years (1939-1942) was a single-bladed Gillette, and I used a similar razor for almost forty years. When Gillette came out with Track II, a twin-bladed razor, I changed, and it has been almost nick-free shaving for over ten years.

Brief experiences with electric razors in the 1960s and 1970s were unsatisfactory.

A Typical Weekly Grocery Shopping List for Us—Grand Union Store
January 3

Crackers	1.89
Paper towels	.89
Prune juice	1.49
Dove soap (2)	1.58
Schweppes Ginger Ale	1.19
Deposit	.05
Kitchen trash bags	1.59
English muffins	1.49
Tub margarine	1.39
Laundry detergent	1.59
Bisquick	1.99
Stick margarine	1.49
Frozen pizza	2.49
Minestrone soup	1.09
Decaffeinated coffee	3.79
White bread	1.49
Tomatoes .41lb. @ 1 lb./1.49	.61
Large eggs	1.19
Bananas 2.03 lb. @ 1 lb./.33	.67
Pork tenderloin	3.44
Ground round 1/2 lb.	1.62
Post Grapenuts	2.39
Croutons	1.39
Macaroni/Cheese 3/1.00	1.00
(one M/C for church basket)	
Jello lemon pudding	.59
Lemons	.40

Chicken cutlets	2.49
Cleaning cloths	1.39
Baked ham 1/2 lb.	2.27
Rolls	.66
Cabbage	.71
New York Times	.50
Dinner napkins	1.29
Fabric softener	2.89
Rice pilaf	.99
Tuna fish	.68
Frozen spinach	.45
Frozen green beans	.73
Salmon	2.49
Mandarin orange slices	.85
Canned baked beans	.59
Broccoli	.99
Apples 1.76 lb. @ 1 lb./.99	1.74
Mushrooms	1.59
Shrimp	3.05
Acorn Squash	.88
Chocolate Hershey kisses	1.79
Chocolate chip morsels	1.25
Carrots	.59
Subtotal	70.55
Coupons	-3.60
Total	66.95
Tax paid	.90

Grand Union store at the Delaware Plaza.

**Renovation and Enlargement
of Grand Union Grocery Store
is Completed
January 4-5**

A beautiful new Grand Union is now attracting dozens of new shoppers to the Delaware Plaza in Elsmere. Bethlehem citizens now have two choices of large, bright, and well-stocked groceries: this Grand Union and a brand new Grand Union of similar size at the new shopping center on the corner of 9W and Feura Bush Road.

Finally, after several years of average grocery shopping, Bethlehem citizens have nice places to shop. In earlier years we had an Atlantic & Pacific, a large Albany Public Market, and a decent-size Star Market, but all of these fell by the wayside, victims of relentless competition. In a sense, Grand Union knocked out the competition.

Many of us were angry about the lack of choice three years ago but the growling has subsided. It is solely Grand Union now, and they are excellent stores.

The Delaware Plaza Grand Union is managed by Art Kane with the help of several assistant managers. They seem to be doing their utmost to please customers and stock their favorite items—no easy task in this age of crowded grocery shelves.

There is now room to pass in the aisles. Objectionable "obstacle" displays have been removed from the ends of most aisles, making it easier for customers to get around.

And it seems that big money is in frozen foods since the new stores have at least tripled the shelf space used for such foods. The choices are overwhelming at times, and it is sometimes hard to find one's favorite brand.

Citizens who are still disgruntled with the lack of choice in the main shopping areas can drive to Albany or go to the Davis Stonewell Market (Routes 85 and 85A) or Handy Andy at the Four Corners (in Delmar). Overall, it is a reasonably good picture for grocery shopping in Bethlehem.

Grandchildren in the Electronic Age
January 8-9

The newspapers complain that fewer people are reading their news—down about 25 percent since 1967. Teachers complain that many of their pupils are computer literate but book shy and parents often report that their children enjoy three or more hours of television each day (71 percent) but only 27 percent read daily for pleasure.

Thus far, our grandchildren seem to be the exception. They both enjoy television and read a lot. However, I wonder if the pattern will persist.

I feel out of touch without the *New York Times* on a daily basis but concede that the electronic age is beginning to transform learning habits and that my grandchildren might get more and more of their general knowledge from TV, computer banks, and various new electronic information sources that are more pleasurable to

Jonathan and Stephanie Brewer.

learn from. What counts, in the end, is not where they get their general knowledge from, but that they get it from somewhere. Naturally, the print media proponents are shaking in their boots. They're losing clientele. Books and newspapers are becoming less and less attractive as sources of information. Jonathan and Stephanie may live to see the demise of print media.

For now, however, those who program information into electronic gadgets must get their information from books and newspapers. Time will tell if this trend will persist throughout the lives of my grandchildren. I doubt if it will...but no one can be sure.

Wayne R. Johnson.

JOHNSON STATIONERS, INC.
239 Delaware Avenue
DELMAR, NEW YORK 12054
Phone (518) 439-8166
Fax (518) 475-0922

SOLD BY			DATE JAN 10 19 91	
NAME BETHLEHEM ARCHAEOLOGY				
ADDRESS GROUP				
CITY				
☐ CASH ☐ C.O.D.	☐ CHARGE ☐ PAID OUT	☐ MDSE. RETD. ☐ PD. ON ACCT.	PREVIOUS BALANCE ▶	
1	INDEX STRIPS		2	75
1	PEN		1	39
10	ENVELOPES	.07		70
16	EXP FOLDERS	.62	9	92
			14.76	
	DISC.		1.48	
Paid			13.28	
	TAX EX. 182634			
Thank You!	RECEIVED BY			

PRODUCT 350 NEBS Inc. Groton. Mass. 01471

Wayne R. Johnson and Johnson Stationers, Inc.
January 10-11

I shop at Johnson Stationers at 239 Delaware Avenue in Elsmere on an average of three or four times a month. You can find everything related to an office there except furniture. It is handy to stop there on the way to weekly grocery shopping at Grand Union, to pick up pens, envelopes, manila folders, erasers, tacks, any form of poster board and, in fact, almost anything one needs for office supplies, from a postal weight scale to elastics or paper clips.

As the slip above shows, Wayne Johnson gives non-profit groups and businesses a discount, rendering his store competitive with the many discount stationery stores throughout the Albany area.

You often say: Why should I drive fifteen or twenty miles for stationery purchases when, for a few pennies more I can go up the street and get the same thing in about ten minutes. Additionally, you find a congenial storekeeper in Wayne Johnson. It is a pleasure to do business there. If he doesn't have what you want, he will order it delivered to his store the next day. He is a perfect example of why it is always better to shop at home *first*.

For all of these reasons, Wayne Johnson does $350,000 worth of business each year—a very successful business by anyone's standard.

Countdown to War in the Persian Gulf—A Sinking Feeling that War is Inevitable
January 14-21

Never before in my memory has there been such a calculated, inexorable march toward a military confrontation as one finds between the United States and Iraq today. President Bush has been relentless and unyielding in his demand that Iraq get out of Kuwait, and Iraq has steadfastly maintained its right to be there and denied that it is any of the United States's business.

Bush rightly does not want to reward aggression, and Saddam Hussein is just plain stupid about the horrible consequences of such a war for his people.

Is Kuwait worth all that much to him (Saddam Hussein)? Apparently so.

Is the principle of stopping a blatant aggressor worth several thousand American lives to Bush? Apparently so.

The United Nations deadline for Iraq to get out of Kuwait is today, January 15, 1991.

On Saturday, the United States Senate approved the use of force in the Persian Gulf by a vote of 52 to 47. The House vote of approval was a little stronger: 250 to 183.

In a word, I feel discouraged. Having served in and observed the death and destruction in WWII, I don't want to see another big war.

My mind keeps wandering over an idea to form a "Moral Death Squad" under the United Nations structure in which a highly trained group of ten or twelve suicide commandos is given the task of rubbing out men such as Saddam Hussein—after careful deliberation by the world body. It is admittedly a crackpot idea, but no other constraint has emerged to control stupid, power-hungry aggressors. Why not try it?

War Comes to the Persian Gulf
January 17

We turned on the television at 6:30 P.M. last night and discovered that there had been "a few indications, as yet unconfirmed, that allied warplanes had struck Iraq and Kuwait," in CBS announcer Dan Rather's words.

Sounds of planes taking off from Allied bases in Saudi Arabia brought the war into our living rooms before it had been officially announced by government officials. Around 8:00 P.M., Secretary of Defense Richard Cheney and the head of the Joint Chiefs of

Staff, General Colin Powell, approached the microphones and confirmed that the attack had taken place. They both referred to President Bush's speech scheduled for 9:00 P.M.

At that time, President Bush reviewed all the main reasons for the attack and said, "It will not be another Vietnam." I hope not. The world cannot take another protracted war right now. Too many economies are already in chaos.

The pride of Dave's Glass. Left to right: Gerald G. Condon, his wife, Theresa, and son, Dave.

"Desert Storm," the Persian Gulf war in progress for some 2 1/2 days, has focused considerable attention on CNN, a relatively new television network. I ordered cable TV several years ago mainly to get CNN and I have not regretted this decision for a moment.

When you turn on your TV, you know that millions of people around the world are watching CNN, even the two key protagonists: Presidents Bush and Saddam Hussein (of Iraq). You think: television has become a prime vehicle for both diplomacy and collecting statistics on a war. Chief of Staff, General Colin Powell, admitted that "I'm watching CNN just as you are."

Dave's Glass, Inc. — A Handy Service
January 24-25

We have traded at Dave's Glass in the mini-mall behind Grand Union (at the Delaware Plaza) for a number of years and appreciate the customer-centered service offered by Gerald G. (Jerry) Condon and his wife, Theresa, co-owners. They live in Voorheesville.

Jerry and Theresa have four men working for them. One of them replaced a four-by-eight-foot storm window covering our living room window a few years ago and a glass panel alongside our front door last year. We've had many panes cut for picture frames including one made of non-glare glass for Jeff and Beth's family picture in December 1990. It does not surprise me to learn that Jerry and Theresa's business is well over $200,000 a year. They earn it!

Brewer home in Delmar, New York.

Hooray! The House is Paid For
February 7-8

We celebrated this evening because this document (shown on the next page) arrived from Home & City Savings Bank today.

A welcome piece of mail!

How I Feel about *The Spotlight*, Bethlehem's Weekly Newspaper
May 14

Once again, a *Spotlight* editor/writer, Deborah Boucher, and her supervisor, Managing Editor Susan Graves, saw fit to publish a story about our progress with bicentennial publications. This one is important to me since Ms. Boucher did a fine job of plugging a benefit garage sale, which we hope will enable us to buy computer equipment.

This has been my usual experience with The *Spotlight* staff. When you need help and have a newsworthy idea, they often are quite willing to help. I suspect that hundreds of Bethlehem citizens feel as I do.

Also, I believe I am a typical reader. I read many of the stories every week and browse heavily through the repetitive features such as the calendar. I don't read all of the sports stories thoroughly because I am not a big sports fan, yet I occasionally run into a fascinating sports story.

Working with Friends of the New Netherland Project
May 25

Several people met this morning at the newly renovated 1735 Nicoll-Sill home in Cedar Hill to plan a fundraising event, "Our Forefathers Day," for June 16. Those attending were Floyd Brewer, Peter Christoph, Florence Christoph, Martha Shattuck, Paul Mulligan.

The group was given a tour of the home by Paul Mulligan, owner and resident, a Schenectady attorney and son of former town historian, Thomas "Ed" Mulligan. There were numerous ohs and ahs as we moved from

𝕶now 𝕬ll 𝕸en 𝕭y 𝕿hese 𝕻resents,
#50323
SATISFACTION

That 𝕳ome and 𝕮ity 𝕾avings 𝕭ank
Formerly known as City and County Savings Bank

A Domestic Banking Corporation, having its principal place of business at 100 State Street, in the City and County of Albany and State of New York does hereby certify that a certain Indenture of Mortgage bearing date the 27th *day of* June *Nineteen Hundred and* Sixty-six (1966) *made and executed by* FLOYD I. BREWER and A. COLEEN BREWER

TO City and County Savings Bank   LIBER **2807** PAGE **901**

to secure payment of the principal sum of Twenty-two thousand two hundred and no/100----------------- ($22,200.00) *Dollars, and interest thereon and duly recorded in the office of the Clerk of the County of* Albany *N.Y. in Liber* 1862 *of Mortgages, page* 275 *, on the* 28th *day of* June *Nineteen Hundred and* Sixty-six (1966).

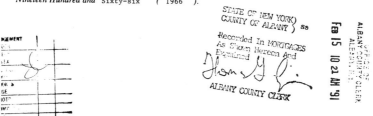

STATE OF NEW YORK
COUNTY OF ALBANY } ss

Recorded In MORTGAGES
As Shown Hereon And
Examined

ALBANY COUNTY CLERK

Feb 15 10 21 AM '91
OFFICE OF ALBANY COUNTY CLERK ALBANY, N.Y.

Is, with the Bond accompanying it, fully paid and satisfied, and does hereby consent that the same be discharged of record.

This mortgage has not been further assigned.

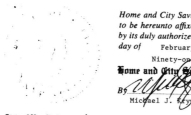

IN WITNESS WHEREOF, *the said Home and City Savings Bank has caused its corporate seal to be hereunto affixed, and these presents to be subscribed by its duly authorized officer this* 5th *day of* February, *Nineteen Hundred and* Ninety-one (1991).

𝕳ome and 𝕮ity 𝕾avings 𝕭ank

By _____
Michael J. Krywinski, Assistant Vice President

𝕾tate of 𝕹ew 𝖄ork, } ss.
City and County of Albany,

On this 5th *day of* February *Nineteen Hundred and* Ninety-one (1991)

before me personally came Michael J. Krywinski

to me personally known, who, being by me duly sworn, did depose and say that he resides at 600 Boght Road, Cohoes, New York *that he is the* Assistant Vice President *of the Home and City Savings Bank, the corporation described in and which executed the above Instrument; that he knows the seal of said corporation; that the seal affixed to said Instrument is such corporate seal; that it was so affixed by order of the Board of Trustees of said corporation; and that he signed his name thereto by like order.*

_____
JOSEPH F. PICKETT, JR.
Notary Public, State of New York
Qualified in Schenectady County
Commission Expires 4/6/91

ResM 35 (11/81)

Brewer mortgage retired.

room [to room] in the twenty-six-room house: many old doors retained, woodwork reconstructed from scraps that were left along the edges of doorways, complete reconstruction of the 1830 wing added by William Nicoll Sill in the early days, gorgeous colors—deep greens and browns, to go with the paneling in some rooms...and much more. The Mulligan family deserves a lot of credit!

Furniture That Lasts:
Green Formica Kitchen Table
June 3-4

We bought a kitchen table at Sears in 1952 that has turned out to be so serviceable that we hate to throw it away (even though we haven't used it as a kitchen table for thirty-two years).

When we moved to 1637 Winchester Avenue in Cincinnati around 1959, it was relegated to the basement where it was used to keep everything needed for our pet guinea pigs—dozens of them!

By 1966, shortly after we moved to 31 Lansing Drive in Delmar, it was placed underneath the basement stairs to keep my books and other precious family relics off a floor that sometimes flooded.

In 1970, Mark borrowed the table for use in his Myrtle Avenue apartment in Albany when he attended SUNY Albany, and for a year or so after he

graduated. He returned the table when he moved to Schenectady.

The table did another tour of duty at the bottom of our basement stairs until 1983. That year it was needed at our Archaeology Lab where it eventually became our main lab, library, conference, and work table.

When we lost the library and two other rooms at the lab in 1990 (because of the conversion of the Waldenmaier building to a trash recycling center), it was placed in storage in a room below the lab.

I dug the table out of storage once again today for use in our "Bicentennial History Benefit Garage Sale" coming up this Saturday. It is still an attractive table—perfect for some of the nicer things that dozens of citizens donated for the sale.

Perhaps some enterprising reader will track down this 58 1/2" x 35 1/4" metal table (with an extra center leaf in place) in 2010 to see if it is still in use. [The table was purchased by Mary Foley of Delmar at the garage sale.]

Lawn Care Service,
Helpful but Expensive
June 19

When and if I stop mowing my own lawn, I'll probably make a contract with Cassidy Lawn Care, 82 Salisbury Road in Delmar. Michael Cassidy

145

handles some of my neighbors' work, and I like everything about his service—which includes snow plowing in the winter. Most people want the twin service. Also, his ad says that he does landscaping, organic fertilization, grub control, and spring and fall cleanups, services that older people often need. Finally, I like him personally. All of these services would add an estimated $800 to my existing lawn care bill. Hence, I'll do my own mowing and plowing as long as I can. Also, I like the exercise.

Little Known Hotel in Bethlehem's History: Beckers Corners Hotel, First Home of Grange No. 137
July 14

We know about the old Beckers Corners Hotel primarily because of a picture taken in 1901 by Emmett A. Terrell. His daughter, Marjorie Terrell, has hundreds of pictures taken by her father around the turn of this century and later.

Bethlehem Grange No. 137 met there from 1874 to 1880 when the present Grange hall was built. The old hotel was located just west of the Grange on Route 396. It burned about 1908.

It was one of those rambling two-story structures with a long front covered porch, and shutters to cover the windows in the event of a violent storm. The Terrell photo shows a spacious building on the right with open-air type doorways (without doors) possibly for tethering horses to get them out of rain or snow.

There are huge trees on the front lawn, one of them with a very long swing, and with John Alan Terrell, brother of Marjorie, enjoying a swing. Elizabeth Winne Osterhout is pictured sitting at the base of the tree.

Bethlehem Scenes from the Seat of a Bicycle
September 13-14

Hudson Avenue begins at Tool's Restaurant on Delaware Avenue near the railroad overpass in Delmar and dead-ends at Gardiner Terrace. It is often a pleasant ride on a bicycle in mid-afternoon as you ride by a mixture of older homes with some new ones mixed in. I rode by North Street (off Hudson) earlier this week and couldn't help wondering what all the commotion was about a few months ago when senior citizens' housing was proposed for this area. There is a lot of open space on North Street, an ideal place for senior citizens' housing. But Hudson Avenue and North Street residents howled bloody murder (and, as I recall, funding was denied) so the housing project was canceled.

I dropped in to see Shirley Schenmeyer, who has built up a large hobby/profit business in ceramics in the years since 1981, when she took over the old Knights of Columbus building at 38 Hudson Avenue. She teaches classes and turns out attractive greenware for sale. She also works as the librarian at the Middle School. Her nephew, Craig Smith, showed me around.

Leaving Hudson Avenue, I rode toward Albany on Delaware Avenue and turned left on Herrick Avenue. This is a pleasant area with lots of trees and nice homes, some of which were designed by architect Walter Pember for Judge Herrick when the two had a real estate partnership in the early decades of this century.

On the way back on Delaware, I paused to push my bicycle up the hill by the Stewart's Shop at 309 Delaware Avenue and watched a very short train go by behind the shop. The engine and four cars all had flamboyantly large CPRail (Canadian Pacific Rail) letters, except the caboose, which had a moderate-sized D&H on it. The historic Delaware & Hudson railroad was absorbed by CPRail last year.

Bethlehem from the Seat of a Bicycle
September 22-24

One of my favorite bicycle rides on a cool, sunny day (like today) is the entire length of Roweland Avenue, right on Albin, left on McGuffey Lane and back home via Westchester Drive South, Betsey Lane, and Roweland.

Today, I stopped to see Arnold and Margaret Foster at 67 Roweland. They live in a delightful old residence on spacious grounds that is probably a pre-Civil War home. They don't know who built the house, but [they] learned that John and Hugh Winne (brothers) probably owned it before the man they bought it from (Mr. Lyons) lived there. I plan to search the records to see if this is the John Winne who was Bethlehem's town supervisor between 1883 and 1885. Margaret will soon do some sketches for the bicentennial history. She is a founding member of the Bethlehem Art Association. Dr. Foster, her husband, is a retired sociology professor from SUNY Albany. We've known them for twenty-five years, since we bought our home from them when we arrived in 1966.

Roweland Avenue homes are surrounded with trees that hang out over the road in places. A car passes bike riders occasionally, but most of the time one rides through a quiet, country-like environment by a mixture of old and new homes.

Passing by 187 Roweland, a stately old mansion set well back away from the road, I spied the owner, Dr. David O'Keeffe, who has a general surgery practice at 632 New Scotland Ave. We talked about the age of his house (about 1830), previous owners (Duncan Martin, Col. Walsh, among others), and the enormous job of keeping up the grounds. He said, "I do it all myself now, the kids are gone...."

At the end of Roweland, I usually turn right on Albin Road, another beautiful tree-lined street, but somewhat more recent. Coleen's minister, Larry Deyss, his wife, Christine, and their children live at 32 Albin Road, and I always think of them as I ride by. He has been pastor of the Delmar Presbyterian Church for the past ten years.

On Roweland last Sunday, I ran into Dominick DeCecco delivering his campaign literature to the homes of Republicans. Dr. O'Keeffe was on his list. Everyone knows Dom. He is on a dozen boards and committees, and has served as the social studies supervisor for the Bethlehem Central Schools for the past thirty-three years. In recent years, he has been moving into town government positions and is currently running for a seat on the Albany County Legislature to represent the 36th district. If he were in my district, I would vote for Dom.

I turn left on McGuffey Lane and find dozens of cars in the lot and on the streets around the Hamagrael School. The attraction: a picnic for kindergarten pupils and their parents from all over the area (judging from the number of cars). Soon I ride by a DAR marker commemorating Lt. John Leonard, a Revolutionary soldier buried in the area. It is a peaceful ride back home via Westchester Drive South, another beautiful street on which it would be a delight to live, to Betsey Lane and back on Roweland Avenue.

A Bike Ride into Historic Elsmere
October 3-4

At least twice a month in summer and fall I pedal my bicycle down tree-shaded Fernbank Avenue to historic Elsmere Avenue and wander through a section of Bethlehem Cemetery. Gilbert O. Drake, president of Bennett Plumbing at 341 Delaware Avenue, is the current treasurer of the cemetery association, maintaining a seventy-year tradition of Bennett management. Gil writes that "on November 4, 1935, my father-in-law, Daniel A. Bennett, succeeded his father, Frank Bennett, as treasurer, [a post] which he held until 1974," when Gil took over the job. The cemetery was founded in 1865. I ride past Bennett Terrace on the way to the cemetery.

For fans of history, there are endless things to see. Today, I wandered up a hill in the cemetery at the corner of Kenwood and Elsmere and came upon the Booth family markers in a configuration rarely seen in places like this. There is a 12' or 13' tall stone for John H. Booth (1811-1876) and his wife, Sarah (1817-1906), with twenty-two small marker stones in a circle around the tall stone. Most of these are Booths, except three. V. Booth (1901?-1916?) apparently married into the Stratton family. Two additional markers are reserved for Jeff Daniel Stratton (born 1914) and Sidney R. Stratton (born 1912). There is a street named Stratton Place near my home. Like all the others, this bike trip produced some new information for me to ponder.

Outdoor Paradise in Bethlehem: from Game Preserve to Classroom
October 21-22

Coleen and I visited the Five Rivers Center last week on a beautifully sunny, cool day. We go there infrequently, but always enjoy it immensely when we do. After walking the Vlomankill Trail, we sat on a bench by the administrative office and enjoyed the birds, petted a brown cat and talked about our memories of this paradise in the woods so close to home.

We knew it was first a game preserve formed from two large (112 acres) orchard farms in 1933. Civilian Conservation Corps workers dammed the Vlomankill with large limestone blocks salvaged from the Watervliet lock of the old Erie Canal. Later, another dam was made downstream on the Vlomankill, to create a beaver pond.

There was a zoo containing a few animals native to New York state when we arrived in 1966. Some people still ask me for the location of "Delmar Zoo." But in 1970, when the Conservation Department was reorganized, the Department of Environmental Conservation was established, and an Environmental Education Center was created here following passage of a $20,000,000 Environmental Quality Bond Act in 1972. Nature trails were created and the zoo was removed. We knew Bob Budlinger, the first director of the Education Center, and his wife,

Carol. They were always at parties given by John and Doris Gold, good friends of ours in the 1970s and 1980s.

Now, everything is changed at Five Rivers (for the better, in my view). It is a relaxing place to visit and learn.

Philosophy of Editing Revisited
October 25-26

As I indicated before, my philosophy of editing can be summed up in two sentences: (1) Select good writers and help them do what they want to do, and (2) insist on adherence to a "bible" (*Chicago Manual of Style*).

This philosophy is serving the bicentennial history project well; however, I have expanded the level of editor involvement in the project by inviting associate editors with special skills to take charge of specific functions.

Peter Christoph helps all members of the writing team search original documents and widely accepted scholarly books for solid historical facts. Further, he often picks up errors in the copy submitted. His years of experience as associate librarian-manuscripts, New York State Library, and his long affiliation with the New Netherland project have served him well in this role. Also, he is a former English teacher.

Joe Allgaier, current town historian, has not had special training in matters of style, but his attention to detail is

Leonard F. Tantillo in Albany at the May 1994 unveiling of his painting, *Return of the Experiment*.

outstanding. He regularly consults the *Chicago Manual of Style* as issues arise, and we are slowly defining our policy for the book.

Hugh Hewitt is an outstanding photographer (with several exhibits to his credit) and is looking with a sharp eye over photos and graphics recommended by writers for their chapters. Additionally, he is a former English teacher.

Chuck McKinney is an exceptionally competent computer operator with a good sense of what is needed in an attractive, readable book. His design

and production skills are strong, and badly needed with this project.

An Afternoon with Artist Len Tantillo: the Ultimate in Meticulous Creativity
November 14-15

Five editors with the Bethlehem bicentennial history project spent a large part of the afternoon in L.F. Tantillo's studio on Irish Hill Road near East Chatham, southeast of Albany.

Len Tantillo greeted us with a smile and a joke or two. He had been going over some experience he had in working with Chuck McKinney in 1979-1980, when the two of them turned out a book for the NYS Energy Research & Development Authority. Chuck ended the experience with considerable respect for Tantillo's skills.

Tantillo's paintings were all around us—on walls, against a piece of furniture, on the drawing (or draftsman's) table. He has done numerous historical scenes in different parts of New York. He said his plan for his artistic life is to document as much of old New York state as he possibly can. Just glancing around his studio confirms that he has made a good start toward his goal.

Tantillo's originals sell for $500 to $8,000 [and up], depending on the size and complexity. He is currently working on a mid-nineteenth century Albany building [old railroad station], long since demolished, that he has gone to extraordinary lengths to document and draw. The tiniest details around the huge building's windows, roof lines, doors, etc. are drawn to scale. We had to agree with him that a record of this kind of architecture should be preserved. It leaves one with a feeling of warmth as opposed to the feeling of coldness some of us get looking at the mostly glass boxes of today.

Len agreed to do a scene for the cover of our bicentennial history—an effort to recapture the detail and mood of the successful Nicoll-Sill farm in Ce-

dar Hill in the eighteenth century. I gave him a book full of research materials on the farm. He will call us soon and arrange to visit the house, which was recently restored.

Is Radio Dying?
November 26-27

With so much electronic competition for the citizen's mind today, one would think that radio has receded far into the background, but such is not the case in our home and car.

Coleen and I both like low, background music (the Muzak variety) part of each and every day, and often have the kitchen Panasonic radio on WROW-AM. This station's music is soft, melodious, and pleasant listening. Also, you get a little news just before the hour. I listen to the same station on another Panasonic radio when I'm in the bedroom dressing or shaving each and every day. We rarely change the dial in these rooms.

The lure of beautiful classical music often wins out as I work at my research and writing downstairs in my study—on compact discs about three-fourths of the time, and on radio station WMHT about a quarter of the time (I'm down there an average of four hours every day). Sometimes I don't want to fiddle with the discs and/or I like the selections in progress on the radio. The radio is built into my Sony CFD454 CD player and the

Woodgate condominiums in Delmar.

sound reproduction through speakers hung on the wall is excellent.

The Chrysler radio (with speakers on the dash and in the back of our minivan) has excellent tone and I often leave the dial on WGY-FM, especially for Rush Limbaugh, a talk show host out of New York whose grasp of the issues of the day is phenomenal. Although I often disagree with his positions on selected issues, I like to hear what listeners throughout the country have to say about such issues and sometimes remain in a parking lot for a few minutes until a particularly fascinating incident or issue is fully aired. Radio adds a great deal of pleasure and richness to my life. If anything, it is more important in retirement than in any other part of my life.

Bethlehem from the Seat of a Bicycle: Scenic, Peaceful Woodgate in Delmar
December 12-13

One of my favorite bicycle rides for a half hour of really helpful exercise

amid pleasant surroundings begins at my home and takes me west on Dawson Road from which I take a right on Carson. Sometimes I wave at or stop and talk a few minutes with a friend, Arthur Ritchko, at 63 Carson Road. Art is a retired football coach— Bethlehem Central High School. His wife, Sue Ann, a former member of town board, now works in Washington, D.C. He "winters" down there with her.

But my real goal is to get to the Woodgate development as quickly as possible and do six or eight laps around the Woodgate Square, as some call it. Coleen and I watched all of the condominiums go up at Woodgate between 1973 and 1982 when the last four of the planned eighty-eight units went up on Leaf Road. The survey work was done by Elliot & Thibault, and the architects were Clark J. Shaughnessy and Everett J. Jenner.

I often say hi to Joan Laffin when she is outside at 21 Willow Drive. We know her through our church. Joan said today that she is the second owner of her condo, and that there are thirty original owners currently living at Woodgate. I'm not surprised. The place is attractive. There is a community pool, lots of original trees, and homeowner association management. The condos range from one to four bedrooms and are now selling for $90,000 to $120,000, depending on the size. J.T. Burns was the original manager when the first units were sold in

1973. My neighbor, Paul Reagan, was one of the sales agents. I like to ride around the square at Woodgate because there is very little traffic over there. On the way home, I sometimes see Harry or Betty Sheaffer at 496 Stratton Place. Harry was town supervisor from 1975 to 1977.

It is a pleasant ride, and I still enjoy it after more than twenty years of cycling over to Woodgate.

FORMER POST OFFICE; FORMER ADAMS HARDWARE.
DELMAR FOUR CORNERS, MARK L. PECKHAM, AUGUST 6, 1994.

10 *Nineteen Hundred Ninety-Two*

People and places of local interest continued to show up in Floyd's diary entries, but work on the bicentennial history had climaxed. As copy was finalized, the book moved into the typesetting stage, courtesy again of local volunteers. While the production team continually consulted Floyd, as editor, his roles as researcher and writer for select chapters ended. He and Coleen treated themselves to a trip to Florida to visit Floyd's brother and sister-in-law. Back at home, they

indulged in country drives and Ben and Jerry's ice cream, all the while keeping tabs on the presidential campaigns and election.

By year's end—just in time for the 1993 bicentennial year—the Bicentennial Commission had set its calendar of events, which Floyd, the commission secretary, duly recorded, modestly listing the history book last in a collection of commission endeavors.

At Long Last: The Land Use Management Survey Results
January 8-9

The sections and conclusions I like:

1) The need to maintain the small-town atmosphere despite a population approaching 30,000 is especially important (a tenuous balancing act these days);

2) The green is going fast. I want to see the town add two or three more parks before developers grab the land for housing (free land is scarce);

3) The town park is a jewel in Bethlehem's crown. Although Coleen and I use it very little, it is easy to see that thousands of citizens do. It should be strengthened and expanded when money becomes available;

4) and 4a) Everyone I talk to wants to add *only* light industry. I don't think a large office building or two in Selkirk or Glenmont would hurt us. They would improve our tax base.

Eva Marie Saint's beginning as an actress, ca. 1939. Left to right: Francine Ardizone, Virginia McCormick, Joan Weaver, Ruth Hafley, Eva Marie Saint, unidentified, Constance Conroe, and Janet Flume.

Bethlehem's Tri-Village
Little League: Lest We Forget
January 20-21

Before the records are lost, let us be sure to acknowledge the leadership of the Delmar Kiwanis Club and the Bethlehem Shrine Club in the organizational phase of Little League teams in our town. Their support led to the purchase of Magee Field (from Harold J. Magee), a three-acre tract of land on Kenwood Avenue where it intersects the Route 32 bypass. The price was $2,000. The year was 1954.

Since that year, thousands of boys and girls have learned to play baseball as well as the fine art of teamwork and such skills as sportsmanship and co-ordination.

1942 Bethlehem Central Grad
Makes Good: Eva Marie Saint
January 24-25

Bob Hendrick's decision to invite Eva Marie Saint to serve as grand marshal of the bicentennial parade in 1993 reminds me to look up a few things about her.

I found her in Alice Boutelle's scrapbook dancing with a group of girls in a musical at BCHS in the late 1930s, and I found the front page of a *Knickerbocker News* story about her (March 31, 1955) in the same scrapbook. Alice kept everything!

The evening of March 30, 1955, must have been a highlight in Ms. Saint's career. A picture showing her holding an Oscar (for Best Supporting Actress for *On the Waterfront* with Marlon Brando, 1955) and smiling broadly, appears with the story. She is described as the wife of Jeff Hayden, and as the daughter of Mr. and Mrs. John Saint, who were living in Bryn Mawr, Pa., at that time.

It was Ms. Saint's first movie after a string of roles in television. She played Marlon Brando's girlfriend in his life as a dockworker, a life of crime and violence, in *On the Waterfront*.

I hope she accepts our invitation to serve as grand marshal. [She did not.]

It would add a touch of class to our parade and it would permit me to tell the rest of her story!

One of My Favorite Homes in Delmar —187 Roweland Ave.
February 5-6

Mentioned in last year's diary in connection with one of my bicycle trips, this beautiful home has been owned in recent years by

The O'Keeffe home in Delmar.

•Edwin and Elizabeth Heinsohn, 1932-1942.
• Mr. and Mrs. Niles Persons, 1942-1949.
• Brig. Gen. and Mrs. Charles E. Walsh, Jr. , 1949-1965.
• Mr. and Mrs. Duncan (Jane) Martin, 1965-1971.
• Dr. David W. and Diane B. O'Keeffe, 1971-present.

Diane and David O'Keeffe took me through their home a few weeks ago. They added a room in the back with a beautiful view of the grounds, flowers, birds, and shrubbery.

Believed to have been built in the 1830s, this ten-room home has a spacious double kitchen, a large living room with a fireplace, and a comfortable family room in the back. Additionally, Dr. O'Keeffe has a study on the first floor. The house has three baths and lots of room for guests.

The O'Keeffes' three children are living on their own elsewhere, a pattern repeated in earlier families living in the house.

Diane works part time in the offices of Drs. Duffy, Leyhane, and Fruiterman. Dr. O'Keeffe has a general surgery practice in Albany.

What Happened to Joey Marotta?
February 9-10

Little Leaguer Joey Marotta hit five home runs (driving in thirteen runs in two consecutive games) at Little League national playoffs in 1960.

At the time, Mickey McConnell, director of the Eastern Region for the Little League organization, wrote that "We do know of one boy who hit eight home runs in eleven times at bat in regional and World Series play in Little League." However, he acknowledged that it was impossible to compile individual records with 5,520 leagues and over a half-million boys participating each year. In short, it was difficult for Mr. McConnell to remember any more than one boy in the Eastern Region who had bested Joey's record.

Upon seeing a record of Joey's performance in Ade Arnold's scrapbook, I had a strong urge to find out what happened to Joey. I called the Marotta family, living at 41 Paxwood Road in Delmar, and Clara and Col. James Marotta said they were his mother and father. Further, Col. Marotta brought some papers to my home about their son. Joey graduated from BCHS in 1967 and earned a B.S. in business administration from the Uni-

The Reverend Frank T. Rhoad.

versity of Missouri in 1971. He worked briefly at the Latham Computer Center in 1971-1972 before his untimely death of unknown origin (in his sleep) on February 5, 1972.

Frank T. Rhoad: Symbol of Longevity
February 11-12

Frank Rhoad was my neighbor for more than twenty years. He lived at 25 St. Clair Drive in Delmar following his retirement as pastor of the Second Presbyterian Church of Amsterdam, N.Y.

He grew up in Bath, Pa., graduated from Yale Divinity School, and received an honorary Doctor of Divinity degree from Marietta College, Ohio, in 1942. Most folks I know around here didn't know his degree was honorary.

I used to kid Frank about being raised as a Lutheran, ordained as a Baptist, doing an internship as a Congregationalist while at Yale, and turning Presbyterian with his second major job. He'd say, "Oh well, the differences are minor."

Frank was at least ninety when I began to visit with him at his home. I provided the intellectual stimulus he needed on occasions. He always wanted to discuss weighty issues and was forever calling me for facts for the booklets he enjoyed writing. Once he insisted on a precise year the world began. I shared what I had learned from Steven Weinberg's brilliant book, *The First Three Minutes* (1977).

He was often a guest preacher at the Delmar Presbyterian Church where his words electrified his audiences.

We loved him for his kernels of reason: "Love without justice is mushiness, and justice without mercy has no power to move the stubborn heart of man."

Marie and Frank Rhoad had one son, Frank, Jr., who died before Frank, Sr., died. Frank, Sr., remained in his home until age 102 (in 1989, if memory serves) and went to Ohio to live with his grandson until his death at 103. God rewarded him with a long, purposeful life.

We miss Frank.

Thomas Edward Mulligan, former town historian.

The Ed Mulligan I Knew: Former Town Historian, Activist, Journalist
February 29-March 1

Ed Mulligan started me on a fascinating retirement career during a casual conversation in the fall of 1980. He took the initiative. I told him about some of my digging trips and he asked, why don't you dig here?

I asked, where? Ed promptly took me on a tour of the archaeological hot spots in Bethlehem and encouraged me to put a proposal in writing.

I learned rather quickly that Ed was not only a man of his word, he backed up his words with action. He invited me to visit with town Supervisor Tom Corrigan where the three of us could review my proposal to dig at the Slingerland vault and around the Nicoll-Sill estate. Both men gave their approval, and I began work at the vault with my continuing education class in 1981.

I was aware of Mulligan's problems with some groups in town, but, for me, he brought good luck and support.

A Necessary Ritual
March 10-11

Dorothy Hinsdale, a member of Coleen's gourmet luncheon group died last weekend, and Coleen attended her funeral yesterday. There was a "viewing" on Sunday at the Meyers Funeral Home at 741 Delaware Ave. in Delmar. Coleen declined to go to the funeral home feeling, as I do, that this is a barbaric custom for all except the immediate family. I can see where loved ones would want a final chance to say good-bye—but why invite others?

The church is really helpful at a time like this, a source of support from friends and significant others. Some churches have a ritual that has been honed by previous experience with bereaved families. The hymn is often the deceased's favorite hymn, the pastor's remarks are often a careful (positive) reflection on the deceased's life, the program at the end is often a meal enabling friends and family to get their feelings out about the deceased.

I often think: What about people who don't have a church? Does this mean a perfunctory service in a funeral home? Probably yes.

Coleen didn't enjoy the funeral (as participants did in the early years of our town's history), but she was glad she went.

Selecting Families for Inclusion in the Family Chapter of the Bicentennial History
March 18-19

Allison Bennett and I have discussed dozens of families for inclusion in the family chapter, and agree that we are limited only by the availability of information and our ability to trace the families selected back to earlier centuries.

In the back of my mind, however, is the thought that the families chosen should have played a significant role in the development of Bethlehem: governmentally, culturally, geographically, socially, and as many "allys" as we can dream up.

John B. Geurtze, ca. 1987.

John B. Geurtze—Farmer, Politician, Administrator
April 13-14

John Geurtze has stopped by my house several times over the past few weeks to share his vast collection of scrapbooks and pictures. He loaned me a picture of the oldest Boy Scout troop (16) in Bethlehem, which he claims was organized in 1912. His father, Harold Geurtze, is in the picture, as is his uncle Raymond Geurtze. John has led a colorful, constructive life.

Over all the years since his college days, John is best known for the ter-rific chicken barbecues he conducts for community-wide events of all kinds—including political get-to-gethers—in Bethlehem.

I have sampled his chicken. Umm um! It is just one small reason why the energetic Geurtze was elected to the town board in 1977, a post he held for around a decade, after which he accepted a position as a supervisor in the water/sewer section of Bethlehem's department of public works. Everyone likes John; they especially like his barbecued chickens.

Approaching Age Seventy-One: More Frequent Need for Rest and Relaxation
April 15-16

Twenty, even ten, years ago, I could do several dozen things every day and drop in bed every night for renewal, ready to do another day with gusto.

No longer. Today, I'm lucky to do a dozen things well, and I have trouble dropping off to sleep at night. The knot in my stomach isn't gone until the next morning.

The reason is my own doing—no one's fault but mine.

My treasured bicentennial history is at a crucial stage—third drafts on most of the fourteen chapters are in, copy is being loaded into the computer, a marketing strategy is under discussion, meetings of the editors and writers are decision-making in character, and a hundred-and-one details must be resolved.

I'm fortunate. Now the people I selected with great care are moving into the forefront, working out the difficult problems and doing the job. Our production team

- Chuck McKinney—associate editor, design and production.
- Ryland Hugh Hewitt— associate editor, graphics.
- Kristi Carr, Ross Gutman, and Emrie LaBarge—assistant editors, copy.

is turning out beautiful copy and meeting separately to reach cooperative agreements on these special problems.

They check with me often, and the net result is a lot of tension.

For some weeks now, I've realized that the only way I can get quality rest is to leave town for two or three weeks; hence, I have decided to drive to Florida to see my brother and his wife, to work on my family history, to swim and walk daily, and, generally, to wind down and enjoy a vacation.

Visit With Calvin and Ruth Brewer, Avon Park, Florida
April 25-26

At sixty-seven, Calvin is a happy retiree from the cold, rainy weather of his home community of Westminster, Mass. They own a villa-type condominium in the River Green golfing resort community in this central Florida town; ideal for Cal and his wife, Ruth.

Would I move here permanently?

This question pops into my mind every time I visit Cal and Ruth. The answer is maybe, if I were alone. But my life with Coleen in Delmar is full and satisfying. We like it there: the people, the opportunities to do some productive work, the culture, and most of the things Cal and Ruth enjoy about this town.

In short, the big difference is the weather. However, their July and August weather is as objectionable to us as our January and February weather is to them. Therefore, on balance, we're better off in Delmar with friends we enjoy, a church (Delmar Presbyterian) Coleen loves, and a community that seems to appreciate my work.

The Democratic National Convention
July 14-15

Coleen and I watched Senator Bill Bradley deliver a keynote speech last night at Madison Square Garden, site of the Democratic National Convention. It was an upbeat speech paving the way for later speeches in support of the Democratic ticket: Governor William

Before White Man Came, bicentennial painting by Colleen Skiff Kriss, 1993.

(Bill) Clinton for president, Senator Al Gore for vice president.

It is a reasonably young ticket that the polls show has a possibility of winning.

The hoopla leaves me with mixed feelings. I want some big changes in the way things are done in Washington, but I am not sure a new team can do any better than the current administration.

Art, Archaeology, and History Groups
July 28-29

A couple of years ago I approached Colleen Skiff Kriss, president of the Bethlehem Art Association, about the possibility of doing some paintings with a bicentennial history theme. She liked the idea, and the art association subsequently turned out eleven paintings, which were exhibited at the li-

brary in June. The plan is to find a permanent location to display the paintings after a series of temporary exhibits over the next year or so. Paintings of historic buildings and scenes were completed by:

- Amelia Anderson, *A Few of My Favorite Things.*
- Eleanor Bolduc, *First Reformed Church of Bethlehem Farmhouse* (1830).
- Linda Bunzey, *First Cross-Country (Glenn Curtiss) Flight* (1910).
- Rita Buttiker, *South Bethlehem Methodist Church* (1848).
- Dale Crisafulli, *Cedar Hill School* (1859).
- Jean Eaton, *Albert Bratt Tobacco Farm* (1640).
- Connie Elliott, *Paddock Store— Four Corners (Delmar)* (1918).
- Sue Gillespie, *Edward Heath Delivering Milk* (1920).
- Edna McCoy, *The Essex House (Feura Bush Road, Glenmont)* (ca. 1850).
- Charles A. Schade, *Nicoll-Sill House* (ca. 1835).
- Colleen Skiff Kriss, *Before White Man Came* (A.D. 1300).

I mailed a note of thanks today to Colleen Skiff Kriss partly to let the group know how we plan to utilize the paintings and to ask for further ideas.

In speeches to local and state professional groups, I have often called for closer and more frequent collabora-

163

tion between art, archaeological, and history groups in documenting local history. Lo and behold, we now have a classic example in our own town.

Founded in 1966 by Margaret Foster and Barbara Wooster, the Bethlehem Art Association has demonstrated a strong sense of community through its many public-spirited projects over a period of twenty-five years.

Summer Sweets
August 1-2

One of our regular habits during the warm months is to follow dinner out on Saturday evenings with a stop at Ben & Jerry's ice cream shop at Main Square, 318 Delaware Avenue in Delmar. Tonight was typical. After a pleasant forty-five minute drive to Coxsackie on Route 9W, and dinner at Pegasus, a popular restaurant, we drove back to Main Square for a cone of ice cream.

Ben & Jerry's is a big family stop. We notice that this is an especially popular place for families with small children. There is practically always a short line waiting for ice cream when we arrive around 7:30 P.M.

At $2.30 per cone for me and $1.60 for Coleen, dessert at Ben & Jerry's costs less than dessert at the restaurant and offers an additional measure of enjoyment as well.

Two Key Issues Influencing My Vote for President of the United States
August 3-4

Appointments to the Supreme Court: I like the trend toward a more conservative court, but want court decisions that favor a woman's right to choose— to have an abortion if she chooses.

It seems to me that we are more likely to get justices with this leaning through electing a Clinton-Gore ticket. President Bush has demonstrated his pro-life leaning time and again. More of the same won't solve this problem for the country.

Need for the re-emergence of a charismatic feminine leader: But a more liberal president can't do the job alone. We badly need another Margaret Sanger, who captivated the nation with her pro-choice pronouncements for so many years when I was growing up. She died in 1966. Where, oh where is there a Margaret Sanger in the 1990s? I don't see one among all these female candidates for public office.

The Statistical Character of Bethlehem in 1990
August 29-30

It is rare for me to photocopy an article from our local paper, the *Spotlight*. Why duplicate a story that's already on the record? However, an article by Mel Hyman in this week's paper is fundamentally important. It should be included in other publications as well, because his excerpts from the 1990 Census describe the character of our town.

No, I wasn't surprised to learn that 90 percent of our residents are monolingual, but I was surprised to discover that the average family income is $64,287. Amazing! That is more than twice my retirement income. Maybe I shouldn't be living here. Rest assured it would be difficult if our house was not completely paid for.

And where are the 535 blacks living in Bethlehem? I am delighted to see this figure, but don't see very many blacks in places like banks, grocery stores, and other buildings used by many citizens.

I was very much aware of the high percentage of residents holding graduate or professional degrees (4,269) and that we are a community of managers and professionals (6,383).

The abysmally small number of farmers (153) is likewise no surprise, a figure Carol Northrup, author of the farm chapter in our bicentennial history, would not dispute. It is an especially ironic figure when placed against a historical backdrop of Bethlehem's sweet success as a farm community in the 17th and 18th centuries.

It looks like many more divorced men (than women) remarry. What else could explain the astounding ratio listed in the Hyman article: 842 divorced women to 478 divorced men!

My Disagreements with the Republican Party Platform
September 14-15

I am an unhappy Republican. The Republican approach to health care for all Americans is sadly deficient. Further, many of President Bush's vetoes have left me feeling frustrated. When will the system begin working for the average American?

But most of all, I am in fundamental disagreement with a number of planks in the Republican Party platform: abortion rights, gun control, artistic freedom, separation of church and state, and government initiatives to create jobs.

These disagreements with traditional Republican positions are so fundamental that I am ready to give Democratic leaders a chance in spite of all the inherent risks and the poor record of some Democratic administrations in the past.

A Relaxing Country Drive
September 8-9

Coleen and I wanted to get out into sparsely populated sections of Bethlehem last Monday afternoon and chose to visit Hollyhock Hollow Sanc-

tuary on Rarick Road in South Bethlehem.

It was a pleasant drive on a beautifully sunny day along parts of routes 32 and 102 south and deep into the woods on Rarick Road.

Robert and Leona Rienow owned Hollyhock Sanctuary from 1940 through the 1970s, if memory serves, but both are dead now. They deeded the property to the Audubon Society of New York State before their deaths.

Dr. Rienow and I worked at SUNY Albany together. I remember well his success with a book called *The Lonely Quest* (for presidential leadership) when I first arrived on campus in 1966. However, it seemed to me that his book *Moment in the Sun* the following year was even more of a hit. I was among a small group of faculty invited to Bob and Leona's home on Rarick Road to celebrate release of the new book.

It was peaceful and relaxed at the sanctuary last Monday. Oddly, few birds could be seen or heard. The rubble from the couple's home has been removed—the aftermath of a fire which took Dr. Rienow's life in the 1980s. Leona had passed away well before the fire.

A new Audubon Society building was closed, but we could examine it from the outside.

Wildflowers so admired by the Rienows could still be seen around outbuildings and along the various trails.

Paperboys: A Dying Breed?
September 20-21

Being an early riser, I often watched paperboys deliver papers to my neighbors after they left our house, sometimes quietly, sometimes whistling as they went. From casual conversations as I put out the trash on Monday mornings, I learned that they made $30 to $35 each week delivering to forty or fifty customers. For years, it was the one job youngsters could count on to stir their entrepreneurial passions, their ticket to a degree of independence from tightwad parents.

We didn't have door-to-door delivery of the Bangor (Maine) *Daily News* as I grew up in Bridgewater, Maine, otherwise, I would have grabbed a route.

With seven children in the family, my Dad couldn't afford to give us an allowance. Delivering papers would have been a perfect way to buy things we needed.

I hear by the grapevine that the *Times Union* has not had an easy time getting boys to deliver papers and this probably explains why Coleen's paper is now delivered by a handicapped adult. When he is off for whatever reason, another adult with a pickup truck substitutes for him.

One assumption might be that publishers are now finding many adults who can't find regular jobs, and can be tapped for paper delivery jobs. Are these adults delivering to hundreds (rather than dozens) of homes today in order to make a living wage? I don't know. It would seem nearly impossible to deliver enough papers daily to make enough money to live on.

Oops, our paper just landed on the doorstep. I hope he didn't ride his bicycle across the lawn again as he dropped off the paper. Adults make fine paperboys, but sometimes take shortcuts as they rush from home to home. We want the service very much. Without her morning paper, Coleen would skip that second cup of coffee and a pleasant morning pastime would go down the drain.

Historic Schools Located on 1910 Map
October 12-13

The crumbling ruins of a number of historic district elementary schools are still visible in various parts of town. A few have been converted into homes, such as the former District 8 school on Elm Avenue South and Feura Bush Road (Houcks Corners).

On a bicycle trip around South Bethlehem a few months ago, I noticed the rather large elementary school building (which probably replaced the old District 3 schoolhouse) boarded up and sitting idle. You wonder why industry or a developer hasn't bought up the land for other uses.

During a trip to the Hollyhock Hollow Sanctuary (described in this diary on September 8), Coleen and I drove past the old District 2 school on Jericho Road and noticed the "for sale" sign on the property—really a beautiful place to build a home but it will more likely end up as an industrial or commercial site.

In his chapter, "Schools and the Library," in the bicentennial history, Tom Collins discussed these one-room schoolhouses at some length but since there were fifteen, he obviously could not include much detail about each. In fact, some of them were not one-room schoolhouses, since they were enlarged at some point in their history to include a second room.

167

District 1 school is a case in point. The Cedar Hill School, now a museum, was expanded to two rooms.

How One Bethlehem Group Got Under Way
October 28-29

I am occasionally asked, how did the Bethlehem Archaeology Group get started, and my memory has always been hazy on this subject until I found an old paper today.

It is a statement written at the height of a lot of interest engendered by my 1981 continuing education class in archaeology, which featured a dig at the Slingerland vault site.

I really didn't want to form a group; I simply wanted to provide a setting in which people who had been in my class could continue to work on local sites. Someone apparently got a $10 prize for suggesting the name Bethlehem Archaeology Group in February 1982. You might say we backed into forming a group. Later, it was apparent that we needed to worry about insurance, a budget, and even the most dreaded thing of all—a constitution.

How I Feel about the Elections
November 3

Coleen and I voted at the library today with a steady trickle of people. The parking lot was full, the people were in a serious but hopeful mood, and the turnout may even exceed the 80 percent for which the local people are justly famous. Our voting average is often higher than similar communities.

The Eternal Quest for Something New and Different
November 9-10

Ten years ago, my idea to arrange for writing a bicentennial history was new and different. It is still a good idea, but it is also a lot of work. About the same time I decided to keep a daily diary of our life in Bethlehem. Now this idea has reached an exciting stage—an editorial team is examining the diary to determine which excerpts from it should be published. I don't want to be editor of this new project, but I do want to be part of the team.

The Beauty and Timelessness of Wildlife
November 13-14

My neighbor Bill Van Valkenburg and I were out raking leaves today when a young deer bounded out of the woods behind Bill's house, hopped gracefully across his lawn, veered around my home, and ran up a small stream that runs by my house.

We gaped at the sight, marveled at the animal's audaciousness, and were thrilled and transfixed by that white tail sticking up in the air.

They are such beautiful animals, and they have as much right to a long life on this planet as we do.

In recent years, deer have been reclaiming their land by moving freely among the homes, nibbling shrubbery and other foliage here and there, much to the discontent of my neighbors.

But all of this is a small price to pay for the sight of a young, sprightly deer, bounding from lawn to lawn, oblivious to people, enjoying a sunny, cool fall day pretty much as we do.

The Highs and Lows in Producing *Bethlehem Revisited*
December 1-10

I stood there thinking, my God, this has been going on in these parts since at least 6500 B.C., when Indians were attracted by limitless hunting in these woods. I have found bones of the white-tailed deer in the Vosburg phase around 3000 B.C. and assume they've been here since post-glacial times.

Such deer are even more common around the lab on Route 32 South where I have seen as many as seven or eight at a time.

My dad always shot a deer near my home in Bridgewater, Maine, just about every year of my youth. We needed it to survive the long winter. Even then I hated to see one shot.

The most exhilarating high I've had relating to producing a book over the past three years stems from a close working relationship with the four associate editors—Joe Allgaier, Peter Christoph, Hugh Hewitt, and Chuck McKinney. It has required dozens of stimulating exchanges with each man, from stubborn problem solutions and discussions of historical facts to numerous exchanges about our families and the small talk that builds camaraderie and friendships. We criticize one another's positions on various issues, but always in a light/serious vein, and from many such meetings, phone calls, and interactions, the policy and copy for *Bethlehem Revisited* has evolved. These are men of principle and responsibility who can

Bethlehem Revisited editors. Left to right: Joseph A. Allgaier, Chuck McKinney, Floyd I. Brewer, Ryland Hugh Hewitt, and Peter R. Christoph, 1993.

be counted on to do what they say they will do and to stick with a project to the very end.

Well, the end is approaching and my respect and appreciation for these talented men have grown steadily, day by day, month by month.

Well over 400 people have taken advantage of the special pre-publication offer of $20 and bought the book sight unseen—about twice the number I expected would buy it at this point in time. There is quite a bit of postage money in the $9,049 collected thus far,

and I have not counted the actual number of books sold.

Equally important has been the slow, incremental progress in building a support team for the actual production phase of turning out the book— each very helpful in his or her own right. Ross Gutman and Emrie LaBarge have been plugging away at their respective computers for months. Kristi Carr has joined us recently to help us through a heavy deadline-oriented schedule. All are volunteers. Any one of them could get annoyed with the frustrations of producing high quality, accurate copy, pick up their marbles, and go home. But they haven't buckled under the pressures. They're still at it.

And the production phase of a book is especially difficult. I have great admiration for people who aren't getting paid to do a job and stick with it until the final drafts have been edited. For them, it must be satisfying to see the product of their labors get translated into copy fit for the most demanding reader.

Looking in on the Bicentennial Commission
December 19-23

My role as secretary is a unique vantage point to ruminate about the Bicentennial Commission's progress over the past year or so.

Overall: The group is moving along nicely under J. Robert Hendrick's leadership. He attends meetings regularly, offers a modest degree of direc-

tion, and attends to details that occupy so much meeting time.

Major events:

1) Celebrate Bethlehem 200—March 12, 1993, has emerged as an exciting evening jam-packed with fifteen events occurring simultaneously at as many locations all over Bethlehem;

2) Bethlehem 200 Family Day—July 4, 1993, at the Elm Avenue Park;

3) Bethlehem 200 Parade—September 6, 1993, is likely to become the event with the most participation by community groups. It will end with a huge fireworks display by Alonzo.

Also, a commemorative booklet, time capsule (to be buried at Elm Avenue Park), bicentennial souvenirs, and a bicentennial history [are all major projects reaching the final stage].

THE O'KEEFFE HOME, ROWLAND AVE.
DELMAR. MARK L. PECKHAM, JANUARY 13, 1975.

111 *Nineteen Hundred Ninety-Three*

This is it—Bethlehem's bicentennial year and the last of Floyd's diaries.

In fact, Floyd penned diary entries for only the first and last months of 1993. The remaining months he turned over to a motley group of five, who had agreed to edit and publish his diaries as a second bicentennial publication in the hope they would prove of interest—both now and in the future—as a record of life in the town of Bethlehem.

Sharing the writing of the diary was perhaps Floyd's way of weaning himself from the daily ritual, but it also showed some thought for broadening the representation of the residents in the entries for Bethlehem's bicentennial year. The other diarists include three women and two men; some conservatives, some liberals; some retired, others with jobs; some single, some married; some young, others older. None were in the habit of keeping a daily journal. For the two months each of them agreed to write, the process sometimes tore at their emotions or proved to be yet another chore, yet, when it was over, they found their written records rewarding and they had new respect for Floyd Brewer, who had maintained his diaries for ten years.

Helpfulness of *The Spotlight* Staff
January 14-15

In recent weeks, Scott A. Horton and John E. Brent of *The Spotlight* production staff have completed several drafts of seventy-five pages of end sections in the bicentennial history. They use Apple (Macintosh) equipment similar to ours and have resolved many technical problems regarding how to present a range of entries from biographical briefs of the authors to long lists in categories such as high school faculty and military.

A few weeks ago, I didn't know where to turn when we learned that the information on Ross Gutman's disks could not be imported by our more recent Macintosh equipment. Finally, I shared the problem with Richard Ahlstrom and his wife, Mary, publishers of *The Spotlight*. The Ahlstroms were both sympathetic and helpful in a tangible sense. Dick took the origi-

Scott Horton at his *Spotlight* desk.

How We Feel About Social Security
January 18-19

In a word, grateful. Our total annual income in 1993 will be a little more than $28,000 plus interest from savings accounts—another $3,000 at best. Therefore, the $13,000 we receive from Social Security is a substantial portion of our income.

It means

(1) We have barely enough income to remain in our middle class home in an affluent community. Without Social Security income, we would have to move to cheaper housing, possibly in a more rural community.

nal Gutman disks to a computer service company and salvaged [much of] the information, although a lot of additional keystroking was needed.

The technical expertise of younger, computer-trained, operators was needed for our project, and Horton and Brent understood the needs. I went back to them time and again over the last few weeks, picking up completed drafts, proofreading their work, and returning the corrected versions for still more drafts. Scott Horton did the lion's share of the work, but left for a vacation in Aruba last week, and John Brent finished the job.

All of the editors are grateful to the Ahlstroms and to Horton and Brent for their help in a genuine, king-sized emergency.

(2) We have enough money to live pretty much as we always have, albeit a little less extravagantly, to replace our car every five to seven years, to take at least one long vacation annually, and to enjoy entertainment events and meals out an average of once or twice a week. Without Social Security, we would have to drastically curtail these pleasurable activities.

(3) that my choice of a career in education (and the resultant modest salaries in return for the joys of teaching) was not an unwise or even risky choice. The system has rewarded us with a

secure life in retirement, due, in no small part, to the Social Security system. For us, it means just that—a socially secure retirement.

How We Have Used Main Square
January 20

We like Main Square at 318 Delaware Avenue in Delmar for a variety of reasons. It is a pleasant place for a meal, for people-watching over a cone of ice cream on a warm summer night, for buying a small gift, and more—all of this in a colonial atmosphere with covered walks, teak benches, and old-fashioned lamplights.

When James Breen and Tom and Dennis Corrigan conceived the idea in the mid-1980s, the plan was to build an upscale shopping center (if memory serves), but renters signed on a little too gradually, and in November 1987, the developers began to accept a professional office or two. Now there is a mix of tenants—some shops, professional offices, services (restaurants, etc.), twenty or so in all.

Some people still wonder—Main Square, what is it? They used to have more shops: flowers, toys, Buster Brown shoes, LeShoppe (ladies clothing), The Daily Grind (specialty coffees), and more. I don't know why each one departed, but it must have been something to do with the location,

high rents, and/or the mix available there.

Despite Main Square's ups and downs, we continue to go there often and expect to have dinner at their new Armadillo restaurant again soon.

Ah For the Good Old Days
When Dried Beans
Were Baked Boston Style
January 22-23

There was a weekend ritual in our home in the 1920s and 1930s. Mom always baked beans all day Saturday in a stoneware crock, and the Saturday evening meal was eagerly anticipated by her husband and seven children. And there was always light brown bread to go with the beans.

In recent years, I have searched for a recipe that approximates my mother's version of Boston baked beans and found one in the 1907 Veronica Club (of the First Reformed Church of Bethlehem) cookbook on page forty-three:

Boston Baked Beans

Soak one and one-half pints of beans overnight. In the morning slice a medium-sized onion into an earthen crock, then add the beans. Mix together two table-spoonfuls of molasses, one tea-spoonful mustard, one-half tea-spoonful baking soda, one tea-spoonful salt and enough water to cover the beans. Place among the beans one-half pound of salt pork. Put cover on crock and bake all day in a moderate oven. Add water if beans are dry.

Mrs. T. R. Brown

The more I searched, the more I wanted the exact recipe used by my mother, to be sure my favorite dishes would come out like the rich brown (but not greasy) beans she baked, and finally found it in a cookbook donated to the Bethlehem Archaeology Group library by Carolyn Lyons, former town clerk. Hood's 1897 [*Practical Cook's Book*, p. 142] recipe contains exactly the ingredients and procedure my mother used. Sadly, that great taste and rich brown

color has gone by the wayside in most Bethlehem homes in recent years with all the emphasis on a low fat diet. Still, one occasionally finds an exception to current trends, tastes, and practices, as I did today while searching through the 1982 Delmar Presbyterian Church cookbook. Apparently, Chris Deyss [pastor's wife] likes beans cooked the old way.

Bethlehem Nurse on the Verge of Retirement
January 24-25

Approaching sixty-five, our good friend and neighbor, Helen Nickel, is thinking of retirement. She is a charge nurse on the evening staff at the Albany Medical Center Hospital. As the various financial emergencies come and go, nurses often have to take up the slack in one form or another. Albany Med developed six teams of heart surgeons in recent years and assigned six of its high tech operating rooms to these units. But new Medicare rules allow them to charge only $35,000 to $40,000 for the average heart operation, whereas they used to charge $60,000 to $65,000. The number of nurses in these units is being reduced. Some nurses had great jobs last year and will be demoted or fired next year.

Further, more and more men are entering the nursing profession throughout the country, a development Helen Nickel approves of, although she complains that the male nurses on her

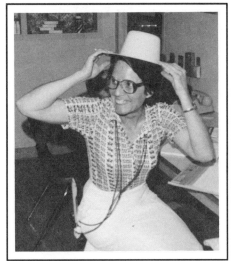

Helen Nickel clowning at her retirement party.

floor move on all too quickly to ICU, coronary care, or the emergency room, all offering them higher pay.

Helen says the higher salaries ($30,000 to $50,000) available to experienced nurses today have not necessarily reduced the so-called "nurse overload" factor. It is still a tough racket. She's tired. The heavy lifting probably contributed to her need for an operation, which she will have in two weeks.

Born in 1928 in Cortez, Colo., the daughter of Robert and Ruth Hightower, Helen graduated from Oklahoma Baptist University in 1951 with an R.N. degree. She married Ardie Nickel in the mid-1950s, and they raised four children—Susan, Stephen, Douglas, and Jeffrey. By 1975, when the children were old enough to permit her to go back to work, she ac-

Nineteenth-century condom container. Sketch by Margaret Foster.

cepted employment at Albany Medical Center and has been on the staff for nineteen years. She has earned the right to retire.

Condoms Then and Now
January 30-31

As I supervised a group of Boy Scouts conducting a surface search near the mouth of the Normanskill in 1985, one ten-year-old Scout rushed up to me holding a small, round metal box discolored from a decades-long entombment in the dark, black soil. "Mr. Brewer, Mr. Brewer," he said, "this must be something important. It

177

rattles...see!" I brushed off the soil and read the inscription to myself. I said, "This is something that should be opened in the laboratory," realizing rather quickly that it was an aluminum box of calcified condoms dating to the nineteenth century, and being a little unsure of how best to explain the artifact to a ten-year-old boy.

In my youth, condoms were sold in drugstores, but none of my friends dared to buy them for fear the pharmacist would tell their moms and dads. In any event, sex among young people in the 1930s and 1940s was much less frequent than it is today.

Last month a Bethlehem Central High School group called for the distribution of free condoms in their school, a notion voted down by the school board following a public hearing. This was not all that irrational an idea, since the subject of free condoms in the schools is on thousands of school board agendas throughout the nation as an action whose time has come. Many feel it is the only way to combat AIDS, an auto-immune deficiency disease that is now a sure route to death.

I favor the distribution of condoms in the schools, and have shared this view with some of my Catholic friends, most of whom are noncommittal on the subject. Privately, I think they want to see it happen, but they are torn between the church's official position espoused in thousands of churches throughout the land, and what they know is sensible policy.

Unfortunately, the Catholic church has slowed the distribution of condoms in numerous settings. Change will come, but it will come slowly.

Diary Entries by Kristi Carr

Teen Drinking in Bethlehem
February 1

A big day—the watershed between a lot of preparation and a finished product. Today's the day we videotaped segments for a message to parents about teen drinking in Bethlehem. The video was prompted, I'm sure, by a terrible auto accident one night at the end of last summer.

Working for the school district has taught me to be skeptical of summers—kids seem more apt to die then. We almost made it through the season, but late in August a truckload of our students careened into a telephone pole at eighty miles an hour. Erin Cox, sixteen, was killed; others were badly injured. The only one who seemed to walk away unscathed was the driver, Christopher Arnold, but his injuries turned out to be of a different nature; he was sentenced last fall to up to four years in state prison for driving while intoxicated [DWI], causing Erin's death.

We've had other DWI student deaths —in fact, David Bartholomew, seventeen, died in an alcohol-related auto accident just last spring—but somehow it's been the Arnold/Cox case that's stuck in people's minds, glued there with particularly strong media coverage.

Groups fighting to contain and beat back teen drinking in Bethlehem have

Kristi Carr.

spawned yet more groups. There's Bethlehem Opportunities Unlimited (BOU), spearheaded by Holly Billings, and endeavoring to provide fun alternative activities—ones without alcohol—for local teenagers. Then there's Bethlehem Networks Project, directed by Mona Prenoveau, which is a joint venture of the community and the schools to develop a safety net of positive role models for teens to emulate or to go to for help. And more recently, there is the Bethlehem Community Partnership. The partnership, a sizable group of community figures and including members from BOU and Networks, broke into task subgroups. The assignment of one of these sub-groups was to reach parents. That led to the video, which then led to me.

Memorial tree on BCHS grounds.

Putting together even a short video can be a lot of work, and it can probably seem pretty intimidating. At any rate, someone thought of me, probably because I'd had some video experience with two projects for the school district—a slide show of Bethlehem Central's first sixty years which was later transferred to videotape, and a video about the work of middle school science teacher Jane Cappiello, a finalist in a national competition last year. I told the sub-group members they might be surprised to find that making a video has a set of steps, not much different from following a recipe or doing most any other task. The all-volunteer sub-group seemed happy

nevertheless to find someone to drive the video through to completion.

Today's taping certainly doesn't conclude the work—we still need to edit two-and-one-half hours of tape down to just a handful of minutes—but it at least gives us tangible material to work with.

I was at the high school's administrative conference room at 7:15 A.M. and Holly [Billings] showed up shortly afterward. She's so giving, willing to take on all kinds of work. Though I wrote the script—a narrative under which we'll group bits of video interviews—Holly's advice helped mold it and keep it on track. I knew I could depend on her judgment as she was the instigator of BOU, well informed about teen drinking, and clear about her own feelings on the subject. It's telling that in one of our many meetings to prepare for today's videotaping, we talked about the Arnold/Cox accident and Holly said, "When it happened, I felt guilty. Maybe there was something I should have done." Here was this one-woman force, chipping away for literally years at teenage drinking, worried that she hadn't done enough.

Holly and I had scheduled all the interviews—two high school students, three school guidance counselors, a physician, a policeman, a child psychiatrist, an attorney, Albany County assistant district attorney, and Nicole Cox, Erin's sister. Luck was certainly with us to get everyone there in one day. And it was probably a relief for our cameraman and editor, Ralph Pascucci, who drove down from Saratoga, battling snow up north and morning rush hour on the Northway.

Except for the Albany County assistant district attorney, Ralph's probably the only non-local person working on this video project. I first met him in December in Ken Ringler's town supervisor office. As a member of the Bethlehem Community Partnership sub-group working on this video, Ken was drumming up funding for the video and got Ralph's name from a representative of Stewart's Shops. Ralph worked for network television, including Olympics coverage, and in our few lulls between interviews told us some good stories.

Holly and I came equipped to the videotaping with legal release forms and questions to prompt responses from the people we were taping, but Ralph came with the hardware—a video camera, tripod, light, cables, and what looked like a little round trampoline minus its stand. It was essentially a big disc of reflective fabric to help bounce light onto our subjects. What I liked about it, though, was that it somehow folded and twisted into a quarter of its full size in order to slip into its own small, round, zippered case.

Every time a new interviewee arrived, we did a bit of set dressing, parking the subject in front of bookshelves one time, a tapestry the next, routinely changing the posters on a large bulletin board to alter our backgrounds. But we couldn't avoid one on-location set of shots, unfortunate since it meant going outside, where it was sunny, very windy, and probably a thirty below windchill. We were videotaping trees, some just saplings and all quite barren at this time of year. Each had been planted in memory of a student who'd died. I hope the chill and that bleakness come across in the final video. Though a touching memorial, a tree is no substitute for a child or a friend.

We finished at about 5:15 P.M. I'm exhausted, both physically and emotionally.

My Birthday
February 4

Today's my birthday—forty-six, on the slide to fifty. I figured this wasn't going to be a day of much celebration. I'd let it be known I didn't expect any presents—I've taken care of that myself with shopping for Seth [my younger son] and my upcoming trip to Florida. But I suppose I was hoping for a little attention, and prospects didn't look good.

[My husband] Brad's out of town—in Boston for the American Bar Association's mid-year meeting. I've been praying to the weather god not to send snow as I really would like to

Brian Carr and friends during rare snowstorm on the University of Georgia campus.

avoid shoveling out a double driveway, besides which I'd feel obliged to shovel the asphalt apron we added a couple years ago to accommodate [my older son] Brian's old jalopy. We want to pamper that "hunk of junk" (as Seth calls it) to see how far it will take us through the teen driving years.

With Brad gone, I had set the alarm for 6:15 A.M., the latest time possible for a non-morning person. Like a fireman, I jumped into my clothes, then woke up Seth so I could chauffeur him on his paper route. We set a new record— forty-one papers in sixteen minutes. I know that'll drive Brad nuts to have bested his top time.

Shortly after seeing Seth out the door for the school bus, I called my mother in Nebraska to check on her health. I'd tried repeatedly to reach her last night, knowing she'd gone to Lincoln for medical tests. I'd given up after 10:30 P.M., but worried the doctor might have admitted her to the hospital. Consequently, I was relieved when she answered the phone this morning. Turns out she didn't get all the medical tests she expected as the doctor felt he knew her problem—something about not being able to absorb bile salts—and could prescribe medication. Forty-six years ago, she had me to take care of; now the roles are reversed. With her living at such a distance, I certainly am not called on daily to help out, but the distance seems to magnify the worry. I used to be after her to move here. Brad said it was like water dripping on a rock, but the rock continues to stand firm and stays in Nebraska.

By evening, my birthday seemed unspectacular. Then, as Seth and I were about to sit down to a supper of macaroni and cheese, I found an envelope as I reached in the cupboard for a dish. It was a birthday card from Seth and just the first find in an evening filled with good wishes. The rest came by phone.

My friend Audrey called from Chicago. We'd met in a hospital labor room and were friends before the nurses ever drew back the hanging sheet dividing our beds so that we could finally get a look at one another. With Seth and Audrey's daughter, Leigh, being born on the same day, birthdays are occasions that will always bind us.

Then Brad called. He usually phones me every day when he's out of town, and the thought of that constancy is a gift—birthday or otherwise—all its own.

But I have to admit, the phone call winner was from my Georgia Bulldog. Calling from a University of Georgia dorm room, Brian held out the phone and the voices of six or so young men combined into a hearty "Happy Birthday, dear Mo-m-m."

Sure, I was now the mom and not the coed. But youth is infectious and their serenade tipped my world—now I was sliding toward nineteen, not fifty.

Boy Scout Dinner
February 5

The Scout family dinner proved to be a good time. It renewed friendships and reminded me of what we'd missed over the months since Brian had turned eighteen and graduated out of the troop.

Brad and I continue to serve on the governing committee, but only Seth and I were able to attend the dinner with Brad out of town on business and Brian at college. I was worried Seth would be bored—he dropped out of Scouting when he was a Webelo—but Seth was occupied with his friend Jeff, whose younger brother is in the troop. Troop 71 is sponsored by St. Thomas the Apostle Church. We're not Catholics, so it seemed a bit odd to us some years ago when Brian was assigned to this troop rather than the much larger Troop 75. Kevin Murray, the current Troop 71 Scoutmaster, told me recently that 71 is down to just nine Scouts now, and that seems a bit thin to me. Still, it is the lower numbers, the intimacy of Troop 71, that is its strength. It certainly afforded Brian many leadership opportunities, plus a closer alliance with the adult leaders.

The easy flow of conversation between kids and adults struck me again tonight. It was fun and pleasant. It was also probably rare, and made Scouting in general and Troop 71 in particular all the more endearing to me tonight. Chris VanWoert, who followed Brian as the senior patrol leader, introduced me to his "honey," Amy, and we chatted about skiing. Seth and I are planning to take the Scouts skiing at Gore Mountain next Tuesday during the school's mid-winter vacation. I talked briefly, too, with Trevor, who last year was a first-time skier and my buddy on the bunny trail. Colleen, Brian Murray's sister, filled me in on her recent accident, a fall that cracked a bone. And we ladies dubbed Father Cribbs—arriving a little late as duty had called him in another direction—a true Irishman and full of blarney for his compliments to the ladies and the cooks.

The night's agenda was familiar. Tables were set up at the back of the St. Thomas School gym, while chairs and a podium were near the stage. In between these two areas was a long table for food. Potluck is one of my favorite types of meals. I contributed a ham, rice, and broccoli casserole. There were Italian pasta dishes, always a staple at these affairs, plus Crockpot meatballs, tossed green salad, and chicken dishes. Another long table was set up off to the side for drinks. It also held a huge sheetcake, iced in white and decorated with the Eagle Scout emblem. I asked Seth to concoct a cup of instant coffee for me. Evidently this was not in his repertoire of culinary skills as quarters could have floated on it. I made a trip to the drinks table myself and proceeded to add hot water, making one cup of coffee into three!

Kathy Murray, the Scoutmaster's wife and thereby hostess-by-default, sliced up the sheetcake, the teens descended on it, and it was gone!

From the meal, we convened in the chairs near the stage, standing at first as the Scouts advanced the colors and we recited the Pledge of Allegiance, the Scouts saluting, others of us pressing our hands over our hearts. Then came the traditional candlelighting ceremony. A birch log holds several candles which the boys take turns lighting and reciting a description of a Scout—"A Scout is trustworthy. A Scout is clean."

Brian had written a letter to the troop, which I was asked to read. He congratulated them on their rank advancements, which they'd receive tonight, and urged them to continue on to Eagle Scout, as he had.

Mr. Murray presented the advancements. Most notable for me was Chris's Life Scout award. Eagle is his next step, and he had asked when Brian would be home for the summer—Chris is planning payback for all the help he gave Brian on his Eagle project. Most Scouts fumble when trying to fasten on the mother's pin, which accompanies each Scout advancement, but Chris had the additional dilemma of simply finding a place for it—Mrs. VanWoert, mother of nine, rivaled any general with her chestful of Scouting medals.

Yes, I miss Scouts. When, as a harried den mother some years ago, a Cub Scout nailed his project into my dining room table, I never thought it would come to this. But today I'm a little bit proud of that nail hole.

Grandma
February 6

Crossgates Mall was on my agenda today. I went to return something. Shopping isn't really my favorite pastime, and I really try to avoid returns.

Seated: Left to right, cousins Lori Leith-Ross, Jan Self, and mother, Melva Rapp. Standing: Kristi Carr.

since I'd even seen my grandmother if you don't count her funeral. That, too, had been at Christmastime, when she, my mother-in-law, and Brad, Brian, and I had all flown in from various locations across the country to gather at my parents' house. For a small family, spread in all directions, it was a rare and wonderful time. Now, my father, my mother-in-law, my grandmother are all gone.

But this was one of the last errands I would run for my grandmother. I was returning a nightgown and bedjacket, a Christmas present for her. I know she saw them before she died, but, of course, she never got to wear them.

The Filene's clerk asked no questions about why I was returning these things; she just applied the credit to my account and handed me a slip of paper as a receipt. I left the store, feeling a little empty.

My grandmother was ninety-four when she died, so it wasn't as if she were cheated out of a long life. Still, I remember when my father died at age sixty-five, my husband's aunt told me that, even though her father lived well into his nineties, she still felt a profound loss. It had been several years

Grandma died just before this past Christmas, and I spent Christmas Day flying back to the Midwest. My cousins had flown in with the body from Oregon and we met at the airport in Sioux City, Iowa, to drive to my mother's home in Nebraska. I wasn't sure I'd even recognize my cousins. Jan, a year younger than I am, had been like a sister when we were little kids, and especially until [her sister] Lori came along. I hadn't seen them since the summer I'd graduated from high school. Jan was dating Leonard at that time. Now more than two decades later there they stood just about as I'd remembered them—Jan, still a real blonde; Lori, diminutive and shy; and Leonard, a gentle giant of a man.

That was a bittersweet gathering of the clan. Mother, always a great cook, hadn't had much of anyone to cook for recently, but she had dinner almost on the table—a good thing, too, as there wasn't so much as a fast food joint open en route on Christmas Day. We sifted through old photos and shared more recent ones (except for me as my luggage hadn't arrived). The next day we drove back into Iowa, stopping at the airport for me to claim my suitcase and change clothes in the airport bathroom.

Gizmo enthusiast Brad Carr trading in high tech for old-fashioned shovel.

Then we drove—back in time really—to Cherokee, Iowa. We drove past the house where my mother grew up and where Jan had had her picture taken as a toddler on the uniquely rounded brick steps my grandfather, a mason, had built. We drove up "on the hill," to the house where my grandmother had last lived before moving out West and where Jan and I, as children, used to conduct elaborate rites for dead birds we'd found.

And then, on a Saturday, the day after Christmas, in bright sunshine but bitter cold and wind, we buried my grandmother next to my grandfather.

My cousins returned to Oregon. I drove my mother back to her home in Nebraska. And the next day, I returned to New York.

The package from my cousins had arrived earlier this week, containing the nightgown and bedjacket which I

returned today. Jan and Lori also sent Grandma's plate which I'd wanted, the one that hung in her kitchen. Painted on it is a girl which I imagined as my immigrant grandmother—a Swedish girl, dressed in a scarf and apron, carrying a bucket. Blue script letters encircle the girl and say, "Välkommen to vår lilla stuga"—"Welcome to our little house." I'll hang it up in my kitchen tomorrow.

The Gizmo
February 7

After almost two continuous weeks out of town on business trips, Brad is back home. But he didn't return alone; he came back with another gizmo.

He's always had this fascination for electronic gadgets. Here's a guy who'll wear his shoes until his toes are practically touching the pavement through the holes, his shirts until the collars are ready to disengage along the frayed line, but he'll be the first in line for the latest invention, so long as it runs by battery or plug, and particularly if it involves TV or movies.

The latest-and-greatest is a voice controlled remote control for TV and VCR. Now, not only do we not have to rise out of our chairs to get to the controls, we don't even have to have the remote control in our hands. All we have to do is speak—"Fast forward!" "Rewind!" "Stop!"

But before this creature comfort will operate, you have to let it get to know you, namely to recognize your voice. So Brad spent the better part of today barking numbers and commands to this inanimate new ruler of our lives. It seems you have to repeat words to it numerous times before it is satisfied. At one point, I was trying to have a long distance phone conversation with my mother, while a few feet away at the kitchen table, Brad was shouting at the gizmo—"One, one, three, eject, eject, eject!"

The gizmo now joins the remotes for both the TV and the VCR in a basket on top of our television set—it's getting crowded in there. I'm not sure where we'll store the gizmo's instructions, but, judging from our continuing inability to be certain we are videotaping anything on our VCR, we'd better keep them handy.

Brian Carr in his dorm room at the University of Georgia.

Call from the Dawg
February 10

When Brian went off to college last fall, we sent him with a telephone, a phone card, and a loose agreement to call us once a week, which has turned out to be Sunday evenings. So we were surprised to hear from him tonight, a Wednesday.

Was he sick? Homesick, maybe? Did he flunk some test? Or maybe he aced it? A love life problem?

So much for parental instinct. He just called to clue us in on the classes he was considering for his spring quarter. The University of Georgia operates on a quarter, rather than a semester, schedule and Brian is halfway through the winter quarter—time to start planning for the spring one, the final quarter of his freshman year. The usual quarter course load is three classes, five credit hours apiece. He told us he is thinking about taking economics, psychology, and another Spanish course.

I love it when Brian calls. He's always got so much to tell us—there's always plenty going on at such a big campus. And he sounds so grown up, so independent. I really like him. A parent always loves a child, but may not always like him. Well, I really like Brian.

We really raz him about being a Georgia Bulldog—ask him if the big Dawg has acquired a taste for grits in the dorm cafeteria, drawl out, "University of Jawja. May ah hep ya?" And truthfully, a lot of New Yorkers, a lot of his high school classmates, turn up their nose at anything outside the Northeast. But Brian's getting the last laugh—he's happy.

Fat Allen
February 11

Time for the big one today—our annual trek to Fat Allen for our taxes. I hate taxes. Who doesn't? Even with a tax preparer, there's so much to track down and to organize. And I'd already figured out our refund was looking pretty slim.

Fat Allen certainly wasn't looking slim. I'm not a good judge, but the guy must tip the scales at 400 plus. And I hate Fat Allen, too. Not because he's fat, but because he's sarcastic. Anyone who thinks sarcasm is an acceptable form of humor should be shot.

Brad was already in Allen's office by the time I got there. I wasn't late, but naturally Fat Allen had some snide remark to make. The office probably hasn't seen a coat of paint since the big WWII. These guys believe in low overhead. They are completely computerized, however.

Allen sat like Jabba the Hut [from the *Star Wars* movie] behind his desk. I started shuffling the papers across to him—W-2s paperclipped together, interest income, deductions. As usual, he found something to chide us about, this year telling us our broker didn't know what he was doing when it came to our IRAs [individual retirement accounts]. Then he launched into his own retirement plans—moving to a wide spot in the desert in Nevada, where he plans to operate a self-service gas station/convenience store, sitting in an air-conditioned glass booth, collecting the money from his patrons. Give me my IRAs and deliver me from the desert.

At one point, Fat Allen encountered no response when he bellowed for the girls in the outer office. Finally, he pushed aside his snack of the hour and hoisted himself to his feet. After banging on a recalcitrant knee, he toddled over to the door to the outer office. Brad turned to me then and whispered, "This guy is going to die." Actually, if he does it will be the second tax preparer we've gone through. The first guy died and his wife sold his client list to Fat Allen, which is how we got hooked up with him.

Bowling partners. Left to right: Min Savoca, Barbara Stiglmeier, and Marge Thurlow.

Allen returned to his desk with great effort and proceeded to do our state taxes. It was then that he started questioning my line of work. I'm not sure why, since he's known how both Brad and I make our living since we started coming to him a few years ago. But I suspect it was because he wanted to let me know that he, too, produced a newsletter via desktop publishing, that it was no great shakes, and I was probably overpaid. I wasn't going to take that without a comeback. So, as Brad looked on somewhat in horror, I proceeded to tell Fat Allen that I would keep my nose out of his tax preparation if he would grant that I might bring more journalistic training to the table than he could.

Just then, he ripped our state tax form from his computer and announced we owed Uncle Mario [Governor Mario] $102. It was probably the first time in twenty-one years of marriage that we've ever owed on our taxes.

My Bowling Partners
February 25

Usually I try not to work on Thursdays, and during the school year spend my Thursday mornings at Del Lanes with the Tri-Village Welcome Wagon bowling league. When I moved here in 1984, everyone urged me to join Welcome Wagon and also to join the bowling league. I've finally managed to slightly exceed the 120 average I was told was respectable. Still, I've thought at times about giving it up, but it's something I do for myself. (Heaven knows I don't go to bowl—I go to socialize.) I also keep going because it's where I find out what's going on around town.

Bethlehem Diary

My bowling partners haven't changed since 1984, and we make a compatible, though odd foursome. Marge Thurlow and Min Savoca have a lot in common—each has three grown and married children, three grandchildren, and part-time jobs (Marge is a Welcome Wagon hostess and Min works before school hours with the School's In program for children of working parents). Then there's Barb Stiglmeier, who has one daughter, Sarah, a high school freshman. Barb's an oncology nurse at Albany Med and sometimes comes to bowling just after getting off from a twelve-hour shift. We're always trying to get Barb involved in our crafts projects, but so far she's been steadfast in her avoidance of such involvement.

I really wanted to go bowling today. My bowling partners were planning a delayed birthday lunch for me. But I still had it in the back from all that snow shoveling. I got in touch with Min and we agreed I'd skip the bowling but meet them afterwards at the bowling alley so we could go to lunch.

We drove together to Nicole's on Delaware Avenue in Albany for lunch. What a treat! I'd heard of the restaurant but never been there. It's small, although I understand there is a room in back for private parties. There's a bar at the front, and on it was an elaborate copper and filagree espresso machine. There were lots of patrons when we arrived, all dressed in business attire. We felt a bit conspicuous in our casual clothes, but we're all too practical to let that dampen a good time.

I could hardly settle on what to order—everything on the menu had its own appeal. The others had the same sort of quandary, so it was funny that when we ordered we chose only two different dishes amongst the four of us. Marge and Barb had an eggplant and chicken dish, and Min and I had grilled chicken with roasted peppers. It was absolutely delicious. Marge asked for a "doggy" bag for her leftovers, and the waitress brought them back to the table in a Styrofoam container, which we began referring to as Wes, Marge's husband and the "doggy" who would get them. We even indulged in desserts, swearing off dinner for the evening.

Next week, bowling will be more normal. We'll bowl three games. Probably lose most of them, as our current ranking is eighth out of twelve teams. The only food we'll see is the dime coffee and doughnut sections provided by Del Lanes. But there's nothing average about my bowling partners. They're gourmet all the way.

Diary Entries by Joseph Allgaier

A Movie We Had to See
March 3

In the evening Jackie and I went to the Spectrum theater on Delaware Ave. in Albany to view the movie *Brother's Keeper*. Ed Brown left a newspaper article about the movie in our mailbox. It is a documentary about the trial of a farmer in Munnsville, N.Y., accused of killing his brother. Since Jackie was born and brought up in Munnsville, we just had to see it. Somewhat disturbing was the fact the film presented a distorted view of the people in the town. One would think they are unkempt, not too smart, use a lot of profanity, and have no teeth. Very little shown of the town. Jackie was upset by the presentation and could understand why her aunt Frances wasn't too enthusiastic about the film. In many respects, an unfair representation of the town and the people in it. We paid $4.00 each, as seniors, versus the normal rate of $5.75—one advantage of getting old.

Bowling
March 5

Bowling this morning at Del Lanes with the Normanside group. Only ten of us there since most others are down South. Had games of 136, 214, and 198—not bad. Another good time with a great group of guys.

Joseph Allgaier.

The Rescue Squad—In Action
March 7

We went to 10:30 A.M. mass at St. Thomas. During the mass a man fell ill. The situation was handled very calmly and with discretion. The rescue squad and police arrived and took the individual to the hospital. I suspect many people in the church didn't even know about the situation.

I have high regard for both the police in our town and the rescue squad. The fact that many are volunteers is amazing. We had only one occasion during our years in Delmar to call the rescue squad. Unfortunately, it was during a dinner party we were having and one

Joe Allgaier and friends, in flight, in their Mooney 201.

of our guests had a choking incident. Jackie called for help and it seemed like only minutes when they arrived and handled the situation in a very professional manner. I regret now that I couldn't find time during my younger years to volunteer with this organization.

Why I Fly
March 9

When I tell people what we do when flying, I sometimes get a blank expression that conveys, why? Guess you need to be a pilot to understand. Each flight is a learning experience as well as a necessary condition to maintaining currency. For the instrument rating, I need to have six approaches and six hours of actual or simulated instrument flight within the past six months to be current. There is a real sense of satisfaction in executing an instrument approach "by the book." In addition, I have always found that when I fly I become completely focused on the task, and no other thoughts enter my mind. A great stress reliever. I guess someone who is a boater would understand. My brother, John, bought a sailing boat for his retirement and spends much of his time on that activity.

History Presented and Received
March 10

Made a presentation on local history to the Second Milers today. I kept it at about thirty-five minutes, which I feel is more than adequate time.

At one point in my talk I made reference to John Blanchard and also the fact he built my house thirty years ago. A comment from the audience let me know that John was there and I saw him after the meeting. I asked him about the Delmar railroad station which he bought in 1955. He said it was sold to others, who tore it down.

The Diary Strategy and a Surprise Call
March 11

The afternoon was spent on the diary project, 1986. The technique I used to evaluate what should be extracted was to record the titles of each diary entry. I then looked over the whole list of topics. I decided to extract topics that were social or political issues of the day, like health care, discount stores, pornography, etc. Then, items linked to the town, like the GOP steak roast and establishment of the bicentennial publications committee. Floyd has a lot of personal entries that I did not use, since I feel they reflect more on his personal life than on providing a picture of the times. For example, a trip to a museum, attending a symphony, or dinner out.

In the evening, I received a surprise call from Tony Pizzitola, who is involved in a long-running legal battle with the town over access to the Slingerland burial vault. It lasted about twenty minutes and I wrote a memorandum about the conversation while it was still fresh in my mind. Tony contends that the land containing the vault is his property. He says he would permit access to the town, for maintenance or visitations, if the town guaranteed insurance. I wonder why he called me on this matter [other than the fact I am the town historian]. But I attempted to seek from him what would be required to resolve the dispute. From his perspective, there is no solution at this stage of the issue. That's too bad, since the community is being denied access to a historically significant landmark in our town.

Bicentennial Celebration— Opening Night
March 12

Tonight was the big night as far as the town's bicentennial celebration was concerned, and the planning of the commission, on which I serve. The weather was ideal, although cool. A blizzard, touted as the worst this century, was on the way, due to start Saturday morning. The commission members met at town hall an hour before the start of festivities to assure that all bases were covered. The best count we had was that about 1800 buttons were sold for the mini-night. I felt it was terrific.

Program cover design, Bicentennial opening ceremony.

Dominick DeCecco, master of ceremonies, Bethlehem 200, opening program.

The stage in the auditorium was set up for the re-enactment of the first town meeting, produced by Pat DeCecco. I thought she did a tremendous job with the setting on the stage. At 5:45 P.M. I wondered if the auditorium would be full for the 6:00 P.M. presentation. That turned out to be a false worry. Not only was the place packed for the first presentation, it also overflowed for the second show at 7:00 P.M. The Adamsville Ancients played for about fifteen minutes (nice to see and hear Carol Willey again), Dom DeCecco acted as master of ceremonies, officials were recognized, the Bethlehem schools elementary choir sang two pieces, and the show presented the act of incorporation in 1793, then 1794 officials [portrayed by town residents] were introduced and spoke of their duties. As an inducement to clear the auditorium for the next show, a mini-fireworks display was held on the lawn.

The audience was very mixed from the elders in the town to the smallest children. I felt proud to be part of the community. It seemed many desirable characteristics of people, such as intelligence, courtesy, respect, good humor, and patience, were clearly evident in the crowd. These characteristics continued throughout the evening at the various events I witnessed. I exchanged greetings with so many people during the night, it is impossible to recount all.

I volunteered to monitor the action at Normanside Country Club. When I arrived, I was surprised at the number of members who were there, and wearing buttons. The Phil Foote dance band, in formal dress, was all set, and along with our redecorated bar room, an elegant setting was provided for anyone who chose to visit.

Jackie and I were able to visit in St. Thomas to hear Jonathan Moak on the organ, I learned the Texas Two-Step in the school hall (with Liz Matterson as partner), and then we went to town hall, where I turned in my money from button and program sales at Normanside. Jackie went home at 10:00 P.M., but I visited the Porters, Irish song group, at the Delmar Reformed Church, then to the Legion Hall to hear the Bavarian Barons (of course, with a beer).

The day after the big blizzard.

A number of people worked long and hard on this event and it certainly seemed to have paid off. In my view, one of the best things the commission did was to spend the (modest) sum of $2,000 to hire Maureen Duda and Bob Girouard, who have been presenting the Albany first night event. They added professionalism and stability to getting it done.

The Big Storm
March 13

The storm (blizzard) of the century, as labeled by the weather bureau, hit us today. Started snowing about 8:30 in the morning and kept up all day. Total fall reported at twenty-seven inches, the second largest fall in a single storm. I really put my old-time Lawn Boy blower to the test. I purchased the unit about thirty years ago from Vinnie Herzog for $25. At the time it was about twenty-five years old. Two years ago I almost threw it away because I couldn't keep it going. But I brought it to Weisheit and asked if it

was worth fixing. Looked like all it needed was a little tune-up and a carburetor part. Been running well ever since.

I tried to keep up with the snow by going out every few hours and doing the driveway. When the winds picked up I had to abandon trying to keep the walk to the front door open.

Because of the snow and winds, I expected a power failure, a fact of life in Delmar. The power company claims the problem is due to the large number of trees in town and the reluctance of the residents to have them cut down or trimmed. So, I went to Curtis Lumber and bought fifty feet of wire so I could run a circuit from the generator, in the garage, to my electric distribution box, to activate the furnace—also for the freezer in the basement. Still haven't gotten around to making a permanent connection for auxiliary power. I bought the generator I have immediately after the October 1987 storm, when we were out of power for a full week. I said never again!

According to the TV, there was a real run on stores for food supplies and items as batteries. Most markets ran out of basic items. I was in the Tri-Village hardware store and two people came in looking for propane (sold out) and wood. I noticed they were out of batteries and the store owner said he was also sold out of lamp oil.

Of course, the storm dominated the coverage on TV and the radio. Couldn't get much of anything else.

Politics As Usual
March 19

I was disappointed to see that [Congressman Michael] McNulty voted for increased spending, along party lines. Business as usual, I fear. The so-called stimulus package is just another pork barrel, as far as I can see. For example, Rush Limbaugh revealed in his TV show that over $10 million was allocated to projects in Puerto Rico. So much for providing jobs in this country.

The announcement that Justice [Byron] White will retire opens up another saga in the continuing story of that sorry bunch of senators on the confirmation committee. Now, we have a different bent to the abortion issue. Will the proposed candidate be required to pass the litmus test of pro-choice? Will questions on the issue reflect the intensity directed to Justices [Robert] Bork, [David] Souter, and [Clarence] Thomas during their hearings? Will Senator [Joseph] Biden get a hairpiece for TV? Will Senator [Edward] Kennedy stay awake? Stay tuned!

The Fat Club and Perot
March 21

Harry and Eunice (Spindler) picked up Jackie and me to go to the Tomlinsons' for brunch. This was a variation of our usual Friday or Saturday night monthly meeting of very good friends for dinner (participants bring a dish, wine, salad, or dessert) and duplicate bridge. Usually more dinner than bridge. Some years ago our daughter, Karen, dubbed the group the "fat club" and it stuck.

The main event during the evening, for me, at least, was the first Ross Perot TV program under the auspices of the organization he started, "United We Stand." I think he gave another excellent presentation of the status of our country and the need for change. His first chart (which has become a hallmark of his speeches on TV) was the most significant, for me. It showed that with the Clinton proposals for taxes and "fuzzy" spending cuts, the trend of increasing deficits remains unchanged over the next four years, growing to seven trillion dollars. He took the most optimistic view presented by Clinton. We are not being told the truth by the Clinton administration.

Brownie Troop #641
March 22

I had a pleasant experi-
ence in the evening meet-
ing with local Brownie
Troop #641. Jean O'Don-
nell made the arrangement
with me for her troop of
eight Brownies. After two
false starts on meeting location, we wound up at 17
Parkwyn Drive, the home
of Jim and Robin Storey.
The children were won-
derful. It really rolled back
the years for me, when our two daughters were growing up and Jackie had
her own troop. Jean had previously
taken pictures of various buildings
around town and each of the girls
made a drawing. I used the drawings
to discuss some local history. Then
talked about some other material that
I had brought. I hope it was interesting for them and their participation
was not a result of the obvious up-
bringing that taught them to be polite
to guests. After our little meeting,
they invited me for cookies and juice
and they even had me participate in a
Brownie "circle." Not bad for an old
man. The children and their parents
personified the best of neighbors we
have in our town. It was a pleasure to
be with them.

Jean O'Donnell's Brownie Troop.

Bicentennial Update
March 27

The morning was spent on a meeting
with the Bicentennial Commission. All
reports indicate that our March 12
opening night was a huge success and
all were encouraged to make sure our
next event, on July 4, is equally successful. I'm impressed with the quality of the people serving on the commission. All seem to be anxious to do
a good job and willing to work to
make things happen. Too often, lots
of talk but no action. This group seems
to be different. Things moving along
very well to July 4, and also, the Labor
Day parade.

My report on the status of the time
capsule project got a few laughs because of the burial vault Peter

The submerged fourteenth green at the Normanside Country Club.

was more than fifty percent under water. Both traps on the creek side were completely submerged. Took a number of pictures.

Applebee has volunteered to contribute. In any event, all agreed with my recommendations and $800 was approved in the budget for a marker stone.

Normanside Golf Course
March 30

Went to Normanside [Country Club] to say hello to our golf pro, Tom DeBerry, setting up the pro shop for the season. His father, Jim, was there along with assistant pros Glenn Davis and Tara McKenna.

Also brought some pictures for Jim Kurposka, our greens superintendent. The other reason for the visit was to see how we were surviving the flooding of the Normanskill. I walked to the fifteenth green and the water was over the bank and about thirty feet away from the bank. Our new trap was completely submerged. Also went to the fourteenth green, which

Diary Entries by Susan Graves

The Melting Pot
April 1

Somehow I've always thought of Bethlehem as homogeneous. Most of the people I know and meet—though varied in talent and interest—have similar backgrounds and values.

But a few months ago that notion was smashed when I started going to the Getty station on Delaware Avenue across from Stewart's. I went initially because someone at *The Spotlight* said cigarettes were cheap there—they are relatively—but continued to go because of the people who run the business. Most often, I deal with the woman who seems to be there a lot. I think she is Indian, though that's simply a guess. I'd like to ask her all about herself, but I don't want her to think of me as a pushy American. The woman has dark hair and eyes and most often wears colorful clothes that you never see in Peter Harris or the L.L. Bean catalog.

She and the others—I think they're related—are always friendly, and they used to hand out a Tootsie Roll with every purchase, be it one pack of cigarettes or $5 worth of gas. Also, even if you buy the exact same thing, they never charge you the same price.

The Tootsie Rolls have stopped, but you still get a free lighter if you buy a carton of cigarettes. I wonder if some-

Susan Graves.

one from the state or the health department threatened to close them down for dispensing Tootsie Rolls unlawfully. They also used to tend to bargain no matter what you bought and that practice has also dwindled. Still there's a little sign on the front of the booth that invites patrons inside "if the weather is bad."

And every so often, I get a surprise. Once the woman called me back to the booth and shoved a T-shirt and hat under the glass promoting some brand of cigarettes to me. "You nice lady," she said. I took the hat and shirt and told her she was nice too. I felt good the rest of that day and still do whenever I think of her gesture.

I hope these people don't lose their native business ways altogether. One thing that struck me as kind of a half-American-half-foreign symbol recently was on one of their cars. A younger man, maybe the woman's son, parked his car near the booth. The car sported the bold bumper sticker "I (heart drawing) Allah."

Kevin DeLong prepping Greta for company.

Lighten Up
April 2

Hanging onto a bad habit isn't easy, but so far I've clung to my addiction unscathed. Well, maybe not unscathed if you consider the medical effects of cigarette smoking, but at least I've learned to cope with the social situations where people seem to act as if cigarettes don't exist or as though people who smoke them belong on another planet.

It's so "in" not to smoke nowadays. At *The Spotlight*, and just about every other work place I guess, smoking is taboo on premises. So, smokers go outside in summer and winter and even the Blizzard of 1993 to satisfy their habit.

How times have changed. When I first worked for a newspaper, almost everyone puffed away happily at their desks, in their cars, in restaurants, and even on the street. Mind you, I started working in Troy, not Delmar, where I suspect even hard-core smokers are more discreet.

Nuts
April 3

As of today, my son Kevin and I have bagged two squirrels, part of a contingent of rodents that have invaded the attic via two holes they chewed in the eaves on both ends of the house.

Kevin, who has been staying with me on and off since he was diagnosed with a brain tumor last October, is recovering from radiation treatment and has devoted his time to "home improvement" projects. Right now, getting rid of the squirrels is number one on the list for me. My solution was to glut the attic with D-con, but Kevin nixed that with a capital N.

We instead are going after the squirrels with a Havaheart trap, which allows you to capture the animal and then drive miles into the country and release it.

And as annoying as the whole thing is, it's been kind of fun, I must admit, since things have been so life and death for us throughout most of the winter. Each morning starting about 5:30 A.M., Kevin and I sit down at the kitchen table watching the birds at the feeder and the trap at the foot of the old maple just outside the window. It has to be a quick waiting game since I like to get to *The Spotlight* early. So far, we've had two lucky strikes. I guess the squirrels just can't resist the allure of peanut butter set on the small platform that triggers the trap's doors. Once we have one, Kevin and I spring into action. He goes outside and covers the trap with a towel, which he insists calms the animal down, and I go out and start the truck. Then it's off to a remote spot in Rensselaer County about six or seven miles away where we hope the animal will establish residence. We returned to the exact same site with squirrel number two, thinking he or she might meet up with his former cohort and live happily ever after.

Bethlehem VIPs
April 4

I am going to miss Ken Ringler when he leaves office. I think he has done an excellent job as supervisor, and I think he will leave big shoes to fill. His business experience has helped Bethlehem through the recession relatively unscathed, and his personable nature has endeared him to many, including me.

Ken also is very open in his dealings with *The Spotlight* and our weekly meetings on Fridays have generated many comprehensive stories on the town and the way it is run. I especially admire the way he stood up for the incinerator that had been proposed for Cabbage Island. Most politicians wouldn't have touched that one with a ten-foot pole. What surprised me was that even though he took such an unpopular stance, his popularity never waned.

Ken is the kind of man who restores faith in the American political system.

Mary Ahlstrom
April 5

I probably know Dick and Mary Ahlstrom as well as anybody in town. They have owned *The Spotlight* for better than ten years, and spend most of their waking hours at the office on Adams Street. Both usually arrive early—about 7:00 or 7:30 A.M.—and both usually stay late. Dick has already received about every community service honor imaginable—the chamber businessman of the year award, and man of the year award from the Masons, and is probably better known in town than his wife.

So for this entry, I'll focus on Mary. Mary is a woman who goes about her life in a quiet, unassuming way. She is kind and always seems to be doing something for somebody else. There

Mary and Richard Ahlstrom.

are countless instances when a card or a cake or a smile or a sympathetic ear have cheered me. And I'm proud to say Kevin is on her "prayer list," which is almost a guarantee of success in my book even though I am not religious myself. I believe in Mary's belief.

Mary is a good mother of six, a grandmother, a wife, and doesn't hold any fancy titles, but she epitomizes everything that is good and rightly deserves woman-of-the-nineties recognition. Mary sparkles and lends a little bit of her glow to anyone she touches.

April is Cruel
April 7

In the last day or two, spring has made a valiant effort to live up to its name. Temperatures have been almost balmy—60 degrees plus—and the sun has melted most of the mounds of snow left over from the blizzard.

This winter was grueling compared to the last three or four years, and it seemed to take its toll on more than just the roadways. Potholes formed in people's personalities causing, as someone recently suggested to me, "an overall low-grade depression."

Role Models
April 9

Reading Floyd Brewer's diary triggers many feelings in me. I marvel at his brutal honesty, his attention to every detail of life, his devotion to his family, and his ability to look at most things with an open mind. As a writer of sorts, I guess I envy Floyd's ability to always tell the truth about intimate personal details that most of us keep swept under the rug most of the time. I think Floyd is a man of true courage. I wish I was more like him, except when it comes to his taste in popular music.

Taxing Times
April 12-13

I finally got around to writing the $52 money order for New York state income tax this year. It galls me to owe the state given my relatively paltry salary, but more so because the state mismanages its fiscal affairs so flagrantly. I sometimes think that if I were not so rooted in the area, I'd pack up and go elsewhere just like many businesses have done in the last few years.

Bethlehem VIPs on my List
April 14

I have known Betty Colyer for many years. We taught together at the Albany Academy for Girls where she was my mentor both in a professional and a personal sense. Betty retired after thirty-five years of teaching, the year before I left the school to take a copy editing job with the _Troy Record_. Betty's husband, Bud, died that year, and Betty and I drifted apart. I thought of her often, but got caught up in my jobs and other things so I was delighted recently when she called. We picked up our friendship in a heartbeat, and have resumed occasional lunch dates and phone calls.

Betty's immaculate, yet lived-in, home on Nathaniel Boulevard is a true reflection of her talents. She always has at least several projects going—be it her latest quilt or her most recent new hobby—and she always makes whatever she does look easy. It's not. She got me hooked on quilting and mine, though passable, were nothing next to hers.

I'm happy that Betty has been able to carry on happily in her retirement.

Money
April 15

I wonder how many single women are struggling with finances. In my case, it seems like I'm always behind—no matter how hard I work to keep a budget. My latest worry is paying the property tax bill, which is already overdue.

If I had small children—or even one child to raise alone—I don't know how I'd ever manage. I freelance for the _Capital District Business Review_ in addition to my _Spotlight_ job, but the money goes out as fast as it comes in. The only thing of substance I have is the house, and in today's market, that wouldn't mean much.

It looks as if there won't be anything close to "retirement" for me. I think women pay a high price for independence.

Bethlehem Women
April 24

Holly Billings is quiet and unassuming, but perseveres like a Sherman tank when it comes to BOU. As founder and president of the organization—Bethlehem Opportunities Unlimited—that works to provide activities and alternatives to town youth, she works tirelessly on a number of events and many committees.

BOU's accomplishments include reopening the Pit, a recreational area in the middle school, and raising thousands of dollars every year in BOU's annual auction for projects the organization sponsors.

Holly Billings.

Marty DeLaney.

Holly has also taken her message on the road and has appeared on local public TV Channel 17. She is working hard against some hard-core traditions — including teen drinking parties held in people's homes and at various town sites.

Holly typifies the spirit of so many town residents in that she works hard and long for something she believes in.

It's probably impossible to measure the success of her efforts, but her cause is undoubtedly worthwhile. Bethlehem has lost ten young people in accidents related to drunken driving in as many years.

More Bethlehem Women
April 25

Marty DeLaney is the executive director of the Bethlehem Chamber of Commerce and works like a trooper to promote town businesses.

She's another one of those Bethlehem people who seem to be everywhere at once. And she doesn't just put in an appearance at the many town functions she attends, she enjoys herself and is fun to be around.

I also learned not too long ago that Marty was the prime mover behind the School's Out program, which provides quality after-school care for children.

Marty has a lot of energy, is productive and professional. Bethlehem is lucky to have her.

Diary Entries by Hugh Hewitt

May Day Past and Present
May 1

Today was the occasion of May "Hay Day" at Delaware Plaza in Elsmere, another event in the half-year-long celebration of Bethlehem's 200th anniversary. There were hay rides, a disc jockey playing country-western music, demonstrations of sheep shearing, yarn spinning, and blacksmithing, and our town supervisor, Ken Ringler, riding in the carriage that was used by our town's first supervisor, Philip van Rensselaer. Some of us who worked on the bicentennial publication, *Bethlehem Revisited 1793-1993*, took part in a book signing outside the Friar Tuck Bookshop: Floyd Brewer, Joe Allgaier, Peter Christoph, Tom Collins, Bill Howard, Carol Northrup, and I. It was good to get together again after a hiatus of several months. During the writing and editing of the book, we had met and talked on the phone very frequently. Some of the writers and editors had been involved for six or seven years. I have to confess that I miss the camaraderie of the weekly meetings we had during the production of *Bethlehem Revisited*.

Perry and Arlen Westbrook
May 2

We had dinner and spent the evening at the Westbrooks' on May Day, and saw slides of their recent trip to Russia. We've known Perry and Arlen for

Hugh Hewitt.

something like thirty years. Perry is professor emeritus from SUNYA (English Department) and Arlen is a practicing social worker. Over the years, we have traveled together to Portugal, Yucatan, Scotland, and Jordan, and Rowena and I have visited them several times at their summer place on Martha's Vineyard.

Every year, Arlen has a birthday dinner for Rowena, and last night's, as always, contained lobster, this time with other fare from the sea in a delicious paella. Pat and George Hartman were there, too. Pat is a part-time secretary-receptionist at Capital Area Speech Center in Albany and George a Fleet Bank vice president.

Book signing at Delaware Plaza. Left to right: Peter Christoph, Hugh Hewitt, Bill Howard, Floyd Brewer, and Carol Northrup.

Photoing
May 3

Yesterday, I went to Magee Park for the opening ceremonies of the fortieth season of Little League. I was very interested to observe the care taken and the attention, warmth, and encouragement given the boys on his team by coach Joe Messina. I'm sure this happens with all the teams; I mention this team in particular because I was taking photographs of it for *The Spotlight*.

Taking photos for *The Spotlight* is a relatively new avocation for me. I've been taking pictures (or, as they say

nowadays, making images) since about the age of five when I won a Kodak Brownie box camera in a contest in my hometown of Elmira, New York. In 1936, my father and I were in New York City and toured the German ship *S.S. Europe*, which was docked on the west side of Manhattan and open for public inspection. Apparently, the German flag, red with a black swastika, flying at the stern attracted my attention because I took a snapshot of it. An enlargement of this early "art photo" won a prize in a photo contest in a school I attended in northern Massachusetts. I looked at it today and wondered how it could have won a prize. But I was so encour-

Prize-winning photograph of German flag, 1936.

Louise Rainer in *The Great Waltz.*

aged that I spent a lot of time in the school darkroom, to the detriment of physics and algebra.

It was at that school that my friend, Sherman Katz, let me use his Leica Model D (or Model II) camera, quite an advance over my Kodak Brownie covered with red leatherette. One of the phases he and I went through was photographing at the movies, and I still have a picture, "taken from the screen" as I labeled it, of the beautiful, fragile Austrian film star, Louise Rainer, in *The Great Waltz,* photographed in Radio City Music Hall. In the fifties I was able to scrape enough money together to buy a Leica M3 and for forty years it has been my favorite camera, outlasting several other makes that I bought during that time. It's an old-fashioned rangefinder camera, not one of those newfangled, single-lens reflex marvels or the kind that does everything for you with the push of a button. But it's solid and well-constructed and has a superb Ernst Leitz lens. The only time it has been separated from me was when another American family and we were sailing down the Gulf of Aqaba in a dhow-like vessel and security-conscious guards at the Saudi Arabian border kept it and our passports while we had our picnic on the shore some twenty kilometers south of the Jordanian border.

My Dog Fergus
May 12

I took Fergus to the vet today because he'd been limping for a week and I was concerned. Dog books and vets warn of possible dire results if a basset hound jumps from a height of even just a couple of feet. The dog's little crooked front legs, as well as his long, poorly supported back, may suffer

Fergus the frisky basset.

[May 23: It's difficult to enforce "taking it easy" when one's puppy is frisky. The recommended regimen had a positive effect and the limp disappeared.]

My Mother's Health Problems
May 15

My sister, Louise, and brother-in-law, Warren, live in Dunwoody, a suburb of Atlanta, Georgia. My mother, who is 94, lives in an adult home a couple of miles from them. They're all northerners, but have lived there for fifteen or so years and are now confirmed southerners. Lately, my mother's physical and mental health have been deteriorating, and now she is in Emory University Hospital. Since she has said that she'd like to live near me, Rowena and I have been looking at nursing homes in this area. We find that a semi-private room in a nursing home costs around $50,000 a year and a private room $60,000-$65,000. We have applications from Villa Mary, Guilderland, Good Samaritan, and Child's, but there is no vacancy in any of them at this time. My brother-in-law also inquired in Dunwoody and found that the cost there is about half what it is here.

serious injury. In spite of my care, Fergus has several times jumped from the couch in the living room when he hears someone approaching. Knowing that he shouldn't get up on the furniture doesn't deter him. Fergus weighs fifty-six pounds, and that weight and his delicate legs and back are a combination which put him at risk for injuries.

After a thorough examination, the vet concluded that probably a strain or sprain in his right front leg was the cause of the limp. Fergus should take three aspirin-like pills each day and stay as calm and inactive as possible for a week to a week and a half. If the limp continues, we should return for X-rays.

The "problem" of what to do when an aging and ill parent needs care faces more and more of us as we grow older. In most instances, it is not possible or desirable to provide care in our own homes, much as we would like to.

And so we have to make the difficult decision of who will provide the care and where. I guess there's no easy way.

Kite Flying
May 17

My Reflex 9000 kite arrived from the store in Boulder, Colorado, in this morning's mail. Bill Burnett helped me assemble it and late in the afternoon we went to the Elm Avenue Park so that I could try it out under his expert instruction.

It crashed several times, which necessitated a lot of walking, untwisting of lines, and checking to see that all the pieces were still attached. After one crash, we found that a whisker, or standoff, was missing. The six-inch-long piece of fiberglass was under pressure, bowed, and apparently sprang out of its fittings and shot away some fifteen feet when the kite hit the ground nose first. We decided that the whiskers could be improved upon. I phoned the store and the representative said that he'd lost dozens of them. His solutions were to buy more standoffs or make them from fiberglass rods or wooden dowels. So Bill made me new standoffs of slender wooden dowels with Rube Goldberg-like ends fabricated from wire. The ends fit nicely into the pockets on the lower edge of the kite...in fact, the whiskers work like a charm and I'm sure they'll survive many crashes.

Crashing properly so that one's kite doesn't disintegrate takes some skill. Probably, my early lessons should be concerned with landing the kite gently, not nose first, which buries it an inch or two into the turf. It should float down gently, as a leaf slips through the air and lands on the grass.

Garden Club's Beautification Program
May 18

Yesterday afternoon we drove over to Shirley Bowdish's house in Delmar to pick up our supply of geranium and petunia plants. Shirley really deserves a medal or a star in her crown for all the work she does getting ready for this spring event. She prepares the soil for the flower boxes, purchases the flowers, makes plans which show where each type and color of plant should be placed, and prepares the plants to be picked up. Each spring, members of the Bethlehem Garden Club have been planting flowers in the boxes in front of businesses at the Four Corners and along Delaware Avenue in Delmar and Elsmere.

Rowena was assigned the boxes in front of the Saratoga Shoe Depot and Skippy's Music Store at the Elsmere four corners. At about 7:00 A.M. today we went over to Elsmere and put geraniums and petunias in the three flower boxes in front of the stores. On the way, at the Four Corners, I noticed Jim Tate taking geraniums and petunias out of his station wagon at the convenience store there. On the same errand as we were.

This is a project of the Bethlehem Garden Club, an organization Rowena has been involved with for the past eleven years. This particular effort, which frequently involves members' spouses or friends, is part of the Garden Club's work at sprucing up Delmar and Elsmere not only for Memorial Day but for the summer. In June, as part of the Bethlehem bicentennial celebration, the Garden Club is having a display in town hall of members' floral arrangements.

Southgate Commons
May 19

Back in April, _The Spotlight_ published a letter from Betty Albright of Glenmont concerning a new shopping mall on Route 9W in Bethlehem Center. [XXXVII, April 28, p.8; "A new shopping mall seen cause to worry."] Her concerns were that a large mall there would increase traffic on Elsmere Avenue, Feura Bush Road, Route 9W, and other roads, such as Corning Hill Road, in the area. She also pointed out that the problem connected with the Route 9W exit/entrance for Glenmont Plaza (constructed in 1990) hasn't yet been resolved. In subsequent issues of _The Spotlight_, letters to the editor have urged construction of the proposed complex: "We need the jobs, the tax revenues, the competition for Grand Union, and the recreational opportunities (i.e., movies, restaurants) that this development could provide." There are many pros and cons. One writer says that "We have great minds in this township. Let's get them working on these ideas. Not more but better." Another feels that "existing commercial space [in Bethlehem Center should] be utilized." The Town Squire center is more than half empty and includes space for a sorely needed alternative supermarket." In fact, there is empty space in the three shopping centers located at the Feura Bush-Route 9W intersection. Inhabitants of Slingerlands are well aware of what Glenmont (or Bethlehem Center) residents are going through now; they have for several years been divided concerning the establishment of a major mall at the New Scotland Road-Cherry Avenue Extension intersection. Public awareness of proposed changes, improvements, and additions is vital. It would seem that when something like a major shopping mall is to be introduced into a residential area, the needs of the inhabitants and the benefits which would accrue to them should be considered. Perhaps, as in debating, proponents of change should be required to prove the need for such change. When I wanted to open a speech center in Albany, the Health Department required an exhaustive need study and statement. Like it or not, we in Bethlehem are in the path of urban and commercial sprawl.

Drive-It-Yourself Historic House Tour
May 22

The drive-it-yourself tour of historic Bethlehem buildings, the Bethlehem Historical Association's part of the bicentennial celebration, was today. Rowena and I drove down to the former Cedar Hill School (built in 1859; redesigned 1907) at the corner of Route 144 and Clapper Road where the Bethlehem Historical Association's museum is located.

The museum in the school building is certainly worth visiting, as is the museum in the carriage house (1851) of the Bethlehem Center tollgate, directly behind the old schoolhouse. The museums contain a rich collection of items from our town's past.

Along the route of the tour, we heard that people were going through the Nicoll-Sill House (ca. 1735). Its owner, Paul Mulligan, is selling it and the real estate people were holding an open house, so Rowena and I drove down Dinmore Road and pulled up at the door. Although the "for sale" signs were in evidence, there seemed to be no one around. We sat for a while, just looking at the house and beyond to the old cemetery and then Mr. Mulligan came out and said that although the open house was over, he'd take us on a tour himself. It was a memorable experience for us to see the beautifully proportioned rooms and windows, the eighteenth-century woodwork, and the former slaves'/

servants' rooms, and to hear about the restoration of the historic house from Mr. Mulligan, who has done a great deal of the work himself.

Thinking Small in a Big Way
May 27

The Voorheesville festival, "Small Town at the Millennium," commenced this evening with a program at the library. This was an opportunity for townspeople to reminisce about their lives in Voorheesville and the Town of New Scotland and to share memories, photos, and stories.

The title at the beginning of this entry is from Susan Graves's article in the May 12 issue of *The Spotlight* where she wrote: "The idea for the small-town celebration came from village resident Lauren Ayers, who said she began thinking about the value of small-town life while watching the riots that hit Los Angeles in the aftermath of the Rodney King trial. 'I got to thinking about why those kinds of explosions happen in large areas.... I think this is as good as it gets', said Ayers of life in Voorheesville. 'The point is to celebrate the good life because towns are the basis of this country. When you get 3,000 people together, you have to work things out!'"

It was a poignant and nostalgic evening for me, listening to stories which paralleled experiences of mine in the small towns of Horseheads and Gouverneur, New York, in my pre-

BCHS band members. Left to right: Tom Dorgan, Mike Leogering, Dave Fisk, Lee Eck, and Rob McKenna.

World War II growing-up years. Many of us have learned from Thomas Wolfe and from our own experience that "you can't go home again." Some of us have tried, and found that the "homes" of our memories are very different from those we go back to in an attempt to recapture the past. For me, the only way to go home again is in memory, in recollections, in re-reading letters, in reminiscing with an old photo album, enjoying thoughts of the past, and from time to time, wiping away a tear or two.

Yet to come in the festival are a parade, art show, dog show, watermelon-eating contest, drive-yourself historic house tour, block dance in downtown Voorheesville, and collection of items for burial in a small-town time capsule to be opened in 2093.

Memorial Day
May 31

Excitement and expectancy were in the air in the front parking lot of the middle school this morning. Most of the space was filled with BCHS pupils and their musical instruments. The band, under the direction of Louise Schwarz, was forming and preparing to march in the Memorial Day Parade in Delmar. A man, who turned out to be Mrs. Schwarz's husband, said that the large group was a combination of the high school symphonic band and the wind ensemble. The members

Shannon Woodley and Scott Hasselbarth.

he enlisted in the United States Army and was sent to France with the American Expeditionary Force. He was killed in action on November 9, 1918, only two days before the armistice was signed...." It was in his honor that American Legion Post 1040 in Delmar is named. The ceremony concluded with taps played by Shannon Woodley and Scott Hasselbarth. The notes that Shannon played, standing near the grave, were echoed by Scott who stood on an elevation in the distance. It was a touching end to a moving ceremony.

looked very good in their new T-shirts which they were wearing for the first time. The design imprinted on the back was the traditional BCHS eagle with a musical motif surrounding it and on the front: BCHS/Bicentennial Marching Band/1993.

While the band was running through a march, I walked along Kenwood Avenue to the Bethlehem Cemetery. There, at the grave of Nathaniel Adams Blanchard, members of the American Legion and Veterans of Foreign Wars were preparing for the opening ceremony of the parade. In his chapter on the military heritage of our town in *Bethlehem Revisited*, Bill Howard wrote: "Blanchard was just a teenager when

Diary Entries by Joseph Allgaier

Our President
June 1

The first workday after the Memorial Day weekend and the national news was dominated by reactions to the appearance of Bill Clinton at the Vietnam Veterans Memorial. The president was vilified with audible shouts of "coward," "draft dodger," and "hypocrite" by veterans who felt it was not appropriate for him to be at the memorial service. It was reported before the weekend that polls indicated only about 25 percent of the population thought it was inappropriate for Clinton to appear, given his record of demonstration against his country while in England, his avoidance of the draft, and his stated disregard for the military. If the poll is true, I guess I am with the minority about the issue.

Normanside Country Club
June 2

Country (golf) clubs tend to allocate time periods for various interests. At Normanside, we have ladies day (Thursday), Tuesday night leagues, Wednesday night working ladies league, couples golf (Friday evening), and seniors golf (Wednesday). The usual format is very informal. Just sign up the week before for a tee time. Some seem to have the same foursome every week, but I prefer, like many others, to try to play with many

Joseph Allgaier.

members of the club. Today, our foursome included Nobi Tanaka, Jack Martin, Jack Elliot, and myself. A great group. Nobi and I teamed up against the "Jacks" and won four dollars for the day.

Sometimes I wonder about the benefits of belonging to a country club. In my case, no business contacts to develop or to entertain. That is meaningful for many members. I never have calculated what the average round of golf costs. It would probably make those Florida greens fees at seventy-five to one hundred dollars seem like a bargain. But club membership, like owning a boat or an airplane, cannot (or should not) be justified with economic reasoning. It just becomes a matter of life-style choice. The fact that Jackie is active and plays golf often is an added benefit. We both think the exercise is very beneficial. I walk all the time, but Jackie usually takes a cart for the back nine holes, walking the first nine. The social aspects of the club also extend into our personal lives. We have developed a number of close friendships over the ten years (or so) we have belonged to Normanside. In any event, if we did not belong, a large part of our daily life, particularly during the non-winter months, would be lost. As far as the cost is concerned, I keep reminding myself that it won't make much difference twenty-five years from now.

Joseph Allgaier with N201 YJ.

A Productive Flight
June 3

Most of the day was occupied in doing a favor for a friend of mine, Harold (Tommy) Tomlinson. He is a local entrepreneur who developed an innovative device to detect extremely small amounts of gas, like carbon monoxide. It has medical applications and is being marketed to the medical profession. He was asked to make a presentation to a group of small business representatives meeting in Bethesda, Maryland, under the auspices of the National Institutes of Health. He asked me if I would consider flying him down and back since I have flown him to Maine on a few occasions. I flew down, landing at Gaithersburg, Maryland, and Bill [Hughes] flew back. Almost exactly two hours for each leg. Such a flight really demonstrates the advantage of general aviation over other forms of travel. The trip is about eight hours by car and a commercial flight would probably take three hours or more, considering travel to the airport and waiting for boarding. In addition, the

airline schedule would probably add hours to the time frame needed to make the trip. In our case, we left when desired and took off when Tommy was finished.

Tax and Spend
June 4

It is no wonder why public trust of elected officials continues to erode. It seems that deception is the norm, even at the local level. Here, in Albany County, we have an excellent example with the sales tax. That was raised to eight percent last year, and promised to be a temporary one-year measure because no agreement could be reached on spending to match revenue. The one year was to give the time to make orderly cuts. Well, nothing has been cut in spending and now the talk is of extending the tax because the county still faces a deficit in the budget. But nothing is proposed to reduce spending. Our supervisor, Ken Ringler, supports extending the tax.

That disappoints me, because I respect Ken, but feel he is wrong taking such a position.

Dullmar
June 7

Sometimes, we do not appreciate the advantages of our region. A reminder came in the form of an article in yesterday's paper by a Siena College professor who pointed out such advantages. I showed the article to Brian [house guest, and husband of my niece, Carolyn] commenting on the use of the phrase "Smallbany" which some people like to use. I do not think it is really a derogatory label. As I mentioned to Brian, many of the young people in our town like to label our hamlet "Dullmar." That connotation changes after being away for a few years, as evidenced by our own children, who now appreciate the wholesome environment under which they developed.

A Quiet Afternoon
June 9

Our Seniors Day at the club and a scramble event. For nongolfers, a scramble is an event that groups four golfers of varying ability (usually based on handicap) into a team. Only one ball is used for play and a score determined. The norm is for all to tee off, then one of the four balls is selected for play. All then hit the next

Golf at Normanside Country Club.

shot, the best ball is selected again, and so on.

I was the top player on our team and played with Frank Lotz, Ray Vorce, and Dr. Howard Netter. We did reasonably well, shooting a seventy-five, which was respectable. In any event, we had an enjoyable day.

Are American Cars Better?
June 10

Up early to keep an appointment at Northway Buick to have our new LeSabre serviced. A plastic cap on a seat rail had to be replaced and the alignment corrected. That disappoints me, somewhat, because it is evidence that the factory released a car that was not properly produced. Such an occurrence was commonplace years ago. The customer expectation was that after buying a new car, one had to maintain a list of items that needed correction and make an appointment about a month later to have them fixed.

When buyers realized that a car made in Japan did not need a follow-up "fix it" inconvenience, the American-made automobile industry went on a slide downhill. Supposedly, the message came through and American cars are equal to if not better than Japanese competitors. That is the reason I bought the Buick rather than another Toyota. I hope I am not the victim of public relations hype. Time will tell.

After getting the car fixed, I went to the Schoolhouse Museum to meet with Julia Kelley and Jim Weidemann, as scheduled. The purpose was to help them in doing something about the basement, which is used for storage of artifacts, books, and other items. It is damp and dirty, and something needs to be done about it. There was also an accumulation of trash. I worked with Jim and we brought a number of artifacts to the toll gate building, storing them in room we created (by throwing out empty boxes) on the second floor. The next step, which I hope to do next Thursday, will be to box a number of fragile books, which will be inventoried.

Helping the Historical Association
June 11

In the afternoon, I went to Curtis Lumber in Delmar to get some information on Bilco doors, for replacement of old wood doors at the Schoolhouse Museum that cover the cellar entrance. I talked to Julia Kelley, the new president of the Bethlehem Historical Association. They obviously need some help in getting things moving. It is the reason I volunteered to help with the problem of storage in the basement, but, I did not want to get involved in a significant project. Well, it looks like I will be the prime mover. Renovation of the cellar entrance appears to be the first priority. Then I will take a look at the feasibility of providing some waterproofing in the basement, after we box up some of the material that is just sitting on shelves.

Charity or Business?
June 12-13

On the New York state level, a current issue involves the separation payment of some two million dollars to the former chairman of Blue Cross/Blue Shield, Cardone, forced to leave his job by the board of directors. The organization is the subject of many mismanagement allegations and reported claims frauds that were undetected by the company. In addition, Cardone is claiming to be entitled to free health insurance for the remainder of his life. I feel that is arrogance that should not be tolerated in a not-for-profit organization. It recalls the tale of the head of the national United Way organization (Aramony) who was paid millions in salary. At the time, I also noted, and saved, a report published in the May 12, 1992, *Business Investor's Daily* reporting that included among the highest paid executives in the country in 1991 was the CEO of St. Jude Medical Center, Lawrence Lehmkuhl, at $7,650,000. I wonder how many people who contribute to St. Jude Medical Center, when Danny Thomas does his TV thing, know that fact. For some reason, the press did not give it the coverage afforded to the United Way scandal. It certainly affected my attitude about the United Way and most other charities. Obviously, it has become a business. I was a very heavy contributor to United Way during all my working years. I ran company campaigns for the fund and also served on the local board of directors for a period of years. Now, and perhaps I am too cynical, I no longer support that organization, as well as many others, only because I feel that the charity business is just that, a business, rather than a service to mankind. A sad commentary on the current status of our society.

Golf Course Stories
June 16

My golf partner for the day, Wes Albright, and I won a net total of one dollar over our opponents, Ed Carlton and Al Simpkins, by winning the seventeenth and eighteenth holes.

Ed Carlton and Wes Albright (both past seventy) have been friends for many years, and both are gentlemen. Wes is quiet and low-keyed where Ed is a nonstop teller of tales and commentator about anything. Wes sug-

gested I ask Ed what happened with his electric garage door opener that caused him to miss a golf date yesterday because he had to wait for an electrician. That brought on the story about Ed's attempt to fix the flickering light. Acknowledging that he doesn't know much about electricity, he nevertheless took off the cover of the unit and proceeded to "poke around." Unfortunately, he was poking around with a nail and caused a short circuit that created a flash and knocked him off the ladder. We asked if he was also dumb enough to be on a metal ladder? He was! But, he said, "I was wearing rubber-soled shoes." If that story wasn't enough, he proceeded to tell about the time in his early married life when to fix a light cord, he cut it with a pair of scissors. The only problem was that he forgot to pull the plug out of the electric socket. He reported that his hair went straight up. "I still have the scissors; there's a burned out notch in the middle."

Our Diary Selections
June 17

This afternoon, we had our monthly meeting of the diary publication group. As we review the material each of us has extracted from Floyd Brewer's diaries, we seem to be reaching a consensus about what should be included for publication. The process we follow is to record, without discussion, our opinion on whether or not an extract should be included. Later, we discuss the reasons for inclusion or exclusion and make a decision. It seems clear that future selections will be made more quickly than the first few we worked on. Our group seems quite compatible, in spite of differences in age and sex, and good humor is the norm. I tested both political views and moral flexibility with my report of the latest bumper sticker: "First Hillary, then Gennifer, now Us." I think it was appreciated by all.

Family Values
June 19

After golf, Jackie and I went to a surprise fortieth anniversary party for our good friends, Bob and Ellen Barker, that was given for them by their children. It was at the home of one of their three sons.

I think Bob and Ellen exemplify the positive image of family life and the benefits of a lifetime commitment of a couple through marriage. Their children were surely influenced by their parents, and they, in turn, seem to be providing the same type of positive values to their children. Bob and Ellen can be very proud of them. It was obvious that love and affection runs throughout the entire family. These days, family values and variations of families are much discussed in the media and by politicians.

A Special Day
June 29

Today is a special day. We have our first grandchild, Margaret Mary, born to our daughter, Barbara, in Brigham and Women's Hospital in Boston, at 8:34 P.M. We were called at Barb and Mike's house at about 9:30 by Barbara. She wanted to be the one to tell us. Labor was induced, but the birth took some time. The baby was big (when Barbara called they hadn't yet weighed the baby) and some difficulty was encountered. But, Barbara was very cheerful and could only talk about the birth in a positive way. Mike also got on the phone and he was very happy. He went through the entire event with Barbara, and I give him a lot of credit for that. Thirty years ago, it was unusual for a father to participate in the birth of a child. Today, it is very common. I have to say each one of my children was born in a hospital operating room after I delivered Jackie to the nurses at the emergency entrance. Even if they allowed me to participate, I am not sure I would have been prepared to witness the procedure. But, if really needed (and I almost was for a couple of our children), I am also quite sure I could have responded to assist in the birth.

A Visit With Our First Grandchild
June 30

Mike had stayed with Barbara and the new baby throughout the night and came home in the morning. We all

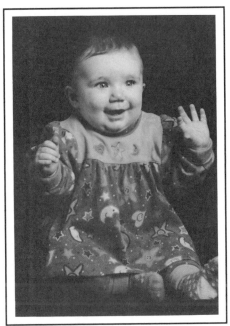

Margaret Mary McGonigle at six months.

our daughter and son-in-law celebrating the miracle of birth.

I am sure other things were going on in the world yesterday and today, but, to us, there was only one event worthy of note.

went back to the hospital, in Boston, arriving at about noon, for a visit.

The hospital just initiated a new procedure called family care for the newborn. Barbara actually delivered the baby in a room setting, and the baby stays with her in a private room. Mike spent all his time with her and the baby. In essence, the "nursery" is no longer used, except in an unusual situation where the mother cannot deal with the new baby.

Margaret Mary is just precious. She weighed in at nine pounds four ounces and twenty inches tall. A pretty big girl, alert and healthy. Took a number of pictures and just enjoyed being with

221

Bethlehem Diary

Diary Entries by Teresa Buckley

Books On Tape
July 1

I like to listen to books on tape when I'm driving. I especially like the longer, unabridged stories. I've always wanted someone to read to me, and, this way, these unknown someones are ready to serve at my whim. I've been listening to Blanche Wiesen Cook's abridged (on four tapes) biography of Eleanor Roosevelt. I am surprised at how little I knew about the Roosevelts, and think that all the fuss over Hillary Clinton would have been magnified if she had done some of the things Eleanor Roosevelt did. Are we that much *more* conservative now, or is it just that the press wasn't so rabid in its coverage of the past lives and daily routines of the rich and famous in the 1920s?

Teresa Buckley.

Blanche Wiesen Cook's biography seems to add little to that already known about Eleanor Roosevelt, with one exception. This biographer seems to be consumed by reporting and speculating on Eleanor's sex life. I'm of the "so what?" school of thought when it comes to whether she had a lesbian relationship with reporter friend and confidante or a heterosexual affair with her body guard.

"Much Ado About Nothing"
July 2

Tonight, [my husband,] Jim [Odato,] and I went to the Spectrum Theater on Delaware Avenue in Albany to see the movie version of Shakespeare's *Much Ado About Nothing*. The show was very funny, and the audience just about filled the movie theater. It's interesting to think that 400-year-old plays can still pack them in. Will Michael Crichton or Scott Turow be able to do the same in 2393?

Bethlehem's Bicentennial
Sunday, July 4

Today is a big day in the bicentennial year. The town always puts on a chicken barbecue and entertainment for the Fourth of July at the Elm Avenue Park, but this year there's even more to do. We went swimming a little after the pool opened at 10:00 A.M., and already the parking lot was starting to fill up. Volunteers were bustling about, setting up tables and directing cars to parking spaces. Usually, Jim and I hang around for the food and festivities, but this year we had guests coming to our house for a barbecue. Some of the members of the diary committee spent time at the park that day selling *Bethlehem Revisited*. The book has had a positive response, especially when people see the attractive cover that Len Tantillo designed. I'm impressed, that's for sure.

The Mohawk River Bike Trail and Lock 7
July 5

Jim and I have been wanting to explore the Mohawk River Bike Trail for some time, and decided to go there today with our bicycles. We parked the car in Niskayuna, and had hardly gotten far at all when we arrived at Lock 7. We were just in time to see two pleasure boats go through the lock. A woman standing nearby told us about the operation just like a seasoned tour guide. She said she visits the locks regularly, carrying along a lunch to eat at one of the picnic tables. Sometimes she eats at Jumpin' Jack's restaurant on the Mohawk in Scotia, and when she sees a big boat go by, she'll jump in her car and race to the next lock to see the boat go through.

After a while, Jim and I headed out on the trail again toward Schenectady, surprised at how little foot or pedal traffic we encountered. Our intent had been to go out toward Amsterdam, but we lost the trail in downtown Schenectady. It follows the streets for a while, but is not well marked in these places. Like our guide, we ended up at Jumpin' Jack's, ate lunch, and decided to head back.

Fayette Walworth
July 6

Jim got a piece of bad news tonight in the locker room at the Elm Avenue Park pool. One of our fellow swimmers told him Fayette Walworth had died when we were on vacation last month. Fay was a retired lawyer, a large man with an ever-present tan thanks to frequent trips to the Caribbean and summers at the Elm Avenue pool. He also was an avid swimmer. I would see him during Lunchtime Laps at the high school, and Jim would see him that same evening at the middle school pool. Lap swimmers tend not to know each other so well; our heads are in the water most of the time. But Fay was known by all by his friendly greetings. I'll miss seeing his distinctive green VW bug in the parking lot.

The Albany-Colonie Yankees
July 7

The Albany-Colonie Yankees had an afternoon double header today, so I decided to go to the first game with a friend from work, Gary Hahn. Jim is always reminding me that the word "fan" is short for "fanatic," especially in June when he's still watching basketball. I'm not a fanatic, but I enjoy watching sports. Today's games were against the Bowie, Maryland, Baysox. Gary's wife, Lauri Cole, thought we wouldn't last long in the bleachers because the day was beastly hot. But we spent an extra dollar to get seats in the grandstand, under the roof, and were quite comfortable. Gary ate a hot dog, and we cheered for the home team, but they lost anyway. It was a great way to spend an afternoon before going to work.

Of Voyagers and Microbuses
July 8

If you want to know something about a place, take a look at its parking lots. As I walked to my car today, at the Elm Avenue Park, I realized every fourth car was a Plymouth Voyager minivan, or its companion vehicle, the Dodge Caravan. What does this say? Family, of course, especially considering the volume of vans parked at the pool during a weekday afternoon; careful consumers—I know the funny and knowledgeable "Car Guys" on National Public Radio recommend the vehicles, and that Floyd Brewer did a

Parking lot, Elm Avenue Park.

lot of research before buying his Voyager; and disposable income, as they don't come cheap.

Funny, I was on my way to Binghamton then, and stopped off in Oneonta for a milk shake at my favorite ice cream store. Of the five parking spaces, two were occupied by Volkswagen microbuses (not the more recent Vanagon) in various shades of primer. As I pulled out, I had to wait for an ancient Chevy van, also multi-colored. Are there sociological studies of vehicle preference? Probably. That's what commercials are all about.

Fife and Drum Meeting
July 9

When I got out of my car on my return to Delmar today from Binghamton I heard what sounded like a parade. An hour or so later, I could hear it still, undiminished. Don't fife and drum corps know about the Doppler effect, wherein sound grows progressively quieter with distance, or was this band stuck somewhere, unable to move forward or quit playing? Finally, Jim and I decided to investigate.

We followed the sound, down Hudson Avenue, across Delaware, down Elsmere and the side streets, Herber, Adams Place, and Oakwood, until we found ourselves at the middle school. The side fields were filled with tents, vans lined the area closest to the street, and fife and drum players of all ages, shapes, and sizes stood in the light playing. "Jamming," I guess you'd call it. As soon as one tune ended, someone struck up a new song and all joined in. It turns out this was part of a regular competition, which was to be held the next day in full dress. The bicentennial celebration brought them to Bethlehem this time. The group members have the choice of staying in motels or joining up at the campsite. Somehow, that seemed more authentic, gathered in the dark (even though battery-powered lights and tents of waterproof nylon replaced campfires and canvas), and I'm sure those evenings are a memorable part of the gathering for the competitors.

Thacher Park
July 10

Jim's company picnic was today at Thacher Park in New Scotland. He works for the *Daily Gazette* in Schenectady, which always seems to do things a little differently. The event isn't really company-sponsored, although I think they kick in a little cash for ham-

View from the Thacher Park escarpment.

burger meat or paper napkins or such things. We met at the Knowles Flat area, and laughed at how it had changed since the last time we were there. That was after the big storm in March, and the snow reached the tops of the picnic tables and came within five feet of the pavilion overhang. This time, the area was green and lush.

Thacher Park is one of my favorite places in this area. I like to go to the overlook and try to figure out what I'm seeing from up there. The trails through the woods are placid and full of trees and wildflowers to identify, or tricky ski slopes in the winter. Being on the Indian Ladder trail is like being inside a geology textbook. I especially like the plaque at its western end, dedicated to the scientists of the first half of the nineteenth century who visited there from around the world. I've taken many visitors to Thacher, and always find something new to enjoy. This year is dry, so more fossils than ever are uncovered in the stream beds.

New Nephew
July 12

My brother and sister-in-law have a new son today. Daniel Patrick Buckley was born at 9:13 A.M. Most of that information was not new to me when my mother called with the news in the late morning. The ultrasound had revealed the baby's sex, so Tom and Joan decided on the name in advance. And complications made a cesarean section necessary, so the surgery had been scheduled for Monday morning at 8:45 A.M. Ultrasound is commonplace, and these days most parents ask their doctors to reveal the sex of the baby in advance. The parents I know say they have a chance to decorate the room for a boy or a girl, and, more important, think of their child as a "he" or "she" rather than as an "it."

Unfortunately, I won't get a peek at little Dan for a while. He and his family live in Phoenix. Tom and my older nephew, John, who is five, will be visiting Binghamton next week for my brother's twentieth high school reunion. I'm planning on driving down to see them on my days off.

An Angry Squirrel
July 14

Today I met Jim in downtown Albany for lunch. I had made sandwiches and iced tea, and picked up some fruit at Bob's Produce on Delaware Avenue, so we took our picnic over to the Acad-emy Park near city hall. It's a quiet little park filled with flowers and trees and ambitious squirrels. One, especially, couldn't be dissuaded from coming by for a handout. This reminded me of an incident last summer when Jim and I and my sister, Bridget, were camping in Rhode Island. It was early morning and Jim was still sleeping, so Bridget and I sat under some pine trees reading. A red squirrel (they're much smaller but much bolder than the gray ones) must have decided we were intruding, so it climbed the tree and proceeded to throw green cones at us. They are much harder than the ripe, brown cones. A few of them hit Jim's tent, and he thought Bridget and I were not so subtly telling him to wake up. He had to stick his head out of the tent and fish out his glasses before he would believe that an angry rodent was causing all that disturbance.

Packing for SPAC
July 15

I drove up to Saratoga Springs tonight to see the New York City Ballet at the Saratoga Performing Arts Center. I try to see them a handful of times while they are close by, but this year my free time is vanishing quickly, so this was my first opportunity to go. Every year, I have to remember what to put in my "SPAC bag," and the contents change depending whether I sit on the lawn or indoors. When I go to the movies, I prefer sitting near the front (I guess that's so there's not so much of the movie theater clogging up my view and reminding me that it's only a movie) but at dance concerts I like to sit back, so I can take in the whole scene. This evening, I sat on the lawn, so I had to pack binoculars, bug spray, sweater, refreshments, and a beach chair. Of course, I forgot something—the chair—and had to return home for it after I had driven a few miles.

Teresa and Jim's garden in Delmar.

City Ballet is doing a tribute to its co-founder and choreographer, George Balanchine, on the tenth anniversary of his death. Tonight, they danced *Swan Lake, Glinka Pas de Trois, Duo Concertant,* and *Brahms-Schoenberg Quartet.* Even if I didn't like dance, or couldn't see the stage, the fun of sitting on the lawn, staring up at the stars, and listening to an orchestra playing Tchaikovsky, Glinka, Stravinsky, and Brahms is more than worth the price of admission.

Giant Zucchini
July 17

Jim mentioned that we have some zucchini ready to pick in the backyard garden. I was surprised, since I thought only the male blossoms had flowered so far, and the female blossoms' appearance was imminent. Sure enough, there were three zucchinis ready for picking—even bigger than I usually like them to get. I'm going to have to monitor the garden more closely, I see. It's funny the way we think we own a piece of property, and it's ours to do with as we wish. Then along come plants growing out of control, and deer chomping on everything in sight, and frost heaving the driveway, and sidewalks all out of shape.

The broccoli has already finished for the summer, but I will plant more seeds for a fall crop. The tomatoes are still flowering, and some are starting to swell into plump green fruits. I refuse to eat raw tomatoes except from the garden. Unfortunately, something else—bigger than an insect, smaller than an elephant—likes my basil as much as I do. It's been eaten right down. I even tried fashioning a make-shift fence around the plant with sharp-thorned branches from the rose-bush I'd pruned. Whatever the creature is, it outsmarted me and found a way to get to the leaves.

A Ride in the Park
July 18

We haven't been riding our bicycles as much this year as in other years. We have certain loops we make that are convenient, and well known to us, so we don't have to put too much thought into our treks. One takes us into Slingerlands and toward Voorheesville, on Route 306. The road is fairly quiet, with little traffic, interesting houses, and a hill or two to get the heart pumping. We also like to ride past the Five Rivers Environmental Center and down Meads Lane to Route 32. Meads makes me think I'm in Scotland or Ireland. I've never been to either place, but those small green hills and cows and a few barns spark my imagination. The funny thing about those hills is their steepness. The cows start to walk down, but gravity takes over and forces them to run. The sight of a cow running always makes me laugh.

This time, we decided to ride through Glenmont on Wormer Road and some of the side roads that curve right up to the Thruway, then back off. I'm sure someone did some creative engineering when they built the highway. There are barns backed right up next to it, with the local road swiveling between outbuildings and houses. We biked past the Bethlehem Historical Association building and down toward the town's Henry Hudson Park. We seem to end up at this park on Sundays, and few people are ever around. It certainly isn't as popular as the Elm Avenue Park. There are picnic tables and swings and softball fields, plus lovely views of the river. This year, the town opened a boat launch at the site, but it's proving to be too sandy. The cars or trucks tend to sink into the soil after launching their boats. Looking out over the river, Jim said, "Wouldn't it be nice to own a house right here?" The river was beautiful and placid today, but the disastrous flooding in the Midwest this summer gives me pause about living so close to the water.

The Endless Painting Job
July 24

One Saturday last fall, Jim announced that we should paint the house. It seemed like a snap decision, but apparently he had been thinking about it for awhile, because he knew he wanted to buy Benjamin Moore paint. We went to the paint store with my sister, Bridget, who was visiting for the weekend. She suggested painting our white house a pale gray-blue, with white trim and darker gray-blue doors and shutters. After forty-five minutes of discussion, we bought the paint. Scraping and cleaning began that afternoon, with Bridget shaking her head in amazement at our can-do attitudes. Ha! Jim spent days asking friends, painters, and real estate agents about what color attracts buyers, even though we have no immediate plans to sell. Would gray-blue be a turn-off?

Jim Odato painting the house.

After two weeks, I agreed to return that color and pick up the safe white paint. The man in the paint store nodded his head; this was a common experience for him.

Several weeks later, friends Betsy Sandberg and Steve Nissen came by and began painting while we scraped and primed and scraped some more. They finished two sides of the house that day. We had a nice reward for them. In late afternoon, we went to a New York state wine tasting at the Delaware Plaza liquor store (I call it the Delaware Plaza wine store, because I think their wine selection is tops in the area). Betsy found some of her favorite wines from the Finger Lakes region, some of which she did not know were available around here.

Weeks went by, we continued painting (Jim on weekends, me during the day before work), but finally got caught by the cool fall temperatures and had to hang up our brushes until spring. Good thing we had stuck with white: small patches at the highest point of the house and portions of the trim were undone, but that was hard to notice.

So, here we are, July 24, 1993. Still undone. There are so many other diversions in summer. We awoke to the sounds of our neighbor, Ann Gunther, and her friend, Joel, painting her house. Scraping and cleaning—done. Priming—done. Covering the white paint with yellow—how daring! It looked terrific! We were shamed into taking one of our precious few days off together tackling the paint job. Trim was done, garage door painted white, blue shutters hung. Progress at last. Of course, there still is that one door... and the trim on the front porch....

Working on Sundays
July 25

Sunday is the beginning of the *Times Union* workweek for me. I don't mind, usually. Sunday evenings can be depressing, thinking about the weekend ending and returning to work. I also have a more responsible job on Sundays, and, best of all, very few people are around. I tackle my job, monitor what's going on in the world, make decisions. It's a nice way to ease back into the week. I don't feel comfortable with the nine-to-five Monday-through-Friday ritual, though that's practically unheard of for newspaper employees. I hate doing the same thing at the same time every day. The thought of it makes me nervous. One of the bonuses of working nights is being able to do errands (banking, shopping) without ever having to stand in a long line. And I accomplish so much more. I remember being tired by the time I'd reach home when I was working days. Now I rarely watch television.

Popular Four Corners Luncheonette. David Heffley, owner and chef.

The Four Corners Restaurant
July 27

I live just across the D&H Railway tracks from the Four Corners restaurant. Though I don't go there frequently, I probably stop in a handful of times each month. Once in a while, Floyd Brewer and I will meet there on *Bethlehem Diary* business; we take turns picking up the tab for coffee and muffins. Some Sundays Jim and I head over for late and plentiful breakfasts with friends. My favorite time to go is on a dreary winter or early spring day, after I'm tired from swimming Lunchtime Laps at the high school pool, for a hearty bowl of soup and homemade bread. Most of the staff has been there since I've been in town. They're always friendly and efficient and being there feels homey, with the fake stuffed moose standing guard over the fireplace and quilted wall hangings decorating the interior.

Diary Entries by Susan Graves

A Momentous Day!
August 4

Today, I drove about one hundred miles to a town called Walton (near Delhi) to look at a Scottish Terrier pup. Needless to say, I never expected to go there and leave empty-handed, so the only hard part of the day was finding the house and then choosing from among the five male six-week-old fur balls.

What made this especially nice for me was that it was a birthday present (even though it wasn't my birthday) from my boyfriend, who had been very fond of my former terrier, Cagney, who died four years ago of cancer.

Susan Graves.

Willie had a tough ride home, and struggled to get out of the box so I kept sticking my hand inside to try to comfort him. Upon arrival at my boyfriend's house, I discovered a bleeding stump where my right arm used to be. The puppy was fine, however, and recovered nicely after a drink of water and a piece of finely chopped-up hot dog.

Dyed-in-the-wool dog lovers never learn, I guess. We are constantly being beaten by the four-footed set.

Dog Days in August
August 5

I called Willie's former owner, Mary Hagele, today, to let her know he was just fine and has made it through the night unscathed. (What I didn't tell her was that I suffered a few more cuts as a result of typical puppy teething practices.) Today, I plan to go to Agway to find substitutes for human flesh and blood. Mary had called *The Spotlight* after I left yesterday to put an ad in for the three remaining pups (one of the others had been sold but she was holding him until his new

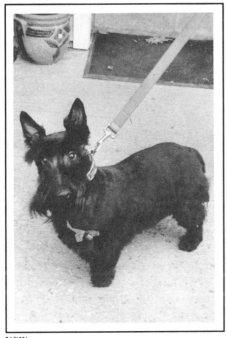

Willie.

Willie Nelson.

owners came back from vacation). I told Mary we'd run the ad for free and wished her luck and promised to call her again and send pictures of Willie as he developed. As much as I really love my job, I found myself distracted today thinking about the puppy and whether or not he was OK at home. My neighbor, a bigger dog nut than I, agreed to run interference with Greta, my resident hound, who I knew would view the new addition as little more than an average sized morsel. Still, I was a little anxious and couldn't wait to get home. As it turned out, all was well—as well as things can go when there's a new puppy and an entrenched canine. I have decided to keep them separated during the day until Willie develops some muscle and Greta some motherly tendencies. So far, all she's shown is a curled lip at the pup, and her most mournful "how could you do this to me" look at me.

Another Willie
August 7

Though I suspect classical outstrips country music in Bethlehem, I had a grand old time watching Willie Nelson and Family at the Starlite in Latham. My friend and I have enjoyed Willie and his music for years, and we try to see as many of his performances as we can. Tonight's was special for me, though, since I got a kiss from the grand old man of country. Willie Nelson is a charismatic person as well as a wonderful singer.

233

I won't go into the gory details about how the Starlite sells one rose for five bucks a pop—but my friend bought me one to do what many other Willie fans were doing throughout the concert—trying to get up to the stage with the hopes of a closeup view of Willie and the chance he might acknowledge your efforts with a kiss. I got both and it wasn't easy. First, you have to screw up your courage to get out of your row. (I got encouragement from an older woman on my right who said: "Go ahead, honey, everyone else is doing it, why not you?") So after a couple of deep breaths, off I went out into the aisle. But that's not the hardest part. You now must encounter and not alienate one of the security men who sit at the bottom of all the aisles leading onto the circular rotating stage. My guard, as it turned out, was plopped right in the middle of the aisle, and his body— he goes about 250, I figure—took up almost the entire space. I played it meek and ever so gently tapped him on the shoulder. "Can I give him this flower?" I pleaded in a whisper. "You're supposed to leave it on the rim of the stage and don't interrupt the performance," he replied. Sure, I thought, that's why everybody else was getting kisses. I stood my ground and waited until Willie almost had to engage in eye contact, and stuck out the flower. I also gave him a Greta look of the "All my life I've been waiting for this moment," and crossed my fingers. Well, maybe Greta's not such a dumb hound. My imitation of her

look worked and I got the kiss. For me this was "gooder than Christmas," as a friend of mine's kid used to say.

Productive Days Off
August 11

Wednesday is supposed to be my day off, but, more often than not, *Spotlight* and/or *Business Review* work and errands take over. Today was especially of the more often than not variety. As it turned out, it was an 8:00 A.M. to 10:00 P.M. stint, which consisted mostly of giving people rides back and forth to places they absolutely had to go. I did squeeze in a few hours in the evening at *The Spotlight* and managed to get quite a lot accomplished. The quiet does wonders for me. During the day, interruptions are the rule, and it sometimes seems amazing that I ever finish writing or even editing a story. I guess the moral is, days off are good for getting work done.

My Balky Lawnmower
August 14

It's been a love-hate relationship for ten years. The Lawn Boy self-propelled electric start mower must have sensed I was a greenhorn as far as sophisticated machinery goes. My former home had a postage stamp size yard, and a trusty push mower. With me self-propelling, it had always been adequate. Back then I was in control, but from day one with the Lawn Boy, I knew I was in for trouble.

The self-propelled mechanism, triggered by squeezing the handles together and pushing down, sent the machine flying much like horses coming out of the starting gate at Saratoga. In that first summer, I hung on for dear life following the machine in whatever direction it was pointed.

I got better at controlling things over the years, but just when I thought I had a problem licked another would crop up. In the beginning, I tended to rush to the Sycaway Bike Shop when the mower wouldn't start or wouldn't stay started. It simply had a mind of its own. The manual I got with the machine was rubbish. I followed instructions religiously, but rarely to any avail. Trying to start the mower on a damp or cool day was futile. The mower has always had apparently a self-stop mechanism that operated at the whim of the machine.

I still fought it, and in the process learned a number of useful things about motors and their ways. I can clean a carburetor filter and make minor repairs without even thinking. I felt real pride one year when a cotter pin broke, causing the mower to stop dead. Today, a simple bobby pin still holds the mower's body and soul together.

More on the Mower
August 20

Despite what I've learned about repairs, the Lawn Boy never ceases to amaze me. The latest escapade—and as Dave Barry says, I am not making this up—involved the mower not stopping as I released the handle. I know I have a thing about the lawn and keeping it clipped in the summer, but anyone watching me remow the lawn the other day would have probably thought I was stark raving mad. Fortunately no one drove by, as I went over row after row of the acre and a half of grass. Aha, I thought. I'll click off the self-start and at least it won't keep moving. I was right about that at least. Then I stared down at the machine still vibrating along merrily. I'll get you, I thought, grabbing onto the battery pack and tugging it off. Lawn Boy ignored this and continued chugging along—the little engine that obviously could and would and was doing what it wanted to do. One full half hour later, it sputtered a few times and finally quit—out of gas.

Ironically, I was only hoping to get through this season and replace my "favorite toy" next spring. I had just been thinking about all the years of ups and downs with my Lawn Boy and decided it was time for a new blade on the block. Lawn Boy's refusal to stop made me think of its really good points over the years. Two years ago, Denny Bailey, who owns Sycaway Bike Shop, had suggested a replacement, but I being financially strapped and convinced I could cope with the existing machine's idiosyncracies emphatically defended it. Denny also usually reminded me of the rough treatment Lawn Boy had endured over the years. "Blade's really bent, whad' ya do, run over a cement block?" is one of his typical remarks.

It's true, Lawn Boy and I have been hard on each other, and so if it's repaired, it will serve as backup to the new mower, which of course will be Lawn Boy II.

Diary Entries by Hugh Hewitt

Convenient Beverwyck
September 1

Beverwyck, the first full-service retirement community in the town of Bethlehem, opened today. It is located on Krumkill Road in North Bethlehem. According to the public relations news release, "The community was designed in response to the Housing Committee of the town of Bethlehem's 1987 recommendation that recognized a need for housing that offered a full range of services for healthy, active seniors." Three Delmar residents moved in today: Mrs. John F. (Dorothy) McColl and Mr. and Mrs. Lewis (Adelaide) Muhlfelder. Rowena and I attended the opening ceremony, I to photograph the ribbon-cutting for *The Spotlight* and Rowena to help me obtain the names of participants for the captions of the photographs.

Beverwyck will help to satisfy a long-felt need in Bethlehem. The living units do not require the work and upkeep that large houses and grounds do, yet they are larger than typical retirement home apartments. And as a new resident said, he could move there from his Manning Boulevard home in Albany and still be near the amenities of Albany and his friends.

Hugh Hewitt and Fergus.

On Wedding Anniversaries
September 3

Rowena and I were married forty-four years ago today. For the most part, our anniversaries have not been memorable. They've been quite uneventful, in fact. The earliest one that we do remember was our second anniversary when we moved from Alliance, Ohio, to Lewiston, Maine. We took off enough time to go to the Polka Dot Drive-in for hamburgers and chocolate milk shakes. That was in the days of driving up to the stand, staying in the car, rolling the window down, and the waitress putting the food and beverages on a little tray hooked over the car door. I guess it seemed so ridiculous to celebrate a wedding anniversary in that way that we've never forgotten it. This anniversary today may live in our memories for some time to come, too, because we went to Ben & Jerry's Main Square ice cream shop in Delmar and splurged—we had medium-sized cones instead of small. Phone calls from our daughters let us know that they're glad we married.

Haircut
September 8

Today dawned gray, cloudy, damp, and foggy, and it looked as though I wouldn't be able to get any painting done outside. Although the deck of the front porch is finished, the steps need caulking where the treads meet the risers and those areas have to be bone dry in order for the procedure to be successful. However, there are three jobs on my permanent "Things To Do" list which can be done regardless of the weather: cleaning the cellar, attic, and barn. None ever seems to appeal to me and so I feel like Damocles, who sat through a feast with a sword suspended over his head by a single hair. Many of us know that feeling—something is pending, something unpleasant is lurking in the background, and the thought of it is there in our subconscious ready to pop out at awkward moments.

One way I can procrastinate profitably is to visit my barber, Ben Boomer, whose shop is on Adams Street opposite the Delmar fire department. I put off getting haircuts, too, but the visits to Ben are the lesser of two evils. I always leave feeling somewhat virtuous. I have accomplished something.

Most barber shops are soothing places where you can read newspapers and

Ben Boomer.

magazines while you wait your turn, talk about politics and sports, or just sit and think or vegetate. And even when you're in the barber chair and he's doing his best to improve your visual image, you may sometimes read, most often talk, or choose to remain silent. I think that by remaining silent, however, you really lose the full flavor of the haircut experience. For it's in the barber shop that you can express your ideas, exchange viewpoints, hear all sorts of solutions to local, national, and world problems, even rant, rail, and rave about something or someone, usually to a studiously silent audience suddenly involved in reading or looking out the window. I find that a visit to the barber is a therapeutic experience. It is intellectually undemanding, and you leave looking and smelling good. Unfortunately, the chores are still there when you get home.

Family Diaries
September 10

Several years ago, my mother wrote a couple of dozen anecdotes or vignettes of times gone by when she was very young and lived in the central New York state hamlets and villages of Delhi, Oxford, Munnsville, and Waterville, where her great-grandparents settled in the 1830s when they came to the U.S. from England and Ireland.

Last November, I visited Mother in Dunwoody, a suburb of Atlanta. Rowena and I drove down, with Fergus, my basset hound, to be there for her ninety-fourth birthday party. We stayed with my sister and brother-in-law, who live nearby. Mother had recently been moved from her apartment in a retirement highrise to a room-and-bath in an adult home. Among her belongings stored at my sister's were chairs, tables, clothes, and everything else that Mother wouldn't need anymore. My sister and I thought we should start the process of sorting through the things. I chose to bring home with me boxes of diaries and letters which Mother's grandmother and mother had written and more boxes and many folders of genealogical material she had collected during sixty years of gathering information

on the antecedents in both Mother's and my father's families.

It would be fine if I had the talent and time to do something with the diaries and letters. I'm sure I'll be able to utilize them in part in the writing for my course in autobiography. Another large group of material already in our Slingerlands attic consists of all the letters I wrote to my parents during World War II and five folders bulging with copies of military records, photographs, and diary entries which document my experiences in the World War II era at Cornell in the ROTC and ERC, in training camps in the States, and during my years in the Pacific theater of operations. Perhaps someday I'll be able to do something with all this material. If not, one of my children or grandsons will. Such descriptions and interpretations and memories become more valuable as the years go by.

Artist Charles Schade
September 17

There was a reception this evening at the Bethlehem Public Library for Charles Argow Schade's watercolor exhibition. Charlie estimated that around 150 people attended. Such a good-sized turnout isn't surprising because, after all, he is well known both as an architect and an artist, he has lived here in Slingerlands for fifty-three years, and he was born in Albany where his architectural firm was

Charles Argow Schade with his painting of the Old Adams Hotel.

located on Ontario Street. There were thirty large watercolors exhibited against the brick walls of the library's entrance hall. Unmatted, the paintings measure 15"x 22".

Charlie has been interested in art since his earliest years; he was awarded the Professor Theodore C. Hailes Prize for excellence when he was in the eight-grade in P.S. #21. He studied architecture at Yale. Since retiring, he's been able to devote himself full time to painting. Lately, Charlie has chosen subjects in the areas of the Normanskill and Helderbergs, local rural scenes, and historical subjects. His paintings are owned by many people in the Capital District. Even Rowena and I have succumbed; my favorite is of "Charlie's," the former well-known Slingerlands landmark at the corner of New Scotland Road and Kenwood Avenue where Mangia is now located. Two of his paintings hang in the Slingerlands Post Office—both are of buildings which housed earlier Slingerlands post offices.

Gays and Lesbians in the Church
September 19

Perhaps the most controversial issue ever to confront the members of the Slingerlands United Methodist Church, of which Rowena and I are members, and members of many other faiths, centers on publicly stating that gays and lesbians are welcome to take part in the life of the church. We have had some small-group meetings of church people interested in exploring the possibility of our church's becoming a reconciling congregation.

This morning, Lillian Venner, a member of a United Methodist church in Burlington, Vermont, spoke during the service. Lil, as we soon learned to call her, is a down-to-earth wife and mother with a message. She spoke to us as the mother of a lesbian daughter who had "come out" several years ago. She described her and her husband's feelings, those of her daughter, and the reactions of relatives and acquaintances. But in particular, she talked about the relationship between herself and her daughter since the "coming out." It has become one of greater understanding, acceptance, and mutual appreciation. Lil is good proof that there is life after the closet door opens.

Lorraine and Tom Smith
September 21

This evening, Lorraine Smith presented a slide show, "Impressions of China," at the Bethlehem Public Library. Her husband, Tom, a local businessman with contracts in heavy railroad equipment in China, takes many trips there each year. A couple of years ago, Lorraine went along and was able to visit Beijing and Qiqihar in

Lorraine Smith in China.

Northern China, unaccompanied, for three weeks. The talk was well attended by an appreciative audience. Lorraine's photographs (slides) are good and include many pictures of people in this carefully and skillfully designed presentation. The slides were accompanied by Chinese music and Lorraine's narrative on audio tape. The narrative explained what we were seeing on the screen and the music augmented and supplemented the experience. Her shots of people, buildings, and architectural details are a visual treat. I certainly hope that Lorraine gives us another audio-visual interpretation soon.

Harry and Alice Howes at the Taj Mahal in Agra, India.

Harry and Alice Howes
September 23

We went to the Sitar restaurant on Central Avenue in Colonie with Harry and Alice Howes tonight for a good dinner of Indian food. We always have plenty to talk about. We've known each other since 1958 and have many things in common in our lives—family, church, travels, SUNY Albany.

On the Sunday after moving into our newly purchased house on Quail Street in Albany in 1958, we attended the nearby Congregational Church. Our plan was to visit several churches before deciding which one to join. We met Alice and Harry that first Sunday, they took us in tow, directed our three girls to their proper church school classrooms, and introduced us to various church members. We felt so at home there that we never "tried out" another church and stayed for more than fifteen years, several years after we'd moved to Slingerlands.

After Harry retired from SUNY Albany in 1984, he and Alice lived in Mussooree, India, for two years. Harry was guidance counselor at the Woodstock School and Alice worked in the school office.

We visited them during their long winter break the first year. They met us at the airport at New Delhi and once again we were under their wing, this time during travels across northern India to Darjeeling and back, mainly by train. I should explain that they've lived and traveled in India before, so they know their way around. We have many images of India: the Agra Fort where we had a picnic in an elevated pavilion, or pleasure dome, and feasted our eyes on the serene Taj Mahal rising in the distance beside the Jumna River; a Buddhist priest approaching us on a path in Darjeeling, chanting, "Oom, oom, oom," as the mist cleared and far off Kangchenjunga, the third highest mountain in the world, between Nepal and Sikkim, glowing white and pink in the early morning sun; a glimpse of Mount Everest's peak rising above us as we flew westward toward Patna; seeing people bathing in the Ganges at Varanasi and bodies being cremated at the ghats a few hundred feet downriver; a memorial plaque at Lucknow: "In Memory of Major General Sir Henry Lawrence KCB and the brave men who fell in defence of the Residency AD 1857," during the mutiny, in Allahabad; meeting Mrs. Roda Gandhi, sister-in-law of Mahatma Gandhi, and stories of Indira, Rajiv, and Meneeka.

How comfortable and satisfying it is to have companionable friends with whom to reminisce and share experiences.

Church's Early Global Concerns
September 25

I spent most of today working on an article for the Slingerlands United Methodist Church monthly newsletter, *The Herald*. As church historian, I try to write something on the church's history several times during the year. For the next issue I'm writing on the Epworth and Junior Leagues, two organizations which over the years did much in the field of missions.

Several well-known Slingerlands families are represented in the membership lists in the 1897-1903 record book of the organizations: Ray F. Arthur, former town clerk and town supervisor, and his wife, parents of Don Arthur, and their daughter, Hestella. Don and his wife, Alice, are long-time members of the church. Mrs. C.W. Frazier, mother of Evelyn and Helen Frazier, who also were Epworth League members and continue to be church members. Ruth Miner and her mother, Mrs. W.H.S. (Mary Ida) Miner. Ruth was a well-known lawyer and,

Ray F. Arthur, town clerk and town supervisor, 1924-1941.

Our Tuesday Outing
September 18

Rowena and I are each enrolled in a class at the new Academy for Learning in Retirement in Saratoga Springs. The academy is affiliated with Empire State College which is part of the State University of New York. Rowena's course is "Indians of the Trans-Mississippi West" and mine is "Writing Autobiography." This educational adventure is for retired people who are not about to sit twiddling thumbs or who do not, when asked, "How are you?" proceed to tell all, detailing aches, pains, medications, sleeplessness, indigestion, and when really warmed up, rhapsodize on diarrhea or arthritis.

My class, with twelve participants, is in the morning from 10:00 A.M. to noon and Rowena's is from 1:30 P.M. to 3:30 P.M., each Tuesday for eight weeks. With this schedule, we can attend classes and have time to read or work in the library, shop, browse in the Lyrical Ballad bookstore, walk around and look at the architecture, and lunch and visit with friends.

Church Exhibit
September 30, 1993

In an unguarded moment during the lazy, hazy days of this past summer, I agreed to organize and install an exhibit in the Bethlehem Public Library having to do with the Slingerlands United Methodist Church, of which I

during the governorship of Thomas H. Dewey, served as New York state's secretary of state. Mr. Charles Darius Hammond, superintendent of the church Sunday school for thirty years and of the Delaware & Hudson Railway, which ran through Slingerlands.

Through sponsoring strawberry and ice cream festivals and sociables and other fund-raising means, Epworth League members were able to help support mission activities in China and India. Through their efforts, two stained-glass windows in the sanctuary were purchased in the 1920s.

am historian. The exhibit will be in one of the display cases during the month of October. I've known about this for a couple of months at least, but am just now getting revved up. My middle initial should be P for, you guessed it, Procrastination, the one thing I do well.

A call for help to Lynn Dunning-Vaughn, friend, neighbor, and church member, was productive. It's amazing what we accomplished with some foam board, photographs, spray glue, a Bible, and candlesticks and candles.

The lesson to be learned is clear: either "just say no" or get on with the project in a timely fashion.

Diary Entries by Kristi Carr

A Sign of the Seasons
October 2

It's pretty hard to ignore the annual autumn show. With September's cold temperatures and wet weather, the foliage has already ignited. But also burning bright is the local politicking.

And in that, it's score one for the Republicans, the first to reach our neighborhood. We came back this morning from some errands to find campaign literature on our doorstep and Sheila Fuller pressing the flesh with one of our neighbors across the street. We know Sheila from her days as school board president and my days as the clerk to that body. She moved on a couple of years ago to the town board when a vacancy occurred there. Now, with Ken Ringler's somewhat surprise decision not to seek re-election, Sheila has thrown her hat in the ring for town supervisor.

Her opposition is Matt Clyne, a Democrat. He hasn't been to our neighborhood and I don't know him, but he wins for most lawn signs—at least on the streets where I travel.

We take a low profile on politics in our house. We never fail to vote, but we resist being forced into one camp or the other, especially in Bethlehem, where the camps are so distinct—the Republicans are a megalopolis and the Democrats a tiny village.

Kristi Carr.

I did read over the campaign flyers which Sheila left and thought they were well done, providing a strong case for staying the course with the Republicans. Our town government, almost exclusively Republican, has delivered good, prompt service over the years, a big reason why Bethlehem is a good place to live. The future holds some thorny issues, however, particularly in the areas of waste management and land use.

So now I'm looking forward to a visit from Matt, to convince us we need fresh ideas. Politics is as timeless—and predictable—as the changing of the seasons.

Education in Bethlehem
October 5

In developing stories for the Bethlehem Central *Highlights*, I came in contact today with several people very pleased with themselves, and deservedly so.

Left to right: Dr. Judith Wooster, Roslyn Faust, Helen and Fred Adler.

The Educational Services Center was buzzing at 10:00 A.M., as the first meeting of a class on Shakespeare assembled in the board room. Normally, ESC isn't used as a classroom, but this week debuts a series of three classes in the new Lifelong Learning program. It's being run as part of the school district's continuing education program, but is different from the usual offerings because classes meet in the daytime (convenient particularly for older, retired citizens) and courses are intellectual pursuits of the humanities rather than crafts or other hands-on activities. Once today's course on Shakespeare, taught by a local college professor, was underway, Helen Adler stopped in to let me know how the program is going. A retired BC teacher, Helen has been an instigator for Lifelong Learning. She told me she approached our assistant superintendent, Judy Wooster, last fall, showing her a brochure targeting retirees and listing card games, teas, and crafts. "Is this how you'd like to spend your retirement?" Helen asked Judy. They rounded up a committee of volunteers to move Lifelong Learning from an idea to a reality. Now that it's up and running, Helen says, "It's like a birthday!" Enrollment was so high, it eventually had to be cut off. A music course has a class size of eighty-three.

After the Lifelong Learning success story, I drove to the high school to take a photo of Lorin Raggio, an engaging high school senior with a terrific smile. He's a semifinalist in the Negro Merit Scholarship Competition. This year BCHS has four semifinalists in the regular Merit program, plus twenty-one students awarded Commended status.

From there, I tracked down English teacher Asta Roberts, who was having her lunch in the faculty room. She's another instigator, also thrilled to see a project reaching a new plateau. Asta helped establish the high school's Writing Center, a place where students can get feedback on writing in any discipline. As a complement to that, she issued an invitation to other teachers—regardless of discipline—who might like to get together to develop their own writing skills. That Writing Group has been going for four-and-a-half years now. Only recently I've become involved to help them get a selection of writing, as well as artwork from BCHS art teachers, assembled into a book. Tomorrow we're going to the printer with it. Several of the teacher contributors stopped by the table where Asta and I were going over last-minute modifications. They seem gratified to have their efforts recognized in a published piece. I even received a personal note from one of them last week, expressing her appreciation to the district for getting the anthology to press.

Seth Carr in Pop Warner uniform.

"Hit 'em high! Hit 'em low! Go, Eagles, go!"
October 10

Today was surely the peak for foliage colors. The reds and golds were handsomely displayed against a crisp blue sky. But at the high school football field there were displays of a different sort as Pop Warner football games matched Bethlehem against East Greenbush.

There were displays of color. Bethlehem was outfitted in traditional Bethlehem Central black and orange. The eighth and ninth grade Eagle Midget boys wore orange pants and white shirts, with black stripes and black numbers. Like a mental game of Pick-Up-Sticks, nervous mothers strained to discern which son was which from the flying heaps of players. The cheerleaders, numbering almost as many as the players, wore predominantly black and white, with flashes of orange outlining the letters on their sweaters and peeking from the folds of their short pleated skirts.

There were displays of allegiance. Volunteer parents sold coffee, hot dogs, and baked goods in the concession stand, or they ran up and down the field with the chain markers (my job for the past two games—talk about the blind leading the blind), or—despite chilly temperatures—they took their seats on cold metal bleachers just to cheer. The Darlington family even decked out their basset hound in a football jersey.

But today, unlike previous games of the season, there were displays of temper. Bethlehem was down by three touchdowns. Starting out with possession on their own forty-five-yard line, the Eagles remained at first down but with every play lost yardage to penalties. Their coach berated the refs—fifteen yards! The players squabbled—offsetting penalties! The coach complained again—another fifteen yards and ejection from the premises! That fired up the players and team star Jeff Linstruth ran eighty-five yards for a TD. But wait! Offsides—no touchdown but another five-yard penalty! Finally, still first down but with forty yards to go to make another, Linstruth sprinted loose yet again. Amazingly, there were no flags on the play. The Eagles scored, but time on the clock had evaporated. Final score: East Greenbush, 34; Bethlehem, 20.

Boss Loomis.

Boss's Day
October 14

Everyone who works at 90 Adams Place showed up at 7:30 this morning, most of us toting muffins, or eggs, or juice, or gourmet coffee.

The occasion was Boss's Day—probably an invention of Hallmark cards—but it's all the excuse we need to add some serious eating to our workday. I'd made a hashbrowns casserole last night, but got up at the crack of dawn to bake it in the oven at home for more than an hour, swath it in newspaper, and still get it to Ed Services by 7:30 A.M. I can tell you, I was ready to tie on a hearty breakfast by that time.

The school district employs lots of people, more than five hundred and most of them living locally. But at Ed Services, there are only fifteen of us now—and of course, no students—so we can fairly easily orchestrate these get-togethers. Our building is old, once the public library, and offices are flung outward around a large, central room, the board room (because that's where the Board of Education regularly meets). Well, this morning it was Cafe BC.

The bosses—Les Loomis, the superintendent; Judy Wooster, assistant superintendent for curriculum and instruction; and Franz Zwicklbauer, assistant superintendent for business—all thanked us and spoke glowingly of our service to BC, but, of course, we'd just fed them.

Eagle Scout Chris Van Woert.

The Path to Eagle
October 16

Today was the culmination of Chris VanWoert's Eagle Scout project. He's worked to organize a food drive to benefit the town of Bethlehem's Food Pantry, and today he stationed members of Scout Troop 71 at local firehouses and the town hall to rake in the donated food.

Brad, Seth, Jeff McQuide (our other son), and I set up shop at Elsmere's fire station, but most of the action was at the town hall. Seth and Jeff aren't even Scouts, but both have brothers in

the troop, and Jeff's social studies teacher requires his students to do so many hours of community service. Brad and I were happy to help, to pay back in some small measure all the help Chris and his family gave to Brian a couple years ago when he was building wood duck nesting boxes for Five Rivers Environmental Center for his Eagle Scout project.

A friend of mine recently made an off-hand remark about Scouting being "uncool" for kids nowadays. From my perspective, that surprised me since so many good things and good people have come to Brian and our family through his involvement in Scouts. Today, Adam Hornick, a high school student who is an Eagle Scout but with a different troop, showed up out of the blue to lend a hand to Chris and his project. I sincerely hope that kind of motivation and service never go out of fashion.

Quilting
October 17

Today was a "veg" day—sit around like a vegetable and do nothing. It was great!

But actually, I'm never content to really do nothing, so while sitting placidly and watching football games on TV with Brad, I worked my fingers raw on the quilt I'm making. This is a star sampler quilt, and I'm determined to have it on Brian's bed by Thanksgiving.

Quilt made by Kristi Carr.

Last spring, I went to a series of Thursday afternoon classes, taught by Pat Bush, to learn how to make the different types of blocks. After each class, before I forgot what I was about, I whipped up four more of the same blocks, so that by the end of May I had a total of twenty-five blocks, five each of five different patterns. The blocks use the same fabrics—a turquoise and mauve paisley on a black base, a beige on beige print for background use, and more prints, predominantly turquoise and mauve. Over Memorial Day weekend, I sewed all the blocks together, separating them with a two-inch black fabric grid, and securely basted together the layers of quilt top, batting, and backing. With the black, the effect is very Amish.

Off and on all summer, I've been hand quilting this full-size spread. Almost all the ladies who take quilt lessons from Pat have her send off their quilt tops for someone else to do the hand quilting, but the hand quilting is actually the part I like best. We have a big basket in our family room where we throw magazines, and most of the time, that's where my current quilt project lives, too.

Pat's classes are always well organized—God bless her family for putting up with so many women carting in their sewing machines, yards of fabric, rotary blades, and rulers. Not this star quilt, but most of the other quilts I've made have been done using a strip technique whereby you chain sew strips of fabric, then cut them—perhaps at an angle—to achieve your pattern. Pat was undaunted when I signed up for my very first class with her a couple years ago and announced I wanted to cut my teeth on a king-size quilt.

The quilts I've made in Pat's classes tend to be strongly geometric and are all in use. A few years ago, I ventured into the spring quilt show at the high school—an intimidating experience! First off, you are given a plastic glove to wear so the oils from your fingers won't damage the quilts. I can see why that's cause for concern. These quilts are works of art, intricately pieced and stitched—a level I'm sure I'll never achieve. But that thought doesn't daunt my pleasure when I snuggle under my first—and king-size—quilt.

Trees
October 19

Feura Bush to Murray to Darroch—that's my usual route to work. I couldn't help but notice on this cloudy, autumn day, however, that the scenes sliding by my car windows are extraordinary. These streets are suburban and residential—and heavily treed. At this time of year, it's as though someone threw open a paintbox. The colors drip from the trees and spill over into the roads, both above your head and below your feet.

I never take the trees for granted (after all, I grew up in the Midwest, where trees are scarcer). Last year, I took fall photos of trees at the end of the Delmar By-Pass and winter photos of trees frosted with snow along Murray Avenue. These I sent to Brian at the University of Georgia (which has plenty of trees to call its own) just to remind him of home, where seasons spin round and round.

Later at work today, I got a phone call from a woman who'd come into town from out of state in order to shop for a house here. She was inquiring about our school system, and, after we'd talked about that, I wished her luck, then suggested that if I were in her shoes today, I would probably be buying a tree rather than a house. Hopefully, she got both.

Upkeep
October 20

Seth and I had back-to-back dental appointments this afternoon. We're pretty religious about dental upkeep in our household—cleanings every six months and both the boys are still in the throes of orthodontia. We're lucky to have health insurance that covers dental work, at least in part. And after battling with Brian over three and a-half years' worth of braces, when they finally came off, it was gratifying to overhear him say to the bathroom mirror, "I LOVE my teeth."

Physical upkeep is a chore. It could be a full time job—eating right, exercising, flossing, brushing, regular exams for eyes, teeth, ob/gyn—not to mention all the safety precautions, the most recent, a law requiring bicycle helmets.

Brad goes regularly to Mike Mashuta's, a local gym, but I dropped out after six months of blood, sweat, and tears, but no weight loss. That type of exercising is just too boring for me. I prefer walking, skiing, swimming, but have to admit I don't do any of that on a very regular schedule. It seems I'm always swamped with stuff to do, yet I know I get a lot accomplished, too. We've got all these modern, time-saving devices, but they obligate us then to go to the gym where we can sweat off on a stair-stepper what people used to sweat off in the course of their daily chores.

High School Open House
October 21

We told Seth, who started high school this fall, that he was going to "the Big House." Well, tonight we found ourselves back in "the Big House" to attend open house after a year's hiatus between Brian's graduation and Seth's arrival in ninth grade.

At least tonight we went early enough to get a decent parking space and to arrive on time for homeroom. That's how it works—parents go through an abbreviated version of their child's

schedule, starting with homeroom. Homeroom remains the same, as do the nearby lockers, for a student's entire four-year stint. Seth is lucky to have Mr. Yeara as his homeroom teacher; at least he can be assured of starting his day with someone laid back, upbeat, and with a sense of humor. Reportedly, Mr. Yeara plays the Beatles' "Yellow Submarine" every day during homeroom—that might get old after four years.

I really liked Seth's teachers. A lot of them were quite young and new to the district. Many I did not know. We had about ten minutes in each classroom, and the teacher generally went over the curriculum. This is not a time to discuss your child's individual progress in a particular subject. For Seth's lunch period, we went to the cafeteria, where the Bethlehem Central Community Organization (like the PTA) was promoting membership (we'd already joined) and dispensing punch and cookies (we were glad to accept). I noticed the teen drinking video I'd worked on playing on a TV screen off to one side.

When Seth was at the middle school, Brad and I always managed to get lost and show up at the wrong classroom at the wrong time. We didn't have that problem tonight. When we got home, we "shared" our impressions with Seth: We didn't know you had an earth science major unit test yesterday. Did you know that homework accounts for thirty percent of your grade in math? We haven't seen you writing in any journal for English. What about this long-term assignment for health?

A Good Place
October 25

Today's weather report was not only too good to be true but it *was* true. Placing great faith in that, I'd arranged to take the day off from work so I could go with a small group, the Vagabonds from Welcome Wagon. This is a group of women who try to take a day trip each month to some place of interest. Last month, we went to Lake George, where we took an hour's boat ride, saw how the other half lived courtesy of the captain's narration, and then nursed our inadequacies by shopping at the outlets. Today's trip was to Schoharie, where we visited the Old Stone Fort.

Despite, a call ahead, we were confronted by a "Closed" sign when we got there, but found a museum worker who not only let us in, but gave us a personalized tour. First built as a church, this stone building was converted to a fort during the pre-revolutionary days when the valley along the Schoharie Creek was routinely raided by Loyalists and Indians trying to curb the food supplies which were raised there and sent to support the Revolutionary troops. Afterward, we had a wonderful lunch at the Parrot House, a local bed and breakfast with an extensive dining room, and polished off our day trip with a shopping stop at a country store.

We are fortunate to be so conveniently located. If you're in the mood for the city, Boston or New York is only 150 miles away, Montreal only 200. To enjoy the great outdoors, the Adirondacks and Catskills are even closer. During the summer, an hour's drive or less will take you to Saratoga to see the New York City Ballet or to play the ponies at the racetrack, to hear concerts at Tanglewood in Massachusetts, to see plays performed at numerous summer stock theatres, or to soak up history and culture at any other number of museums and such. With two sons, we've had lots of sports-motivated trips—the Baseball Hall of Fame in Cooperstown, or to New York to watch the Mets, the Knicks, and the Giants. That's probably why I enjoy a chance like today, to sample a different kind of day trip, with the ladies.

Halloween
October 31

A witch stood at the Moriaritys' door—must have been a party brewing, because the guests' broomsticks were clogging up Dover Drive. The garage door was open at the Mooneys'—looked pretty spooky, too, with all the cobwebs, skeletons, and such. Driving into our subdivision, it was barely five o'clock, but already dark, when we encountered a pint-size Dracula. It must be Halloween.

Weather was lousy—cold and rainy—so we thought the trick-or-treat turnout might be light. No way! We always keep a tally, and tonight we treated eighty-seven goblins. They did seem to start a little early and finish a little early, but the numbers were still there.

The first year we lived here was the best. The night was mild for the last day in October and we accompanied the boys, who were, of course, much smaller then. Everyone seemed to be out on the streets. I remember the Suparmantos serving hot cider from a big black cauldron in their front yard to all the adults. That year, I ransacked the Capital District, searching for black and white striped fabric to make a convict suit for Brian. I finally found some in Scotia.

This year, we didn't go all out. Usually, Brad dons his fake fingers (werewolf, I guess) plus a rubber witch's mask, queues up the music to Michael Jackson's "Thriller," and scares little kids silly. We didn't even get our pumpkin carved up into a jack-o-lantern. Seth went out with some friends, but sans costumes.

Of course, we can't "hold a candle" (pardon the pun) to the McGraths. They'll have night visitors for days, so long as they keep lighting their elaborately carved pumpkins, which they set out all over their yard.

Even with all our trick-or-treaters, we could have used more. We still have some bite-size candy bars left over and they look awfully tempting.

Bethlehem Diary

Diary Entries by Teresa Buckley

First Snow of the Year
November 1

It's only the beginning of November, but already we have seen two snow-falls. The snow didn't accumulate here in Delmar, but I saw the flakes flying on my way home from work on both Saturday and Sunday. The hilltowns got several inches, up to a foot and more in some places. The sleds and skis came out for another year. Still, I hope November isn't chilly all the way through. I love snow, but not cold, dry weather.

Election Day
November 2

I've always been a big fan of election day. I enjoy getting up early and going to the Elsmere Elementary School with Jim. It is one of the few reasons we have for leaving the house together early in the morning, since we normally get a later start on the day than most people with day jobs and families. The elementary school smells the same as those everywhere—a mixture of crayon wax, cafeteria food, and kid sweat. Seeing the people working at the polls makes me think of my mother, sitting with a similar group in another setting in Binghamton. I'm sure this is a social occasion of sorts for many of the workers. They see friends and acquaintances, and catch up on their co-workers' lives.

Teresa Buckley.

This year we have a real race for town supervisor for the first time in decades, from what I hear. Matt Clyne, the Democrat, is challenging board member Sheila Fuller. Since Bethlehem has been a Republican stronghold for so long, the incumbent usually has no problem winning re-election. If he decides not to run, the Republican primary really decides the winner; the general election is more of an exercise in democracy—a foregone conclusion. But this year was different. Why? Perhaps it was that Clyne won the Conservative line on the ballot. Or that Fuller wasn't as well known townwide as the incumbent would have been, or that she was too well known by parents unhappy with some of her decisions during her tenure as school board president. Maybe the Democratic organization is getting stronger in Bethlehem. We'll see how close it comes.

A Close Race
November 3

Election day in a newsroom is akin to New Year's Eve. Most of the staff is working through the evening and into the night. The normally subdued evening hours are filled with social eating: A table of sandwiches and salads in the conference room replaces the usual quick meals eaten at various times at our desks or at local fast-food places. We try to complete as much non-election coverage as possible early on. Slowly, after 9:00 P.M., the results begin trickling in. This year, two clerks in a corner of the room kept tabs on numbers from computer terminals linked with the boards of elections. Phone calls came in from all corners of the circulation area as reporters dictated their stories in stages. The uncontested races reach the copy desk first, then early results from the other races, and, finally, the close contests. The tension and shouting increase as deadline approaches. When all the copy for the first edition is finally shipped, we jump into the next edition (there are three in all). Sometime around midnight, I slipped out quietly. I had been in since early afternoon, attending to the advance copy.

Sheila Fuller, town supervisor.

I felt as if I were leaving the party just as it was hitting its stride. The others on the copy desk remained until almost 2:00 A.M.

When I left this morning, the Bethlehem supervisor's race was still too close to call, with Clyne trailing Fuller by only a handful of votes. The result rests on the write-in ballots.

Sheila Fuller Wins
November 4

The write-in votes went Sheila Fuller's way. As the candidates watched the election officials open the ballots, they realized that most were Fuller's. Bethlehem will have a woman as its supervisor [historic first] beginning in January. Still, the Democrats are hopeful that the close election is a sign that Republican domination is waning in the town.

Blodgett Hill
Nov. 6

A few weeks ago, Jim and I went for a walk at the Hollyhock Hollow sanctuary run by New York Audubon in Feura Bush. We noticed on a map there that the Department of Environmental Conservation has a lookout on land just over the border in Coeymans, so we decided to go down and check it out. Today, we returned to the spot with our friends Rick Williams and Karen Roach. The land is Blodgett Hill, for which Blodgett Road, off County Route 103, is named. The DEC has a sign and a small parking area on the road. Getting to the top requires a short, steep climb through pines and oaks still holding onto their leaves, some of which are gigantic. Unmarked trails crisscross through the woods, so getting to the top means following whichever trail heads up. But after only ten or fifteen minutes, we were at the top—where someone has dragged a couple of lawn chairs for hikers to rest up and enjoy the view. We could see eastern Albany County, including the Empire State Plaza in downtown Albany, and into Rensselaer and Columbia counties, with the Hudson River showing up as a depression in the landscape marked

Rienow Memorial Garden.

by a bridge or two here and there. Next time we go back we'll try to find a lookout south or west. We had to cut short our walk so I could get to work on time.

Bicentennial Publications
November 18

Today was the monthly meeting of the committee that is editing *Bethlehem Diary*. This group's meetings are among the few I've ever enjoyed. They are lively, and time passes quickly. The three men and three women speak our minds about whatever the topic is —whether to select a particular entry, how to edit a long piece—and enjoy each other's company. It is unlikely the six of us would have known each other if it wasn't for this experience.

The Old Vacuum
Saturday, November 20

Jim and I try to squeeze in errands on the fly on our way to or from work. Neither of us is a retailer's dream. We hold on to possessions for years and

Bridge at Five Rivers.

years. Jim still fits into the size he wore in high school. Although he doesn't wear those clothes, it means that he has bits and pieces of twenty years' worth of wardrobe. And, when I reluctantly sold my 1981 Chevrolet Malibu two years ago, it had 153,000-plus trouble-free miles. I had bought it from my father with almost 100,000 miles on it.

Today's errands included a stop at the vacuum cleaner business in Menands. The hose on our vacuum was shot, which wasn't a surprise, considering it's a circa 1961 model. We had an even older model, from the late 1950s, that Jim had inherited from his father. The engine went on that one, but we managed to trade in the unit with a man who fixes vacuum cleaners. He wanted it for parts, and had our current model rebuilt and ready to go. We have had occasion to go to the vacuum cleaner store only twice in the five or six years we've been here, and both times they have tried to encourage us to buy a new model. This one will have to blow up first, I guess.

I don't think Jim and I are extraordinarily cheap, nor are we unable to afford new things. I think it goes back to our upbringings. Our parents were young during the Depression, and instilled the sense of saving and not wasting in both of us. Jim's dad was raising three children on his own, so Jim knows what it's like to do without. I also think we are not much on accumulating. We always lived in small apartments before we bought our house, and the junk really piles up fast, especially when you're reluctant to throw it away. So, if you don't have it, you can't keep it.

At Five Rivers
Sunday, November 21

We have delightful company this weekend. Jim's college friends, Weber and Diane Torres, and their three daughters, Lindsay, 11, Lauren, 8, and Kelsey, 4, are staying with us for a few days. They are driving from their home in Columbus, Ohio, for a Thanksgiving week with their families in New England. They all love the outdoors so we took them to one of our favorite Sunday spots, the Five Rivers center. We walk or ski there in all seasons. Today, the ponds had a thin layer of ice coating them. The few ducks that remain keep the ice broken up by swimming around at one end. Some of the smaller wet areas had a thicker layer of ice, which the girls spent time trying to crack with rocks.

The Sales Pitch
Friday, November 26

Jim recently filled out a card for a drawing to win a free carpet cleaning. Of course, everyone who fills out a card wins this prize—they're trying to sell carpet cleaners, or cleaning service. When we "won" a few days later, I protested that I didn't want to spend several hours trapped with a salesman. Jim agreed to hang around, but the timing just didn't coincide with his work schedule, and he convinced me that the pitch would only take about half an hour. The salesman/cleaner, Rich, showed up at 9:30 or so, just in time to say hello and good-bye to Jim. Then we settled in for the morning. I did laundry, and tried to read, but at every step Rich wanted to show me what he was doing. Naturally, our old vacuum cleaner was not performing up to snuff, so he pulled out the new model from his van and proceded to vacuum my carpet. Then—yes, they still do this—he emptied out the vacuum cleaner bag on my kitchen floor, with a "not to worry, I'll clean it up" for good measure. He vacuumed again. And again. Six times, all told. Each time, he methodically emptied the bag until a pile of grit and fuzz filled the floor space between us, and assured me that I'm not a dirty person, just one who owns an inferior vacuum. Finally, he shampooed, then fluffed the carpet. Oh, and cleaned up the piles of dirt from the kitchen.

Before leaving, Rich offered to inspect our old vacuum. He had a list to check off (wear and tear, cord and hose condition) before The Ball Test. He told me my vacuum should be able to pick up three small metal balls if the suction was working properly. These were no small balls; they were one and one-half to two inches in diameter. Dramatically, he placed them on the carpet, fitted a plastic hood over the hose, turned on the vacuum, and held it over the first pull. Pluck! It swept into the hood. Now the second. Again, it picked up and held. Now the big test—it'll never work, I convinced myself—but it pulled the final metal ball into the hood. What a feeling of pride. Poor Rich, he seemed rather downcast.

Lunar Eclipse
Sunday, November 28

Tonight we are having a lunar eclipse. I've been checking it on and off throughout the night. (Another bonus of working nights is being able to stay up late enough for eclipses to finish eclipsing.) The day was incredibly windy, rainy, and warm. As late as early evening, people coming into the building were complaining about the storm, so I was not very optimistic about good viewing when I first went outside at 10:40 or so (the eclipse was to have begun at 10:27 P.M.) But the sky was clear, and the moon shone like one out of the movies, bright, full, and round and perfectly situated for viewing outside the door by the security guard's cubicle. I had to use my imagination to believe that even a fraction of it was covered by Earth's shadow. I hurried back into the office, excited to tell the others about it. One asked, "When will the next one occur?" (Was he trying to decide whether this one was worth leaving the security of his chair?) Another pointed out that she'd seen a lunar eclipse previously. (Seen one, seen them all?) I was disappointed, but, gradually, they all trickled out to catch a peek.

By the time I drove home from work, about 11:30, there was a definite change. Shortly after midnight, I coaxed Jim outside, and the change was unmistakable. There we were, old Earth, casting a shadow.

Diary Entries by Floyd Brewer

The Albany Institute: Long-Lasting Source of Knowledge and Culture
November 30 —December 1

Floyd Brewer.

Our long love affair with the Albany Institute of History & Art began with Coleen's volunteer role as a docent (tour guide) years ago, and blossomed into regular visits several times each year. I would sometimes browse in the McKinney Library while waiting to drive her home or, if the timing was right, we would sometimes have lunch in the Luncheon Gallery in the Rice building. Later, as I worked on parts of *Bethlehem Revisited*, I returned to the McKinney Library time and again where, it seemed to me, they had the only copy of a special ceramics book or precious original document.

When we finished our book, they placed it on sale in their bookstore. Their bookstore manager, Christina Lamarque, bought five more from me today during our annual trek to the Institute's beautiful Festival of Trees.

We often go for special exhibits and, on occasions, I go for some advice on the identification of an antique or artifact recovered from one of my sites. Year after year, I took ceramic fragments to Charlotte Wilcoxen, McKinney librarian and ceramics specialist, from whom I eventually took a class in ceramics in the Harmanus Bleeker building, where most of the Institute's classes are offered.

When all of these pleasures and sources of skills are added together, I find the Albany Institute of History & Art an enormous boon to scholars, as well as a very pleasant place to visit— a gem of a museum, and a treasury of past life-styles of interest to all age levels in the greater Albany area.

When Good Friends Come for Dinner
December 2-3

Harry and Alice Howes and Hugh and Rowena Hewitt came for dinner tonight, a four-hour round of good conversation and food with friends

Alice S. Howes.

Rowena F. Hewitt.

we enjoy very much. Both couples have lived in Slingerlands for many years. Harry and I worked in the same department at the University at Albany, and Hugh worked there as well.

I asked the group to critique a video-tape of my interview with Joanne Kimmey regarding some of the highlights of _Bethlehem Revisited_, a tape produced at the [Bethlehem Public] library on November 22. They made good suggestions, which will be considered as I do more tapes about my work in Bethlehem over the past twelve years: (1) more close-ups are needed, (2) explanatory props (artifacts, maps, charts) would be helpful,

and (3) more animation would add to viewer interest. Other comments ranged from improving the color of my facial features (which were too dark) to having a dry run of each interview, which might reduce errors in my responses to Joanne's questions. It was a helpful critique from friends known for sharing honest opinions.

It was especially significant to hear that Hugh will take over the diary project in January, keeping a diary like this on a regular basis. He is serving on our _Bethlehem Diary_ editorial committee and understands very well the value of such diaries to future historians.

Coleen, Alice, and Rowena are very active in their church work. All three women have made significant contributions of time, money, and energy to major programs in their churches, especially their educational and mission activities, over the past quarter century.

**Writing in Science:
Satisfaction Par Excellence**
December 10

When my speech, "Albert Bradt, Tobacco Planter, and the Smoking Pipe Story in Early Bethlehem, New York," was published in the *Rochester Science Museum Series* last April, I remember feeling good about adding a few more planks of knowledge to our historic platform in a town Coleen and I have enjoyed living in for twenty-seven years. It is a great feeling because I am sure of my conclusions and scientists everywhere are happy to share conclusions they are sure of. Further, they are continually building on earlier published conclusions and can easily see where they have added something new.

Such feelings of satisfaction were even stronger when my nineteen-page article, "700 Years of Ceramics on the Nicoll-Sill Estate, Bethlehem, New York," was published in the fall 1990 issue of *The Bulletin—Journal of the New York State Archaeological Association*. The editor, Dr. Charles F. Hayes III, used a picture of one of our reconstructed stoneware jugs on the cover.

Prior to the publication of this article, very little was known about pottery used by the various families living there over the centuries. A careful analysis of some 12,733 pottery fragments recovered from the estate, elicited conclusions relating to pottery usage by Indian families all the way down to Marian and Harry Dinmore who lived there from 1927 to 1960. Now, scholars everywhere have this knowledge to use in future books and articles.

I used similar information turned out by earlier scholars and scientists [working on other sites] in my chapters in *Bethlehem Revisited*. Now it is time for us to repay the favors and add a few more planks for others to build on in future years.

The Al Restifo I Know
December 12-13

In some ways, Alfred Restifo can be regarded as "Mr. Bethlehem." Although he was born in Albany in 1928, his family moved to Elsmere in October 1931, and he has been here ever since. The son of Dorothy Wilke and Sebastian Restifo, Al's roots go back to Sicily through his grandparents, Don Giuseppe Restifo and Carmela Ferrara.

We've talked several times about his tenure in the Bethlehem Central School District—beginning with work as a student in the Elsmere Grade School in 1932, graduation from Bethlehem Central High School in 1945, and forty

Alfred P. Restifo.

Hamilton Bookhout in September 1951. He remembers Bookhout as "an administrator with strong convictions, a straight-forward style of relating to others, and a distinguished educator."

Al's love of classical music, local history, and theology, and his vast reading, shine through in every conversation I have had with him. His 1990 conversation with Kristi Carr concerning BC's sixtieth anniversary that year, inspired the district to produce the video *B.C.: A Part of our Lives*. It is an excellent review of highlights of the school district's history.

In addition to all of the young lives he has influenced, Al's lasting legacy will come through his seven children from his 1950 marriage to Valerie Swirzcki. All told, his professional and family life have been unusually productive, a credit to his resourcefulness and high intelligence.

years of teaching—the first half at Clarksville Elementary, the rest at the middle school, a role he enjoyed immensely because he loves kids. Kids in the sixth grade are a particular joy for him, and former students have told me that his enthusiasm for teaching, sense of humor, and exceptional knowledge of his subject (math) were displayed regularly. Many ended their year with Al with "both love and respect," in the words of one student I spoke to in 1992.

Naturally he had to get some training for his life's work. A year at R.P.I. (1945-1946), a B.S. [degree] in chemistry at Siena College (1950), and a year of part-time teaching in Albany schools, preceded his acceptance of a teaching contract from the legendary

An Interim Report on the Results of our Bicentennial Dig
December 16-17

Mosher Dairy Site
Route 9W - Glenmont
May-June 1993

Bethlehem Archaeology Group
and the
Glenmont Elementary School

Partners in Science

Mosher Dairy farmhouse, ca. 1840s. Sketch by Margaret Foster.

The suggestion to do some archaeological work around the old Mosher Dairy farmhouse on Route 9W at Bender Lane originated with Cliff Wright and was approved by Glenmont Elementary School principal, Donald Robillard. He appointed art teacher, Gale Derosia, to work with field director, Floyd Brewer, in supervising work at the site. More than two hundred pupils, parents, and faculty did the bulk of the work with help from Bethlehem Archaeology Group regulars Chester Bolen, Clark Galloway, and Bernard Lamica. Bolen assisted with supervision in the absence of the field director. Thanks are especially due Mary Capobianco, Debbie Carpenter, Heidi Hauf, Dave Ksanznak, Sue Lamora, Gayle Lawrence, Judy Parry, and Barbara Riegel, who brought their classes to the site for periods ranging from a few hours to several days. Most of the participants did their work carefully and followed standard ground rules for archaeological excavations.

Purpose

To provide fourth- and fifth-grade pupils with instruction in basic archaeological practices, with attention to everything from the proper use of tools and temporary identification of artifacts to excavating in thin layers within a grid system of ten-foot squares and recording objects found at particular levels, in a field notebook.

Objective of Site Work

To re-create the life-styles of the various families who lived in the farmhouse since the building was built in the 1840s.

Early Observations

Although firm conclusions can be reached only after extensive work with the artifacts in the laboratory, a few educated guesses can be made about the collection of objects recovered from the site:

1) Age of the farmhouse—Work on the paper trail (deeds, wills, etc.) has not been completed. However, an 1838 large penny was found by Colleen Brewster some seventeen inches below the surface down the foundation of the original building underneath the old porch, which was removed in recent years. It had about five years of wear before it was dropped by one of the builders, suggesting that the home was built in the early 1840s;

2) How they lived in the nineteenth century—Even without their names, we know that the earliest residents used machine-made square nails to secure inner boards to beams, placed their kerosene lamps on metal wall brackets, served daily meals on plain whiteware with beef as a frequent item on the menu, relaxed over games of Chinese checkers played with brown, clay marbles, while men smoked their long, white, kaolin clay pipes. Sometimes the men had cold sodas delivered to the barn on hot, sweaty days. It is likely that the soda was cooled in an icebox, a fashionable appliance of the day. It was also a time when men with mustaches drank from special cups designed to keep their extra growth of hair in one place, and when medicine for horses was sometimes labelled "homeopathic," meaning full of natural ingredients. Buckles, horseshoes, and other metal objects, found in the barn and wagon shed areas, suggest that horses did much of the hard work.

We know that the building was used as a hotel in the last century, since the word appears under the name G.R. Mosher on an 1866 map of Bethlehem. This may be a partial explanation for the fragments of an elegant chandelier, fancy stair rail, and nicely carved living room furniture recovered from the debris on the first floor.

Further, there are hints of church attendance. Religious medals, fragments of fine jewelry, buttons, beads, and other finery, suggest dressing for special occasions, which was often for church in the nineteenth century.

One early resident owned a glass slipper, which may have been used for holding small items (hairpins, buttons, etc.) and placed on the top of a dresser. Numerous finds of large and small copper pennies dating to the last half of the 1800s hint that these coins were commonly used to purchase everything from newspapers to candy packed in glass-topped barrels. The storekeeper sold such candy for a penny a piece from a barrel in front of his cash box. He did the same for pickles, peanuts, and a wide range of products intended to be eaten in homes;

3) How they lived in the twentieth century—After George and Ella Mosher rented the farm in 1900 and established a dairy business, the pace of life picked up a little. Milk was first delivered by horse and wagon in the early 1900s, but the business grew by leaps and bounds when it became possible to deliver dairy products with a small truck in the 1920s. The Mosher Dairy was a small operation in competition with the larger Normanskill Dairy next door on Route 9W, and Heath's Dairy in Glenmont.

Hot, hardworking farmhands still drank soda, but it came in the familiar Mae West green bottle under the brand name Coca-Cola. Chinese checkers was still a fun game, but gaily colored glass marbles were used for this and related games. Further, children played jackstones, which required a measure of manual dexterity as they competed with others by picking up increasing numbers of the many-pointed, metal objects.

Candy bars and related goodies often cost a nickel or dime, and coin finds reflect a gradual transition from pennies to nickels and dimes for small purchases. Food was served on transfer-printed whiteware, which had an attractive blue design. Beef continued to be a favorite food of farmhands, but chicken and lamb were served more often.

Electric power brought a range of small gadgets after 1910, and glass bulbs replaced kerosene lamps. Pearls and costume jewelry were worn frequently by women and girls. Lost keys, ground into the topsoil over the years, provide clues to the kinds of cars purchased by the residents. They were mostly General Motors cars, although one family owned a Toyota late in this century.

When the age of plastics arrived in a big way in the 1940s, a lot of items were made in Japan and shipped to this country. Some ended up on the Mosher Dairy farm. Later, the plastics revolution took the form of toy guns, cars, soldiers, building blocks, and just about everything children liked to play with. Dozens of plastic toys were recovered from all parts of the land around the farmhouse;

4) Mission accomplished! From many comments made by participants since the close of work at the site, it is clear that this was an excellent educational experience for most who came to dig. The participants deserve considerable credit for the care with which they followed standard archaeological methods. The record of past life-styles they exhumed from the soil around the old farmhouse is now being studied in the laboratory and promises to result in a scholarly review of the Mosher Dairy farm story in a future publication.

Interim Report:
Jones/LaGrange Site
December 18-19

Background—Arrangements were made with Adrienne and William Jones, current owners of the former LaGrange estate, to conduct an excavation around the foundation of the old farmhouse on their property on LaGrange Road in Slingerlands. The building is near an old family cemetery in which Christian I. LaGrange (1779-1848) and several members of his family are buried. The property was owned by the LaGranges until soon after the death of Ella LaGrange McBride in 1955. Field director Floyd Brewer, and associate field director Chester Bolen were assisted by Clark Galloway, Bernard Lamica, Marianne Purcell, and occasional short-term volunteers with the Bethlehem Archaeology Group. Dorothea LaGrange served as a consultant in the records search.

Purpose of the site work—This was an effort to determine the age of the home in which the Jones family is currently living, while their new home is being completed nearby. A careful examination of construction features and building hardware suggested the possibility that the home was built in the eighteenth century, and since the paper trail is unclear, it was necessary to look for builder's trench artifacts. On occasions, builders of ancient homes would drop a datable object in the trench surrounding the foundation.

Eighteenth century finds—One underglaze, hand painted, pearlware fragment, found eight feet down the foundation along the front of the house, suggests that the house was built after 1795 since this type of pottery was not made until that year. Several additional fragments of pearlware were recovered, but not from locations that would help date the construction of the house. A few fragments of a late eighteenth century, blue-edged, hand painted pearlware plate were recovered, but the dish could have been handed down to Christian I. and Jamima LaGrange, who lived there most of the first half of the nineteenth century. One large fragment of lead-glazed slipware and several fragments of lead-glazed redware all date to the late eighteenth century, but they were recovered with a large group of nineteenth century artifacts from disturbed soil and offered no help in dating construction of the house.

Age of the house—No "smoking guns," such as coins, kaolin clay pipe fragments containing the maker's cartouche, or precisely datable pottery fragments were found. However, as tiny as the above pattern of evidence is, it suggests that the house was built for Christian I. and Jamima LaGrange around 1800, give or take a few years.

Nineteenth century finds—Several dozen objects, ranging from pottery and bottle fragments to machine-made nails and metal household possessions, were recovered from a layer of disturbed soil along the foundation on several sides of the old section of the house, suggesting some major repairs to the foundation in the nineteenth century. When a full analysis of these artifacts becomes possible in our laboratory, they should provide a sketchy picture of several LaGrange families who lived there throughout the nineteenth century.

The paper trail—Dorothea LaGrange has been working on LaGrange family records for a number of years. She points out that:

Johannes De LaGrange was born in 1630, in France. He was a Hugenot who fled from persecution to Amsterdam, Holland. From there he came to America in 1656. He settled in New Amsterdam and left four sons, Johannes, Omie, Isaac, and Jacobus.

Omie, second son of Johannes, born about 1625, came to Albany in 1665. He was a trader and landowner in Albany.

In 1716, Omie De LaGrange and Johannes Vedder purchased the remainder of the [Van Baal] patent for 250 pounds and [in the same year] Omie and his brother, Isaac, settled on a tract of land [just south of the Normanskill] with Omie selecting for his own farm a large tract along the Normanskill, near or perhaps the same yet held in the family.

Some support for Dorothea LaGrange's version of LaGrange family land transfers can be found on maps. The 1767 Bleeker map of Rensselaerwick shows "Christina LaGransie, Isaac LaGransie, and Omie LaGransie," relatives of Christian I. LaGrange, living in the area that would become Slingerlands—obviously related families despite the different spelling. Further, the 1866 Beers map of Bethlehem lists "J.O. LaGrange" living in the same area which would seem to confirm Dorothea's mention of Jacobus as the second generation of LaGranges living in Slingerlands. Finally, there is a listing of Christian C. and Mary LaGrange on page 256 in _Bethlehem Revisited_, where the reader's attention is directed to a 1916 map of Bethlehem showing this couple living on the land described in this story.

A final report on this historic family will require additional research into deed transfers and more archaeology of promising sites to acquire life-style information on a larger scale than this limited research made possible.

The First Reformed Church of Bethlehem Today
December 20-23

In the last ten years, hundreds of volunteer hours have been devoted to ferreting out the rich history of Bethlehem's oldest church, but what about the church today? The evidence shows that the church is alive and well, and is engaged in a variety of mission, education, and pastoral-related activity especially relevant in a modern age.

One merely has to examine a 1993 flier issued by the church to get a sense of the programs currently underway. Mission activities range from projects

First Reformed Church of Bethlehem Manse now occupied by Mr. and Mrs. Allan Janssen.

in Japan, the Middle East, and Albany, to badly needed rehabilitative services such as Project Hope, Alcoholics Anonymous, and aid to various shelters and camp programs.

In a similar vein, the church's education programs touch the lives of every age group from "Creative Play" preschool activities and youth programs to adult study groups and new member classes, a mix that changes regularly to meet the latest set of needs expressed by lay officials in the church.

The heart of church activity, listed under "Worship" in the flier, involves Sunday worship and special music, along with summer vespers, special services, and such important events as weddings and funerals, which foster lasting memories in the minds of the participants. The central figure in all of these activities is Pastor Allan Janssen, who has served the church for fifteen years. It is likely that he learned a great deal about the role of a minister in a church from his father, who was also a minister, as was his grandfather on his mother's side. Allan graduated from the Western Theological Seminary in Michigan in 1973.

One big reason why the First Reformed Church of Bethlehem is playing a significant role in the lives of modern parishioners is the help the pastor receives from dozens of families who have remained with the church for decades. Jean Lyon has been a member for more than forty-two years and has helped the church in a number of crucial roles. Members for many decades, Ralph and Muriel Wood regretted leaving the church last year when they moved to Cape Cod. Andrew and Elizabeth Koonz have held several key positions over many, many years, as have more than thirty members who received sixty-year pins during a recent anniversary celebration.

Readers of this diary are well aware of my bias, hence, I have to admit that my highest accolade to church members and Allan Janssen has been for their cooperation with me in completing a dig around the church farm in the late 1980s. There was barely room for the highlights of this story on pages 199-201 in *Bethlehem Revisited*. The real fun will come when the church decides to publish a third and updated version of its well-known *History of the First Reformed Church of Bethlehem*, and provides me with an opportunity to do a chapter on the church farm.

When and if such an opportunity comes, I will have dozens of significant photographs of objects used by the families living on the farm between 1800 and 1946, to illustrate how they lived and served the church. It is an interesting story of one phase in the life of an important church, which has been an anchor for many Bethlehem families over the ages, and a source of help with difficult human problems in modern times.

The Joys and Pitfalls in Genealogical Research
December 26-27

Most amateur and professional genealogists are full of stories about really special finds that provided an exciting link between two key people or shed light on where and how members of their families lived. As I begin a serious draft of my family history for publication, it is clear that my own collection of stories has grown tenfold. It has been a thirty-five-year search filled with both joys and pitfalls, an experience that has left me with thousands of papers, hundreds of pictures, and dozens of maps—enough to fill a small library. I am not happy with most of the family histories found in the average library and hope to do better with mine. Conversely, one of the best I have seen in recent years is *A Dutch Family in the Middle Colonies 1660-1800*, by Firth Haring Fabend, and I hope to emulate some of the best features of her book.

Floyd I. Brewer, 1994, working on his next book: *A Dutch-English Odyssey.*

It is both scholarly and readable, a genuine contribution to the literature.

My story, tentatively called *A Dutch-English Odyssey*, will chronicle the aftermath of the marriages of two pioneers in American history—the Dutch immigrant Adam Brouwer (1620-1693) and the English immigrant Jeffrey Estey (1586-1657). My mother and father, descendants of these two pioneers, eventually met in Bridgewater, Maine, in 1909, married, and raised seven children there.

Joyful moments during the search came thick and fast, particularly after I decided to employ professional genealogists to help me with the fine points. Flo Christoph, a local genealogist, helped with the Brouwer line.

Betty Sewell, a Canadian genealogist, worked on the Estey line in Canada. Their suggestions led to special collections in the libraries that contained excellent materials—a map of early Breuckelen with Adam Brouwer's flour mill clearly identified, a map of 1785 land grants in Sheffield, New Brunswick, listing Richard Estey, Sr., great grandson of Jeffrey Estey, another step in the chain of evidence in which the descendants migrated from the United States to Canada in the last quarter of the eighteenth century, and back to the United States in the late nineteenth century.

The pitfalls were numerous, particularly the attempt to do all the work myself out of pure interest. Special training is badly needed if one hopes to make a contribution to the literature as opposed to doing a routine family history. Experienced historian Peter Christoph is now reviewing drafts of my history intended for publication in two or three years. William and Raymona Bogardus of Wilmington, Ohio (his mother was a Brewer), are providing resource materials from their vast library. Even now, after thirty-five years of searching, official records linking two of the Brouwer-Brewer generations cannot be located. Still, I have a solid direction for this family story and have managed to piece together a picture of the main characters, and their meandering route to Bridgewater, Maine, where my father and mother fell in love, married, and kept the chain going.

NATHANIEL ADAMS HOTEL , DELMAR.
MARK L. PECKHAM , AUGUST 22 , 1994.

Credits

Chapter 1. 1983

2.* Courtesy Development and Alumni Affairs Office, University at Albany.

3. Photograph by Chuck McKinney.

4. Map by Kristi Carr.

8. Courtesy *The Spotlight*.

9. Courtesy Shirley Sargent.

11. Courtesy Delmar Presbyterian Church.

14. Logo design by Gale Derosia.

Chapter 2. 1984

19. Courtesy Albany Institute of History and Art.

24. Photograph by Benjamin French.

25. Photograph by Ryland H. Hewitt.

26. Photograph by Ryland H. Hewitt.

30. Photograph by Jon Jameson.

31. Photograph by Benjamin French.

Chapter 3. 1985

35. Courtesy Charlotte Wilcoxen.

36. Courtesy Kay Hendrick.

*Note: Numerals refer to page numbers of illustrations.

37. Photograph by Jon Jameson.

40. Courtesy Marjory O'Brien.

42. Photograph by Floyd Brewer.

44. Courtesy Floyd Brewer.

46. Photograph by Floyd Brewer.

Chapter 4. 1986

52. Courtesy State of New York Education Department.

54. Photograph by Jon Jameson.

57. Courtesy Allison Bennett.

60. Courtesy Bernard Kaplowitz.

61. Photograph by Ryland H. Hewitt.

63. Courtesy Bethlehem Public Library.

64. Photograph by Jon Jameson.

65. Photograph by Jon Jameson.

Chapter 5. 1987

69. Photograph (left) by Chuck McKinney; photograph (right) courtesy Stephen F. Bub.

71. Photograph by Chuck McKinney.

72. Photograph (left) courtesy Dorothy Hosey; photograph (right) by Ryland H. Hewitt.

74. Courtesy Floyd Brewer.

77. Courtesy Lynn Corrigan.

78. Courtesy Ken Hahn.

Chapter 6. 1988

85. Courtesy Main Brothers Oil Company.

86. Courtesy *The Spotlight*.

87. Photograph by Ryland H. Hewitt.

89. Courtesy Key Bank, Delmar Branch.

91. Photograph by Jon Jameson.

94. Photograph by Floyd Brewer.

Chapter 7. 1989

98. Courtesy Tom Knight.

101. Photograph by Chuck McKinney.

102. Courtesy Floyd Brewer.

104. Courtesy Kathleen Newkirk.

106. Courtesy Siena College Public Relations Office.

112. Photograph (top left) courtesy Kay Hendrick; photograph (top right) courtesy Lynn Corrigan.

Chapter 8. 1990

116. Courtesy Lynn Corrigan.

118. Courtesy Allison Bennett.

119. Courtesy *The Spotlight*.

120. Courtesy Ruth Oliver Bickel.

124. Courtesy Patricia DeCecco.

125. Photograph by Floyd Brewer.

128. Courtesy Floyd Brewer.

131. Photograph by Floyd Brewer.

Chapter 9. 1991

138. Photograph by Ryland H. Hewitt.

139. Courtesy Beth Brewer.

140. Photograph (left) by Ryland H. Hewitt; photograph (right) by Chuck McKinney.

142. Photograph by Ryland H. Hewitt.

143. Photograph by Susan Lambert.

150. Courtesy Leonard F. Tantillo.

152. Photograph by Ryland H. Hewitt.

Chapter 10. 1992

156. Courtesy Alice Boutelle.

157. Photograph by Ryland H. Hewitt.

158. Courtesy Sam and Kay Youmans.

159. Courtesy Paul Mulligan.

161. Courtesy John B. Geurtze.

163. Photograph by Chuck McKinney.

166. Photograph by Ryland H. Hewitt.

169. Courtesy Five Rivers Limited.

170. Photograph by Tom Knight, Knight Photographic Services.

Chapter 11. 1993

174. Photograph by Ryland H. Hewitt.

175. Photograph by Ryland H. Hewitt.

177. Courtesy Helen Nickel (top left).

179, Photographs by Ryland H. Hewitt.
180.

182, Courtesy Kristi Carr.
185.

186, Photographs by Kristi Carr.
187,
189.

191. Photograph by Ryland H. Hewitt.

192. Courtesy Joseph A. Allgaier.

194. Bethlehem 200 program cover design by Joyce VanBurgh; photograph (right) by Ann Patton.

195, Photographs by Joseph Allgaier.
197,
198.

199. Photograph by Ryland H. Hewitt.

200. Photograph by Susan Graves.

202. Courtesy Mary Ahlstrom.

204. Photographs courtesy Susan Graves.

206. Photograph by Teresa Buckley.

207. Photograph by Elaine McLain, courtesy *The Spotlight*.

208. Photographs by Ryland H. Hewitt.

209, Photographs by Ryland H. Hewitt, courtesy *The Spotlight*.
213,

214.
215, Courtesy Joseph A. Allgaier.
216.

217. Photograph by Joseph A. Allgaier.

221. Courtesy Joseph A. Allgaier.

222. Photograph by Ryland H. Hewitt.

224, Photographs by Teresa Buckley.
225,
227,
229.

230. Photograph by Ryland H. Hewitt.

232. Photograph by Doug Persons.

233. Photograph (left) by Susan Graves; photograph (right) by Norman Seeff.

237. Photograph by Teresa Buckley.

238. Photograph by Ryland H. Hewitt.

240. Photograph by Ryland H. Hewitt; courtesy *The Spotlight*.

241. Courtesy Lorraine Smith.

242. Photograph by Ryland H. Hewitt; courtesy Alice and Harry Howes.

244. Courtesy Donald F. and Alice M. Arthur.

246. Photograph by Ryland H. Hewitt.

247, Photographs by Kristi Carr.
248.

249. Courtesy Kristi Carr.

250, Photographs by Kristi Carr.
251.

256. Photograph by Ryland H. Hewitt.

Chapter 11. 1993 (continued)

258, Photographs by Teresa Buckley.
259.

262. Photograph by Ryland H. Hewitt.

263. Photograph (left) courtesy Alice Howes; photograph (right) by Ryland H. Hewitt.

265. Courtesy Alfred Restifo.

271. Photograph by Ryland H. Hewitt.

273. Photograph by Tom Knight, Knight Photographic Services.

Biographical Notes

EDITORS

Joseph A. Allgaier, associate editor and author of the chapters on government and business in *Bethlehem Revisited*, is associate editor of *Bethlehem Diary*, compiler of the index, and author of diary selections in March and June 1993. A thirty-year resident of Delmar, Allgaier and his wife, Jacqueline, have raised three children, Joseph G., Barbara, and Karen. Retired from a business career with NYNEX, he has been town historian since 1990, and is also an active pilot and golf enthusiast.

Teresa Buckley, editor in chief of *Bethlehem Diary*, wrote the July and November 1993 entries. She and her husband, James Odato, have lived in Delmar since 1988. Buckley is a layout/copy editor with the *Times Union*. She is a graduate of the University at Binghamton and is pursuing a master's degree in geography at the University at Albany.

Kristi Carr has lived in Delmar with her husband, Brad, and sons, Brian and Seth, since 1984. She is director of information for the Bethlehem Central School District. She was an assistant editor of *Bethlehem Revisited* and is associate editor and author of the chapter introductions, copy for the dust jacket, and the February and October 1993 entries in *Bethlehem Diary*. She holds a bachelor's degree in journalism from the University of Missouri.

Susan Graves is managing editor of *The Spotlight* in Delmar and is a free-lance writer for the *Capital District Business Review*. Before joining *The Spotlight* in 1989, she was a reporter and copy editor for the *Troy Record*. Prior to that she was a teacher at the Albany Academy for Girls for ten years. As associate editor of *Bethlehem Diary*, Graves wrote the April and August 1993 entries.

Ryland Hugh Hewitt served as associate editor-graphics for *Bethlehem Diary*, and wrote the May and September 1993 entries. He and his wife, Rowena Fair-

child, have lived in Slingerlands since 1966. They have three daughters and four grandsons. Hewitt was born in Elmira, New York, educated at Cornell University (A.B., A.M., Ph.D.) and taught in colleges and universities in Ohio, Maine, and New York. After retiring from the University at Albany, he founded and was director of the Capitol Area Speech Center, Inc., in Albany. He was associate editor-graphics for *Bethlehem Revisited*, for which he wrote the chapters on hamlets and religious institutions. He is currently a photographer for *The Spotlight* in Delmar.

PUBLICATION AND DESIGN

Charles D. (Chuck) McKinney served as associate editor-publication and design for *Bethlehem Revisited*, and coauthored the pre-history chapter. He held the same title,

and was in charge of design, layout, and publication for *Bethlehem Diary*. He has lived in Delmar since 1978 with his wife, Barbara-Ann, and two sons, Mark and Ryan. McKinney was educated at Southern Illinois University (B.S., M.S.) at Carbondale. He is an advanced amateur photographer and prepares desktop publications for several organizations. He is presently employed as an economic development specialist by the New York State Department of Economic Development.

Barbara Stoddard grew up in Amsterdam, New York, and moved to Glenmont where she married Arthur Stoddard in 1960. After her husband's death in

1982, the couple's home in Glenmont became the gathering place for their nine children and many friends and relatives. She is presently employed as a secretary at Bullard, McLeod & Associates in Albany. Barbara is a publication assistant for *Bethlehem Diary*.

ILLUSTRATION

David Coughtry was born in Albany and grew up in Delmar, in the neighborhood of the 1838 Adams House hotel, the subject of his cover painting for *Bethlehem Diary*. He holds a B.A. from

Principia College and M.A. and M.F.A.

degrees from the University at Albany. His career in art was launched with two solo exhibitions at the Bethlehem Public Library in 1977. David lives in the Schoharie Valley village of Middleburgh with his wife, Sue Ellen, and daughter, Hannah.

Margaret Foster  grew up in Chicago and studied art at the University of Wisconsin at Madison, where she earned both a bachelor's degree and a master's in art education. Margaret and her husband, Arnold, a retired University at Albany sociology professor, have lived in Delmar since 1964. They have three children, Janet, Ruth, and David. She worked as an artist and college teacher and for the New York State Education Department at the higher education level for thirty years, and was a founding member of the Bethlehem Art Association. She did a number of sketches for *Bethlehem Revisited* and *Bethlehem Diary.*

Mark Lawrence Peckham,  whose sketches of buildings and scenes in and around Bethlehem enliven *Bethlehem Diary,* was born in Albany. He attended Bethlehem Central schools, earned a B.S. degree at the State University College at Brockport, and an M.S. at the University of North Carolina in Chapel Hill. He and his wife, Shauna, have two children, Christopher and Jaimee. Peckham is a historic preservation analyst with the New York State Historic Preservation Field Services Bureau. The family lives in Elsmere.

281

VICTORIAN HOUSES, ON-LOCATION SITE FOR THE
FILM "IRONWEED". NEW SCOTLAND ROAD,
SLINGERLANDS. MARK L. PECKHAM, DECEMBER 1981.

Index

A

Abele, Sally 126
Adell, Jean 14, 37
Adler, Helen P. and Frederic B. 247
Ahlstrom, Mary and/or Richard 173, 201
Albright, Betty 211
Albright, Mildred 104
Albright, Wesley A. 219
Alford, Charles E. and Evelyn 61
Allgaier, Joseph A. 130, 149, 169
    diary: 193, 215
Ammerman, Paul 69
Anderson, Amelia 163
Applebee, Peter 197
Archaeology
    education: 3, 264
    Goes farm site: 23, 30, 46, 67, 71
    Jones/LaGrange site: 269
    Lyons site: 24, 27, 97
    Map of excavations: 4
    Mosher Dairy site: 265
    Nicoll-Sill site: 3, 8, 20, 101
    Winne site: 25, 41
Ardizone, Francine 156
Arnold, Ade 158
Arthur, Ray F. and family 243
Atkins, Dr. Richard A. and family 122
Automation 89
Ayers, Lauren 212

B

Bailey, Denny 235
Bardwell, Mary 104
Barker, John 76
Barker, Robert A. and Ellen 220
Becker, Kathleen 104
Beckers Corners Hotel 146
Bennett family 117, 148

Bennett, Allison Chesbro 40, 117, 128, 160
Bethlehem Archaeology Group (BAG)
    charter: 52
    finances: 33
    laboratory: 12, 117
    organization: 11, 13, 27, 37, 168
    report: 64
    volunteers: 29
Bethlehem Public Library 62
Bicentennial—diary publication 99, 168,
    193, 219, 258
Bicentennial—events 194, 197, 223
Bicentennial—history publication
    committee: 54, 56, 167
    publication: 91, 103, 107, 134, 149,
    160, 161, 173, 206
Bickel, Ruth Oliver 109, 112, 119, 133
Bicycling 146, 152, 223
Biggs, Donald 2
Billings, Holly 179, 203
Birthdays 73
Blackmore, May and Dr. William P. 126
Bogardus, William and Raymona 273
Bolduc, Eleanor 163
Bolen, Chester 266, 269
Boomer, Benjamin 238
Booth—burial markers 148
Bork, Rev. George Christian Frederick 58
Boucher, Deborah 143
Boutelle, Alice 157
Bowdish, Shirley 210
Bower, Mr. and Mrs. Sylvester J. 133
Brent, John 173
Brewer, Floyd and/or Coleen family 8, 10,
    44, 73, 83, 85, 94, 102, 107, 126, 128,
    137, 139, 162
Brewster, Colleen 267
Brouwer, Adam 273
Bub, Stephen F. 69
Bub, William 129
Buckley, Daniel Patrick 226
Buckley, Teresa
    diary: 222, 256

283

Q

Quay, Charles 132

R

Radio 151
Raggio, Lorin 247
Reagan, Paul 153
Reid, Miss Marjorie 129
Religion and Church 55, 57, 243, 272
Restifo, Alfred P. 264
Restifo, Valerie 86
Rhoad, Rev. Frank T. 158
Richter, Nanette 126
Riegel, Barbara 266
Rienow, Dr. Robert and Leona 166
Ringler, Kenneth J. 106, 115, 121, 127, 201, 206, 216, 246
Ritchie, Dr. William 20, 35, 67
Ritchko, Arthur 152
Ritchko, Sue Ann 79, 85, 88, 103, 106, 135
Roach, Karen 258
Roberts, Asta 247
Robillard, Donald 266
Ruckerstuhl, Robert 126
Ruslander, Claire 85
Ryan, Lee 124

S

Saint, Eva Marie 156
Saint, Mr. and Mrs. John 157
Sandberg, Betsy 229
Sargent, Dr. Edward H. Jr. 9
Schade, Charles A. 163, 239
Schaeffer, Morris 133
Schenmeyer, Shirley 146
Schoonmaker, William 124
Schrempf, Jeanne 76
Schwarz, Louise 213
Scott, Helen 124
Scouting 250

Secor, Bruce 105, 110
Sexual issues 7, 43, 177, 240
Shattuck, Martha Dickinson 91, 131, 143
Shaving 135
Sheaffer, Harry H. and Betty 153
Shopping 15, 51, 92, 135, 175, 211
Sill, William Nicoll 145
Silverman, William 134
Simpkins, Alfred 219
Simpson, Donald 98
Singer, Susan 126
Skilbeck, John and Janice 7
Small town life 74
Smith, Craig 147
Smith, Elaine and Martin 126
Smith, Helen 104
Smith, Lorraine and Thomas H. 241
Smoking 87, 108, 200
Smolinsky, John 110
Souk, John 132
Spindler, Harry and Eunice 196
Sports activities 124, 132, 190, 191, 215, 217, 224, 248
Sports organizations 126, 156
St. John, Claudia 14
Stella, Mrs. Joseph 129
Storey, Jim and Robin 197
Storm problems 79, 195, 198, 202
Stratton—burial markers 149
Substance abuse 20, 40, 58, 179
Sussman, Yale 104
Swirzcki, Valerie 265

T

Tanaka, Nobumasa 215
Tantillo, Leonard F. 150, 223
Tate, James G. 210
Taxes 188, 202, 216
Taylor, Betty 133
Terrell, Marjorie family 146
Thompson, Valerie 130
Tibbetts, Dr. Ralph 106 Tilroe, George and Connie 134
Tomlinson, Harold W. 216
Torres, Weber and Diane 259
Turner, Eleanor 54, 64, 71

U

Utilities
   telephone: 12, 99
   cable TV: 13

V

Vadney, John 16, 80
Van Derzee, Pieter and Jay 31, 86
Van Oostenbrugge, Mary Elizabeth 24
Van Rensselaer, Philip 130
Van Rensselaer, Stephen 58
Van Valkenburg, William 168
Van Woert, Chris 250
VanWoert, Irving, M.D. 126
Vedder, Johannes 270
Vogel, Jeanne 104
Volunteers 53, 262
Vorce, Raymond B. 217

W

Walsh, Brig. Gen. and Mrs. Charles E. Jr.
   147, 157
Walworth, Fayette 223
Wasserstrom, William 29, 37
Watson, Mr. and Mrs. Everett 129
Weaver, Joan 156
Webster, Frederick C. 60
Weir, Ruth 129
Westbrook, Dr. Perry and Arlen 206
White, Claude 130
Wilbur, Ruth 133
Wilcoxen, Charlotte 19, 34, 262
Willey, Carol 194
Williams, Bill and Alana 8
Williams, Rick 258
Wilson, Cynthia 85
Winne, Adam 41
Winne, Barent Staats 26, 29
Winne, John and/or Hugh 26, 147
Wock, Carol 14, 34, 101

Women 39, 203, 204, 222
Wood, Ralph and/or Muriel 6, 12-14, 25,
   33, 35, 37, 39, 58, 67, 80,
   99, 112, 131, 272
Woodley, Shannon 214
Wooster, Barbara 164
Wooster, Dr. Judith 247, 250
Wright, Cliff 266
Wright, Stephen R. 60

Y

Young, Sally 104

Z

Zdgiebloski, Dorothy 68
Zick, Sue 85
Zimmerman, Peggy and Joseph 126
Zimmerman, William E. 133
Zomback, Tina and Selma 3
Zwicklbauer, Franz K. 250